Leisure Policies in Europe

Leisure Policies in Europe

Edited by

Peter Bramham, Ian Henry,
Hans Mommaas and Hugo van der Poel

CAB INTERNATIONAL

CAB INTERNATIONAL
Wallingford
Oxon OX10 8DE
UK

Tel: Wallingford (0491) 832111
Telex: 847964 (COMAGG G)
Telecom Gold / Dialcom: 84: CAU001
Fax: (0491) 833508

A catalogue record for this book is available from the British Library.

ISBN   0 85198 819 9

Printed and bound in the UK

Contents

Contributors

Peter Bramham, *Senior Lecturer in Leisure Studies at Leeds Metropolitan University, England.*

Julia Gonzalez, *Lecturer in Leisure Studies and Director of European Relations, Universidad de Deusto, Bilbao, Spain.*

Ian Henry, *Senior Lecturer in Leisure Studies and Recreation Management, Loughborough University, England.*

Bohdan Jung, *Professor, Research Institute for Developing Economies, Warsaw School of Economics, Poland.*

Hans Mommaas, *Lecturer in Leisure Studies, Katholieke Universiteit Brabant, Tilburg, the Netherlands.*

Wolfgang Nahrstedt, *Professor of Leisure Education, Universiteit Bielefeld, Germany.*

Hans-Erik Olson, *Lecturer and Researcher in Leisure Studies, University of Stockholm, Sweden.*

Fouli Papageorgiou, *Director, Centre for Development Studies, Athens, Greece.*

Geneviève Poujol, *Researcher, Laboratoire du Changement des Institutions, CNRS, Paris, France.*

Jim Riordan, *Professor, Department of Linguistic and International Studies, University of Surrey, Guildford, England.*

Aitor Urkiola, *Independent Leisure Researcher and Consultant, Bilbao, Spain.*

Hugo van der Poel, *Lecturer in Leisure Studies, Katholieke Universiteit Brabant, Tilburg, the Netherlands.*

Preface

This text represents the second project of the European Consortium for Leisure Studies and Research. The Consortium aims to bring together European academics working in leisure studies, and to generate literature of a comparative and/or transnational nature for the leisure studies field. This sounds to be a simpler task than it really is. There are important differences in the state of the art in the field of leisure studies in the various European countries. There are also important differences in the way in which leisure policy, the topic of this particular book, is conceptualised and dealt with in different European nation states. The text bears witness to these differences, but represents, we hope, a step forward in the work of the Consortium.

The bringing together of contributors was only made possible by working in the context of conferences organised by institutions other than the Consortium. We would like to thank the organisers of the European Leisure Studies Winter Universities in Brussels (1991) and Bielefeld (1992), and the ELRA Conference in Bilbao (1992), for having offered the Consortium the facility to meet during these events. In addition, we wish to express our gratitude to the Board of the Faculty of Social Sciences of the Katholieke Universiteit Brabant, for their financial support for a Consortium seminar on European Leisure Policy and Research, held in Tilburg, in the autumn of 1991. Finally our thanks to Jacquie Stokes (of the European Leisure Studies postgraduate group working at the universities of Brussels, Tilburg, Loughborough and Deusto, Bilbao) and to Lester Faleiro (of Loughborough University) for their assistance in the 'anglicisation' of material contained in this text.

> Peter Bramham, Ian Henry,
> Hugo van der Poel and
> Hans Mommaas
>
> April 1993

List of Figures

List of Tables

xi

Chapter 1

Leisure Policies in Europe: an Introduction

Peter Bramham, Ian Henry, Hans Mommaas, and Hugo van der Poel

Many find the idea of 'leisure policy' a contradiction in terms. How can one promote government intervention in an area of life which, almost by definition, is self-governed by the autonomous citizen? However appealing the idea may be that citizens should be left to themselves to decide independently how to spend their leisure, this notion is nonetheless misleading. One should recognise both that leisure is invariably subject to intervention, and that intervention not only restricts leisure opportunities, but also creates new opportunities. Watching television, taking a holiday, visiting a museum or ballet performance, going fishing, camping or cycling, are all leisure activities which people more or less freely decide to do or not to do. However, they require governments and banks, companies and voluntary organisations to consider trends in leisure participation, and to develop the necessary infrastructure, to invest in leisure provision, and to foster the training of personnel and the marketing of products and services. All organisations involved in leisure aim to influence our behaviour. Not only governments, but organisations as varied as MacDonald's, Disney, Greenpeace and groups promoting Sunday observance, seek to influence decision-making in leisure, directly or indirectly. Furthermore, government intervention in leisure is widespread, and is seen as essential. Certainly in Western Europe, 'natural' outdoor recreation areas can only exist because governments intervene, deliberately protecting these areas. Such decisions to protect the natural environment are made by 'democratically' controlled government bodies. Similarly in the built environment, if local authorities do not protect the scenic beauty of their city, tourists, and those who cater for them, may end up destroying the very features which attract tourists to their city in the first place.

Government regulations are not simply restrictive. It is more accurate to say that they redistribute freedoms and leisure

1

opportunities. By restricting opportunities for tourists in vulnerable, small scale historic towns, opportunities for later generations of visitors are preserved. By closing lakes and beaches to powerboats, those who prefer more tranquil forms of leisure activity can enjoy greater opportunities. Employment legislation restricting employers in their treatment of employees, creates or preserves the leisure of those employees. To understand the thrust of a book like this, it is essential to comprehend that freedom and leisure are not the logical consequence of the absence of regulation, and that deregulation does not necessarily mean greater autonomy. Whether regulation is enabling or constraining, depends on the content of the 'rules' and to whom the rules apply. State intervention in leisure may well reduce the number of options available to particular groups, but absence of government intervention will equally constrain the choices of others. Indeed the more one advocates freedom from state intervention, the more one lays oneself open to the accusation of promoting existing constraints on leisure choice, and protecting entrenched interests.

The development of government policy presupposes problems that need to be solved collectively, such as the 'negative externalities' which may result from some types of individual leisure decision. Elements of leisure may also be considered to be 'merit goods' or to be instrumental in reaching other policy goals. The rationales for government intervention in leisure may therefore vary from one policy decision to another. We can perhaps identify five groups of reasons why governments may care to intervene in leisure. The reader will find most of these reasons spelled out in more detail in the following chapters, in varying combinations and with specific weights attached to them, which express the existing differences between the respective national policies and national policy-systems.

A first legitimation for leisure policies can be found in the political and organisational aspects of leisure behaviour. The most important of these factors include the use of leisure activity for nation-building and enhancing national prestige, for forging social integration, and for the protection and promotion of (democratic) citizenship. Pre-war Italy provides a good example of the use of leisure in the creation of a fascist state. The use of sport in the former USSR to boost national prestige is another example. While social integration may overlap with the construction of national identity, it may also be evident in measures directed at specific groups, such as unemployed youth or ethnic minorities. The British case provides examples of the use of sport in attempts to reintegrate particular target groups into 'mainstream' society. Certain elements of leisure have also become subject to government intervention because they are linked to disturbances, indecency or crime. Regulation of drinking, prostitution, gambling, media, and the use of public space fall into this category. The protection and promotion of (democratic) citizenship is also evident in measures taken to protect the right of assembly and of free speech. Measures to preserve pluralism in the media, and public subsidy of libraries are also in part designed to safeguard access to information relevant to democratic decision making. The word 'democratic' is placed in inverted commas here, because although the concept of citizenship implies that politics are democratically organised, nevertheless, many non-democratic governments (for example pre-war fascist and post-war communist regimes) have sought to use leisure activities in order to promote some forms of 'citizenship'.

A second major reason for state intervention stems from a recognition of the economic significance of leisure. Most tourism policies, for example, in the 1980s and early 1990s, were primarily directed at creating jobs and business activity. In the Netherlands, the development of job security for artists was one of the justifications employed in the 1980s for the development of subsidy for the performing and plastic arts. In addition to the creation of jobs and business opportunities directly within the leisure industries, (the use of leisure facilities to create a favourable business environment is another economic reason for state intervention in leisure) For this reason leisure plays an important role in many plans for the economic regeneration of inner city areas.

For most people the idea of leisure policy is primarily connected to a third type of rationale for state intervention in leisure. This relates to the socio-cultural goals of government policy; with the elevation of taste, with education and with the right of self-expression. Positively formulated, these policies seek to enhance people's ability to make sense of a variety of symbolic systems (literature, music, paintings, architecture, etc.), to enjoy them, and to increase people's own participation in these types of symbolic production. Governments seek to achieve this through education in schools, art education in museums, subsidies to amateur art groups or to music schools, and subsidised tickets for the performing arts. This type of policy is now under attack from two different directions. Some critics claim that these policies favour particular symbol systems, notably those of established élite culture. What is felt to be wrong is that most government money, and educational effort are geared toward the élite pastimes of the relatively affluent, neglecting the culture(s) of lower income and less well educated groups. What is required in place of this form of cultural élitism, these critics argue, is a form of 'cultural democracy', with greater attention and funding given to forms of popular culture. Thus it is argued there should be more equal opportunities for all groups in society to express themselves, and governments should distribute their subsidies more equally among these groups. Another group of critics suggest that to view leisure as a merit good is itself inappropriate, when governments are confronted with a chronic shortage of funds. Some benefits may accrue from public sector investment in leisure, but there are opportunity costs to be considered since investment in leisure will deprive other service areas (such as housing, or health care) of funding, where needs may be more urgent.

A fourth group of arguments for developing leisure policies relate to the time-spatial characteristics of leisure. An illustration of this is the increasing interest shown by governments in the staggering of holidays, in order to lengthen the tourist season and prevent congestion in tourist areas during high season. A wish to relieve the pressures of spatial congestion often underpins policies directed at improving the accessibility of the countryside for recreational purposes. The Swedish tradition of 'everyman's right' (sic) illustrates how competing spatial claims may be resolved by the state. This custom, which dates back to the Middle Ages, permits access to forests irrespective of ownership for all walkers who conform to a basic code of conduct .

The fifth set of reasons which one might identify, relates to the physical aspects of leisure. Sport and recreational policies in all countries are, at least partly, legitimated by claims concerning their contribution to people's health resulting from the provision of opportunities for relaxation and 're-creation' of the work-force. Recreational policies may also used as an instrument for creating awareness of environmental issues and promoting public support for conservation of areas of natural beauty. Increasingly local and national authorities realise that leisure can be problematic in its impact on the natural environment in which it takes place. The obvious example is the damage tourism may cause in vulnerable areas of natural beauty. Policy-makers often find themselves confronted with protests from nature conservation groups with regard to the leisure pursuits of others, when these pursuits involve, for example, the use of powerful and noisy power boats and jet-skis, the use of mountain-bikes or the development of extensive golf-links in ecologically sensitive areas; or where they simply involve the increased use of cars and planes for leisure transport.

Thus one can identify a range of reasons for government intervention in leisure. However, many of the problems and opportunities associated with people's leisure activities have a 'transnational' character, in that they are not necessarily restricted to the boundaries of a particular state and may not therefore necessarily be the object of national policies. Thus, the factors which affect leisure cannot be understood by focusing solely on the level of the nation-state. Some account must be taken of the changing trade-relations in the world-economy and power shifts within the 'system of nation-states', to be able to make sense of political and economic developments within particular nation-states.

In the period since the 1970s, Europe has witnessed important but divergent developments in the mutual relations between nation-states, and in the internal relations between state, voluntary and commercial sectors, with far reaching implications for patterns of leisure participation and leisure provision. In southern European countries there has been a move towards democratisation and increased industrialisation, a development closely connected with their integration into the European Communities. In north-western Europe the economic crises of the 1970s and 1980s were accompanied by policies of retrenchment, deregulation and privatisation in the sphere of social welfare, and a stricter enforcement of 'law and order'. In the mid-1980s these countries experienced a new cycle of economic growth and developed the project to establish a single market. By the beginning of the 1990s the 'Swedish model' of the corporate state, the pre-eminent example of successful social democracy, was under severe pressure. However, the most striking and significant political changes had taken place in Eastern Europe. These changes may have opened the way for increased political, economic and cultural interchange between Eastern and non-Eastern European countries, but they also heralded the disintegration of existing states, the onset of virulent forms of nationalism, and the revival of religious orthodoxies.

Clearly, leisure patterns, problems and policies are influenced by these international and transnational developments. Nevertheless they have a 'situated' or 'localised' character too. The way these transnational phenomena are experienced, presented and handled, is expressive of local circumstances, and the local response is part and parcel of what makes a 'locality', a specific situation in time and space. For instance, most governments (be they local, regional, national or supra-national) in order to legitimate their very existence, will be interested in policies promoting leisure activities that are in one way or another prestigious and expressive of the 'local (regional, national, supra-national) identity'.) They may therefore subsidise museums, monuments and other aspects of cultural heritage; they may promote the use of the local language in schools, films, television and literature; or they may appropriate the victories of 'local' sports clubs. Although these policies may not differ much in terms of their goals, they vary substantially in content, or the relative weight given to various aspects of these policies, and the means, financial resources and drive with which they are executed. Furthermore, given the 'local' character of these policies, they will also vary in the scale of the problems to which they are addressed, in their respective 'policy context'; and in the policy alternatives available to a particular government given its place in a particular policy system.

It is in the nature of a book like this that the variety in 'local' features of a particular phenomenon - in this case national leisure policy - is what the book is about, providing its main 'raison d'être'. But anyone glancing through some of the introductions to the various chapters of this book will soon discover that most authors find that their national language does not have a suitable translation for the word leisure and, even worse, that in many nation-states no coherent body of policy, defined as (national) leisure policy, actually exists. The editors are fortunate that this has not prevented the authors from writing their respective analyses, but obviously this point deserves some clarification. It is true that leisure policy as such is rarely recognised in an holistic sense by governments. It seems that only in the north-western corner of Europe (Netherlands, Germany, France) have there been significant initiatives aimed at formulating a national leisure policy, but even here such initiatives have not met with success. This is perhaps partly because of the paradoxical nature of the term 'leisure policy' or 'free-time policy' discussed earlier in this introductory chapter. It may also partly reflect the fact that the idea of a 'leisure policy' was contaminated by the attempts of totalitarian regimes to regulate and use leisure. Nevertheless, although there may be no explicit leisure policy as such, there are, in all nation-states, policies which are directed at leisure. The authors of the following chapters were therefore asked to do three things. First, they were asked to establish whether an explicit, holistic 'leisure policy' existed within their own nation-state. Second, they were invited to describe the extent to which tourism, (outdoor) recreation, sport, cultural, and media policies are considered to be policies directed at different 'leisure sectors', or, to put it another way, to establish the extent to which concern about people's leisure has inspired these policies. The third element of the authors' brief was to give the reader some idea of the topics associated with leisure or free time policy, which are typical of the country under study. The first of these questions follows logically from the title of this book. We were however well aware that the answer in most cases would be negative, so that further questions were needed. The second question was meant to introduce an element of comparison. One thing that has become very clear while working on this book is that linking 'leisure' or 'free time' to all five major leisure 'sectors' (tourism, recreation, sport, culture, and media.) is certainly not common to most of the countries we have studied. As far as one can discern a pattern, the media in particular, and to a lesser extent the arts and tourism, are not commonly understood as 'leisure sectors'. The most frequent links are with sports; (outdoor) recreation; community activities and art education; and youth. It is also clear that these links in policy-making are reflected in academia. The study of leisure appears to be as 'sectoralised' as the state bureaucracies, and this made it difficult to trace analysts with a full overview of the different leisure sectors in their respective countries. The extent to which experts in sport, tourism or media consider themselves to be working in the leisure sphere varies from country to another. This relates to the third question we asked. By establishing a clear view of the different ways in which governments conceptualise and deal with leisure, we sought to avoid the danger of imposing a spurious homogeneity in the picture of leisure policy in European states which this book has developed.

Nevertheless, we should acknowledge that there was an element of pragmatism involved in leaving authors relatively free to develop their own argument. For instance, it was decided that the emphasis in the chapters should be on the post-war developments, but the contributors were given freedom to extend historical analysis if they deemed this necessary to be able to sketch out the dominant features of (leisure) policy making in the nation-state under review. This flexibility is, to some degree, inevitable given the state of affairs in the field of leisure studies in general and comparative leisure policy analysis in particular. Although there are books with a comparative perspective on the various leisure sectors or aspects of leisure (e.g. Szalai *et al.*, 1972; Riordan, 1978; McQuail and Siune, 1986; Hantrais and Kamphorst, 1987; Arbena, 1988; Williams and Shaw, 1988; Browne, 1989; Richter, 1989), there are very few which attempt to compare leisure policies in different nation-states. Wilson's *Politics and Leisure* (1988) incorporates a comparative element, but focuses predominantly on sport and draws only on English-language sources. What is even more significant is that most of the chapters in this book contain the first sketches of the respective countries' sets of policies concerned with leisure. The authors could not fall back on established overviews and histories, but had to write these chapters from scratch. Given the fact that there are as yet no established national (or international) traditional views on the subject matter, the various contributions should, above all, be looked upon as the first attempts of a group of academics, each of them with his or her own disciplinary, national-historical and particular 'leisure sector' background, to explore the vast terrain of national leisure policies.

Nonetheless, flexibility and freedom also have another, more positive side, which has been stressed from the beginning of this project. No attempt has been made to provide a 'template' which might exclude all sorts of inconvenient external variables, to allow 'direct comparison' of policy systems to take place. To the editors this seems to be a futile exercise. Instead, what is stressed in this text is the situating of the (national) policies directed towards (aspects) of leisure, in wider contexts, that is in the cultural, economic and political developments within the country and the relevant global-cultural, geo-political and world economy developments with which the country as a whole is confronted. In other words, the editors do not think that it is very useful to consider nation-states as 'independent variables', but rather regard it as more appropriate to treat individual nation states as elements of the context within which other states exist and operate, and as integral parts of 'systems of nation-states', an integrated world-economy and a globalizing culture. For this reason authors were asked to provide some basic information about the prevailing leisure patterns, the (changes in) the general policy structures and political organisation, and the 'external' relations of their respective countries.

Given all these difficulties in delineating the topic of the book - the absence of any clear-cut leisure policies, the lack of 'tradition' and of an established body of work in this field, not to mention the well known controversies about what leisure itself is supposed to mean - given all these problems, why have we engaged in this venture? If governments are so obviously uninterested in developing leisure policies, why expend the effort involved in writing a book on this topic? And why, in a book on leisure policy, should we adopt a European perspective ?

Perhaps the first response to this type of question is to re-emphasise that (governments already do intervene in leisure in substantial and important ways, but that they do so under other policy labels, such as tourism policy, sport policy and so on.) These interventions need to be identified so that they can be evaluated in public debate. Depending on the outcomes of these debates, such policies can then either be continued, revised and improved, or discontinued because they are found to be ineffective or unnecessary. The rationale for analysing this group of policies together under the heading of leisure policy derives from the gains that can be made by adopting a coherent view on leisure, instead of more fragmented views on leisure sectors. For instance, one cannot fully understand what happened to leisure activities such as reading, radio listening, going to the cinema, or television viewing taken alone, if one ignores changes in the other activities identified on this list. The same is true for sports participation, sports spectating and the media coverage of sports events. To put it crudely, (all leisure activities are to some degree in 'competition' with each other in terms of time and money spent, the status they imply , and so on.)(Any policy directed at a particular leisure activity is therefore likely to be more effective if the relationship with other 'competing' leisure activities is properly understood.)

A second factor to consider is that social inequality in general is still reflected in unequal participation rates in leisure activities and provision. More often than not this means that groups with lower income and lower participation rates in education, are less likely to profit from state subsidies for leisure, than their more affluent counterparts. This is true for most government spending on the arts, but generally also true for expenditure on plans to revitalise inner city areas or whole economies. Governments throughout Europe are in need of money and compete with each other in order to attract capital to their city, region or country. Obviously, this competition is likely to be fuelled by the creation of the single market in Western Europe, by the breakdown of the Comecon system and by the failure of the European Free Trade Association (EFTA) to create an alternative free market alongside the European Community. The more Europe moves in the direction of a single European market, and thus the more freely capital, labour, goods and services can move around Europe, the more important this inner European competition for capital (and labour) will become. Some leisure facilities, such as golf courses, tennis courts, opera houses, parks, galleries, luxury shopping areas, museums, etc., represent important instruments in policies aimed at attracting capital, particularly 'service' capital, to particular localities, because they supposedly provide the atmosphere and living conditions to which decision-makers and 'cultured' professional personnel will be attracted. Other facilities, such as soccer grounds and public swimming pools, allotment gardens, supermarkets, less expensive restaurants, cafés and cinemas, which lack this association with cultural capital, are literally being marginalised and squeezed out of urban centres. These dynamics are difficult to control by any government in a national market economy, let alone in an integrated European market economy. On the other hand European governments have been very active in creating this integrated European market, and therefore bear a (political) responsibility for the changes that occur in leisure patterns as a consequence of this emerging market structure. It is thus intended that this book will help to sensitise readers to the links that exist between changing economic, political and cultural relations between and within nation-states on the one side, and patterns of leisure participation on the other, so that the advantages and disadvantages of leisure policies can be evaluated in a more fruitful way than has to date been possible.

The third factor to consider is that leisure is not, as it might seem at first sight, a separate sphere of social life, devoid of political significance. When, for instance, Vaclav Havel, the former President of Czechoslovakia described the birth of the dissident movement *Charta 77*, he reminded us that this was not the consequence of a 'political' incident in itself. In fact it was the trial for sedition of members of a rock-group, 'The Plastic People of the Universe', that shaped the climate in which *Charta 77* was created. This trial was not so much a clash of differing political views, rather it was a clash of differing views on how life should be lived. If one is not even permitted to make the music of one's own choosing, to sing about the things which make life worth living, then what is one to be allowed to do?

How important were the media (particularly television) and tourism in the recent changes in Eastern Europe? Is it too great a claim to make to argue that freedom of travel was one of the levers which prised open the iron curtain? The Italian, Spanish and Soviet chapters demonstrate that authoritarian regimes have been well aware of the significance of these 'everyday freedoms', and have dealt with them carefully and pragmatically. For instance, the communist regime in the USSR tolerated activities such as horse-racing and card-games which were officially frowned upon, while it prohibited travelling abroad. Thus, leisure activities should be understood as part of the bargain struck between governors and governed. Indeed trespassing on the borderlines between what is allowed or tolerated in everyday life, and what is not, becomes a political act, even if it is not intended as such, as perhaps was the case with 'The Plastic People of the Universe'. The example of Madonna makes it clear that the same mechanism operates in the West, although the level of tolerance may be greater than it was in communist Eastern Europe. In some 'free democracies' her videos and shows are forbidden and banned from the television screen because of her 'lewd' and 'salacious' performances. Music, card-games, even clothes, are not simply unimportant aspects of daily life, when compared with fundamental issues such as the 'free market' and 'political democracy'. It is precisely because they are features of everyday life that they reflect the ability to practise freedom, to experience the free market 'at work'. As a consequence, not being able to buy a ticket for a Madonna concert is indicative of a free market that is not operating in all sectors of social life, and betrays a government that clearly does intervene in people's leisure.

Thus, if Europe really is moving towards a unified free market, this will have an effect on the ability of governments to intervene in the operation of markets which have to date been organised on a national basis. The single market will limit, or at least alter, the scope and effectiveness of various forms of (national) leisure policy, such as media and cultural policies, which now more often than not, support artificial and/or monopolistic 'home markets'. In this situation, a comparative perspective on leisure policies may provide some insight into the ways in which a variety of countries organise their policies with regard to leisure, giving greater or lesser emphasis to market mechanisms in leisure provision. It may perhaps be possible to discover some common elements in leisure policies throughout Europe, which it may be important to preserve while constructing a single market .

Finally, although there is a generally accepted view that problems should be dealt with at the lowest possible tier of government (the 'subsidiarity' principle), nevertheless there are some problems which can only be dealt with adequately on a supranational level. As we have already noted, many leisure phenomena clearly are inter- or transnational, and their external effects are not confined to state-borders. Tourism is a prime example, but it is equally true for the media, the more spectacular aspects of sports (World Championships, Olympic Games), and successful products and productions in the spheres of the arts and popular culture. Policies in these areas will have to be co-ordinated, in order to be effective. Currently, for example, the EC is trying to co-ordinate national policies directed at the staggering of holidays, because it has become clear that uncoordinated policies in this sphere may even be counter-productive. Here again a comparative perspective can be useful, informing (future) policy makers about the types of problems which countries other than their own have had to deal with, the conditions under which such problems have arisen, the types of policy developed to counter these problems, and the experiences of other countries in terms of the effectiveness of these policies. We do not claim that we can provide clear answers to all these questions. But we do think that they are important questions, and have tried to make a start in answering them.

REFERENCES

Arbena, J.L. (ed.) (1988) *Sport and Society in Latin America: Diffusion, Dependency, and the Rise of Mass Culture*, New York: Greenwood Press.

Bramham, P., Henry, I., Mommaas, H and van der Poel, H. (eds) (1989) *Leisure and Urban Processes: Critical Studies of Leisure Policy in Western European Cities*, London: Routledge.

Browne, D.R. (1989) *Comparing Broadcast Systems: The Experiences of Six Industrialized Countries*, Ames, IA: Iowa State University Press.

Hantrais, L. and Kamphorst, T.J. (eds) (1987) *Trends in the arts: A multinational perspective*, Amersfoort: Giordano Bruno.

McQuail, D. and Siune, K. (eds) (1986) *New Media Politics. Comparative Perspectives in Western Europe*, The Euromedia Research Group. London: Sage.

Richter, L.A. (1989) *The politics of tourism in Asia*, Honolulu: University of Hawaii Press.

Riordan, J. (ed.) (1978) *Sport under Communism: the U.S.S.R., Czechoslovakia, The G.D.R., China, Cuba*, London: Hurst.

Szalai, A. *et al.* (eds) (1972) *The Use of Time: Daily activities of urban and suburban populations in twelve countries*, The Hague: Mouton.

Williams, A.M. and Shaw, G. (eds) (1988) *Tourism and Economic Development: Western European Experiences*, London and New York: Belhaven Press.

Wilson, J. (1988) *Politics and Leisure*, Boston, MA: Unwin Hyman.

Chapter 2

Leisure Politics and Policies in France

Geneviève Poujol

Reference to government policy relating to leisure in France is not as straightforward as it might seem, since the notion of *leisure* was discarded politically in the early 1960s. However, just as in other European countries, certain elements contribute to policy designed to influence the organisation and the practice of leisure activities. These are usually termed *cultural* policy, a term which derives from a peculiarly French notion. However, before we begin to describe the various elements of this policy, it is important to emphasise certain factors which have constituted significant aspects of the social, cultural and political context in France over the period since the Second World War.

Factors Influencing the Leisure Policy Context

The Centralisation of Power and the Secular State

In France, there has traditionally been a centralisation of economic, political and administrative power in and around Paris. This was a phenomenon inherited from the French monarchy, continued by Napoleon and subsequently fostered by the five successive Republics. Even though decentralisation of the powers of the state had been required by law, it is only after the introduction of further legislation by the Socialists in 1982 that real attempts to decentralise became evident. As such the organisation of leisure activities, either in terms of popular culture or art, has mainly been undertaken by institutions dependent on central state organisation, with regional professional organisations playing a relatively insignificant role. The authority of the central state is also manifest in the economic sphere, and even in its most liberal aspects, French capitalism has been a form of capitalism firmly directed by the state.

13

A Catholic Majority

In addition to the power of the central state, the Catholic church represented a force counterbalancing the strength of the Republic until a constitutional separation between the Church and the State was established in 1905. Nevertheless, both the Church and secular forces have continued to be significant in the world of education and leisure in France.

The Disappearing Working Class

Before the Second World War, the working class formed a considerable proportion of the French population, whose interests were staunchly defended by strong trade unions. However, throughout the post-war period the size and significance of the working-class population has continued to decline, while tertiary sector employment has brought into being intermediate social categories, new middle class fractions, which form a much larger proportion of the population in contemporary French society.

Political Bi-polarisation

The bi-polar opposition of left and right, until recently, dominated the political scene in France. On the left, the existence of a Communist Party (Parti Communiste Français - PCF) which was supported until recently by approximately a quarter of the electorate, has been a significant feature of French politics. Although the appeal of the PCF is in decline (receiving less than 10 per cent of the vote in elections at the beginning of the 1990s) nevertheless the significance of the right-left dichotomy should be borne in mind, especially since polarisation continues with the recent growth of the vote for the far right under Jean-Marie le Pen.

Stages in the Development of Leisure-related Policy

Perhaps three significant periods in the development of leisure related policy can be distinguished in the period since the last world war.

1945-1959 Post-war Reconstruction

This was the era of reconstruction in France in political terms as well as in terms of repairing the physical infrastructure. In the political sphere, the French needed to erase the memory of the Vichy period of collaboration. They found themselves united very briefly under the banner of General de Gaulle during the Liberation. In terms of ideology those who were in power pursued the line of the pre-war *Front Populaire* in matters concerning the organisation of leisure. The *Front Populaire* was a coalition of political parties of the left (communists, socialists and radicals who came to power in 1936). One of the achievements of this pre-war government was a new law granting the workers the right to paid holidays. In fact in 1936, the theme of the 'right to leisure' played a major role in winning over the working classes. The office of the Secretary of State for leisure and sport was entrusted by Léon Blum to Leo Lagrange, whose ministry set about the task of organising leisure, breathing new vigour into existing associations.

> The principle of the 'organisation' of leisure took its
> inspiration from a tradition which goes back to the
> nineteenth century to Popular Education ("Education
> Populaire"), where the term Popular Education represented
> a 'socio-political ' project which went far beyond the reaches
> of mere adult education organised during leisure time.
> (Poujol, 1980)

As the historian Pascal Ory has pointed out, this period under the Popular Front, also encompassed the creation of a 'cultural policy', for the first time in France. According to information unearthed by Ory, the idea of setting up a Ministry of Culture had already been aired in a confidential paper. However, the tradition started by the Popular Front which fostered leisure activities, was simply taken over, by the Vichy regime. The regime encouraged, at least at the outset, the French youth movement *Jeune France* which in its turn spawned clusters of cultural performers in the world of theatre, music and literary publications.

In 1946, the post-war state incorporated a department of 'Popular Culture' (Culture Populaire) within the administrative structure inherited from the Vichy period. Jean Guéhenno the first minister to head the department, and others who succeeded him pursued the policy direction established by the Front Populaire in the year 1936. Youth movements banned by the Pétain regime were reborn and other new movements were created, among them that of *Maisons des Jeunes et de la Culture* (Youth Cultural Centres). Elsewhere new theatre troupes appeared outside Paris, backed by the *Secrétariat aux Beaux-Arts* (the forerunner of the Ministry of Culture). In 1951, the *Théatre National Populaire* was created, and theatre decentralisation initiated by Jeanne Laurent with groups in the provinces (mainly in Toulouse and Lyon) represented the first steps in a policy of cultural decentralisation (Laurent, 1982).

The *Académie des Beaux Arts* an institution which had been very active throughout the nineteenth century continued to impose its hegemony in the areas of painting, sculpture and music. All artistic innovation was rejected and new schools of painting summarily dismissed. Their works were refused entry into museums in general and into the Louvre in particular. As a consequence the National Museum of Modern Art is poorly furnished with the work of contemporary masters. Works of Bonnard, Matisse, Braque, Rouault and Picasso left France in spite of the efforts of those, such as Jean

Cassou, who sought to protect this heritage, as New York began to replace Paris as the focal point of the art world.

Elsewhere the State gave considerable impetus to the extensive development of *colonies de vacances*, (holiday camps for children) and the number of children experiencing a holiday increased steadily up to the 1960s when it began to decline. Finally legislation introduced in 1946 placed an obligation on companies to create *Comités d'Entreprises* (in-company work committees). The activities of the *Comités*, even though leisure-oriented (providing vacations, theatre visits, and libraries for workers), were mainly social rather than sporting or cultural activities. In 1958, when the *Haut Commissariat à Jeunesse et aux Sports* (the High Commission for Youth and Sport) was created the youth and popular education associations rebelled in an attempt to resist centralised control or influence. Given the painful experience under the Vichy regime, any centralised policy favouring youth was regarded with suspicion. In spite of this resistance the new Sports High-Commissioner Herzog, aided by an efficient cabinet member, Olivier Philip, was able to devise a genuine policy of support for these associations which were devoted to leisure activities not only for the young but also for adults. This policy brought with it considerable financial resources enabling the development of a large number of facilities for sport and leisure, and, in particular, providing funding for the establishment of *Maisons des Jeunes* (Youth Centres). The supportive role of the central state in the financing of these sectors seemed to have had the effect of reassuring the National Sports and Youth Federations and the system gained widespread approval and acceptance. This acceptance of state funding developed into something of a dependency relationship so that when the state began to reduce financial support the national organisations were left at the mercy of local clubs or associations. As a consequence by the early 1990s these Federations were experiencing a crisis of confidence because in the eyes of their local associations they were perceived as powerless, having become too reliant on the central state.

1959-1980 Centralised State Planning and Economic Prosperity

In this period France began to flourish and the future seemed assured, thanks to state planning. Between 1966 and 1979 four laws were introduced reducing weekly hours of work. A major policy initiative to promote community projects was introduced in the Fourth National Plan. The building of numerous Social Centres and *Maisons des Jeunes* (youth centres) and some *Maisons de la Culture* (cultural centres) was undertaken. Funding from the central state allowed playing fields and spaces to be developed. Along with the burgeoning of these leisure facilities, in the 1960s, professional education and training of people in charge of *animation* at these centres was also promoted, and several new professions came into being, including, that of the *animateur socio-culturel*.

Eventually General de Gaulle created an exclusive personal Ministry for the writer André Malraux, establishing a new Ministry of Culture (Poujol, 1991). During the early period of the Fifth Republic the concept of *culture* replaced that of *education* which had been a key theme of the period of the Third Republic. This was the era when any project described in terms of *leisure* was excluded as being antipathetic to *culture*, Malraux denounced 'the grossly false idea that cultural problems are those which relate to the utilisation of leisure...' (speech in the National Assembly in 1963), even though Malraux had been a personal friend of the politician originally in charge of the policy for leisure in 1936, Leo Lagrange. For the grand new Minister of Culture, leisure was only a means, not an end in itself.

In 1962, Joffre Dumazedier, founder of the movement 'People and Culture' wrote the book translated and published in 1967 as *Toward a Society of Leisure*. This book was widely publicised by the media and in the academic community because of Dumazedier's influential role in the founding of the sociology of leisure. In this publication he argued that :

> the idea of leisure is far from being integrated in thought
> processes which guide intellectual reflection or militant
> action, whether on the left or on the right, for partisans or
> adversaries of the capitalist system. Right minded people
> argued as if the notion of leisure did not exist. Clever
> intellectuals deliberately avoided the idea, justifying this
> omission in their search for a new system, by arguing that
> they were reflecting contemporary thinking.
> (Dumazedier, 1967)

Opinion was far from unanimously in favour of this multi-faceted approach to culture and to the problem of the organisation of leisure. However, from the early 1960s onwards the notion of culture was increasingly idealised in public debate and progressively replaced leisure. Thus 'culture' began to be used in political discourse in much the same way as 'leisure' had been used at the time of the Front Populaire and even under Vichy.

A decree of 24 July 1959, defines the mission of the new Ministry in the following terms :

> The Ministry for cultural affairs is committed to making
> accessible to a large number of the French people, firstly,
> the masterpieces of France, as well as those of other nations,
> to assure the maximum audience for our cultural heritage,
> and secondly to promote the creation of works of art as well
> as of the spirit enriching (art).

To 'render accessible', and to 'promote the creation of works of art' represent two apparently complementary goals. In fact the predominance given to one or the other of these goals was to lead to a debate splitting cultural administrators into two factions, a debate which was still going on three decades later and which went far beyond the competence of the Ministry for Cultural Affairs.

One of the key concerns of policy makers was with how to render art accessible. This was certainly not, Malraux argued, to be accomplished by pursuing the approach of high school education. An education-based approach to the project was promoted but Malraux fended this off. What then, was the difference between *cultural action* and *popular education*? In Popular Education paradoxically the cultural content was based on traditional notions of high culture, mostly presented in written form, and so the model for popular education was peculiarly pedantic and elitist. Popular education in France could boast of having invented a certain pedagogical style which in turn served as an example for schools. However little attention was given to art in popular education. If art there was, it was academic, declamatory, classic drama, and interpretations of classical musical works.

In its early days, the new Ministry of Culture experienced growing pains. On the one hand the new ministerial department inherited a management levered away from the Ministry of National Education. This Ministry though wielding considerable power, did nothing to help facilitate the task of its organisational off-shoot. In fact few people in government believed that this ministry was anything but a temporary toy for Malraux. As a result, there was a substantial reduction of funds allocated to it by the Ministry of Finance. At that time it was difficult to perceive a grand master plan for culture in the creation of this ministry. However, due mostly to General de Gaulle's faithful support of Malraux over more than a decade, and to the tenacity and the imagination of some top civil servants, this ministerial structure not only survived, but in the period after Malraux's term of office, it came to maturity as a ministry in its own right (Poujol, 1991). Having gained in size and substance, the organisation was regionalised to develop its work along a wider front. Pompidou inaugurated the tradition of presidential involvement in art and culture, maintaining close privileged links with his Minister of Culture and thus bypassing the Prime Minister. A similar relationship developed between President Mittérand and his Minister for Culture, Jack Lang, from 1981 (with a break in office in 1986 when Jacques Chirac was Prime Minister).

Malraux seemed to wish to break away from 'official art' (although some authors would disagree; Laurent, 1982; Fumaroli, 1991). He played a role in neutralising the conservative *Académie des Beaux Arts*. This was deemed necessary since, for some people, art was still to be measured against standards of reference derived from the aesthetics of ancient Greece. In the first part of the century some held that art, by definition was dead. In the second half of the century others were able to argue, not only that it was alive, but also that it had reached a new high point in terms of the recognition of its significance.

Support for the strategy of democratisation of culture was, at this time, unanimous. But for some, especially Malraux, a clear line had to be drawn somewhere. The Minister, for example, was against the idea of democratising the Opera, and of presenting classical performances, under the aegis of his ministry, at the Palais des Sports (a sports stadium). The assembling of several paintings for an exhibition inside the Renault car factory, exasperated him. From an early date, the controversy raged even within the *Maisons de la Culture*. It is not easy to reconcile the two objectives of promoting both 'accessibility' and 'creativity' which imply sliding between the requirements of quality and popularism. This debate between 'cultural action and/or socio-cultural action,' divided the two chief administrators of the Ministry of Cultural Affairs and became a key debate throughout France in the 1970s (Poujol, 1980).

There was a further tension in the Ministry's remit between the promoting of artistic creation, and promotion of the 'enriching spirit of the arts'. In the 1960s, in the milieu of the *Maisons de la Culture*, promoting the creation of art meant bringing the public into contact with art (Poujol, 1991). If the attention of the art crusader in the early 1960s was on the public and the way in which it relates to art, by 1980, the promoters of culture seemed anxious to shift the emphasis towards giving the artist the opportunity to be creative. The *Maisons de la Culture,* hitherto concerned with generating a wider audience for the arts, now became concerned with 'promotion of artistic creativity'. It was no longer the done thing to stage Brecht for the political education of the public at large, but instead, unpublished creative works from the public, or unpublished interpretations of established works, were to be staged (Poujol, 1986). It seems therefore that there was a radical shift from promoting the artistic work to promoting the act of creativity.

By the early 1990s, however, the emphasis had returned to the work of art, not simply as an aesthetic product but also as a marketable commodity. As a consequence of this shift, cultural decision makers have been able to reassert the importance of the public in their policy, marking a return to the Malraux approach. Jack Lang, the Socialist's Minister of Culture for most of the 1980s has not departed from the line taken by his illustrious predecessor in this respect. Thus, there is a certain continuity between the policy put in place by the two ministers who occupied the same privileged position in relation to the President of the Republic. Both de Gaulle, and Mittérand were, in their own way, promoters of what some people denounce today as a 'Cultural State' (Fumaroli, 1991), that is the paternalist guardian of 'appropriate' culture.

1981-1991 Policy Development in a Period of Economic Uncertainty

The economic prosperity of France began to be seriously threatened in the 1980s and unemployment and social costs in the public sector were deemed to be far too heavy. But the left picked up the reins of power after 25 years of exile when the Socialists gained power in 1981. The government of François Mittérand affirmed that economic progress was to be subordinate to cultural aims, and substantiated his words by giving the Ministry of Culture much increased means. Contrary to the other European countries which tend to limit their public cultural expenditure in such circumstances, France has held its own original point of view in this respect. If we consider the index for central government spending on culture to be 100 in base year 1979, by 1983 it had dropped to 92 in Sweden, 94.8 in the Netherlands, 95.1 in the Federal Republic of Germany (spending of the Federal government and Länder), and risen to 109.1 in Great Britain and 207.3 in France. (This represents Ministry of Culture expenditure excluding spending on libraries, monuments and art teaching.) The gap is narrower but still significant if we count total spending on culture (by central, regional and local government): taking the index for base year 1979 as 100, the index for 1983 was 98.7 in the Federal Republic of Germany, 101.2 in Sweden, 102.6 in the Netherlands, 120.9 in Great Britain and 140.9 in France (in 1984).
(Council of Europe, 1988)

Thirty years after its creation the budget of the Ministry of Culture had increased in real terms by 250 per cent from that of 1959. The growth in its budget was 40 per cent more than the growth of the state budget as a whole, which was itself quite substantial. People, performance and education had begun to benefit less (through subsidy of artistic productions, schools of art, cultural animation) than buildings (subsidy to ancient monuments etc.). This trend has been accentuated in recent years by the costs associated with the opening of the George Pompidou Centre and the acquisition of public reading libraries by the Ministry.

At this stage we must note that the Ministry of Culture devoted nearly half of its expenditure to conservation in addition to the promotion of 'cultural heritage'. Investment was heavy in this sector. 'Grands Travaux' or extensive public works such as those of Musée d'Orsay in 1983, of the Louvre in 1985, more recently that of the Bastille-Opera, and the projected construction of the Très Grande Bibliothèque (the mega library) project, continue to burden the budget of this Ministry. Thirty per cent of the Ministry's budget is devoted to artistic production and 10 per cent to the education and training of artists and administrators.

In 1982, legislation was enacted granting a fifth week of paid vacation while at the same time, the age of retirement was to be lowered. As with other developed economies, the annual working hours of the French, have decreased, and free time is on the increase. Leisure was by no means a key theme when the Socialists were returned in 1981, though a brief attempt was made to return to the tradition of Front Populaire by creating a short lived *Ministere de Temps Libre* (Minister of Free Time). Charged with the responsibilities of the traditional ministerial department of Youth and Sport, this ministry contributed little to the organisation of leisure activities, with perhaps its single, significant act being the creation of the *Conseil National de la Vie Associative* (National Council of Voluntary Associations). This body was set up to advise the government on what should be done to facilitate the relations between the associations, either at the local level or the national level, (notably those of the Popular Education movement) and government administration. The office of the Secretary of State for Youth and Sport took over what was left of the functions in these fields when the legislation promoting decentralisation was introduced in 1982.

Leisure and the Process of Controlled Liberalisation

As we have noted in the French case there is no unified body of policy called leisure policy. Indeed, even in the form of a *cultural* policy, leisure-related policy has rarely been the subject of discussion, a fact which surprised the European Council experts when they reviewed French cultural policies (Council of Europe, 1988). Even though the vote on the budget for Youth and Culture has been a subject of parliamentary discussion, the Députées have rarely instigated a debate on the theme. Once laws have passed through the National Assembly, the Executive has been almost the sole power to govern the cultural domain. An occasion such as the development of Disneyland, has led the National Assembly to argue bitterly over economic, urban and regional issues. However during the debate there was virtually no consideration given to the consequences of such facilities for the organisation and the practice of leisure activities. Even when the Députées have debated laws concerning tourism, the 'cultural industries', or the organisation of the Olympic Games, they have concerned themselves with the problems of foreign trade or employment rather than those of leisure. Qualitative, rather than economic aspects of the problems of leisure and cultural provision are seen as part of the Administration's (the Civil Service's) responsibilities, except in those areas where they involve political decisions affecting the prestige of France. The Députées were thus very eloquent in articulating their concerns over the aesthetics of the Louvre Pyramid and over the Buren Columns of the Palais Royal. In the area of leisure the Administration operates virtually under its own discretion, if only because there is no official policy to follow. The Administration generally controls, institutes, and establishes its own rules. In the field of the organisation of leisure, through its various ministers, the preoccupation of the central state has been to guarantee the security of its citizens and of public order (Comte, Luthi, and Zananiri, 1990). However, if there is one area in which a more conscious approach to policy has been adopted, it is in the planning of professional qualifications in the leisure field, through the organised granting of diplomas.

Professionalisation of Leisure

One of the effects of the institutionalisation of the planning of leisure and the commitment of the state in this sector has been to 'professionalise' a certain number of functions which had traditionally been performed by volunteers working according to the principles of 'Popular Education'. In the early 1960s the Popular Education project was superseded by that of socio-cultural animation. A new ideology was born, reflecting rejection of the approach to education adopted in the school system. Animation consists of focusing on groups and analysing their social and cultural needs. From 1965, *Jeunesse et Sports*, traditionally the guardian of the Popular Education associations, assisted in the propagation of the idea of animation, emphasising its aims of fostering communication, and giving priority to group activity.

From the moment that demand for professional animateurs began to grow servicing all the newly created institutions such as the *Maisons des Jeunes* and *Maisons de la Culture*, the principle of professional education and training, and the awarding of diplomas to trained animateurs, became the main preoccupation of the state's central administration. In the Ministry of Culture professionalisation was given short shrift, particularly by those cultural workers working in the theatre who were keenly opposed to state interference on this issue. By contrast, *Jeunesse et Sports* promoted professionalisation heavily in the field of animation, the socio-cultural sector. Successive experiments in collaboration with the Ministry for Social Affairs gave rise to the DEFA (the State Diploma for the Practice and Administration of Animation) while the Ministry for National Education prepared its own separate degree. For the last twenty years there have been professional diplomas, as well as a whole gamut of diplomas following the training given to paid volunteers who participate in the running of leisure centres and holiday centres.

Animation as an area of work was viewed positively by the unemployed who were attracted by its novelty. A lot of young people were drawn towards animation because teaching did not appeal to them, and also because this sector at one time seemed to be teeming with jobs. Thus the separate profession of 'animateur' was born. The animateur is a social worker, who works *in* and *on* the free time of others, whether it be in the social, cultural, or socio-cultural field. Apart from this common feature it is quite difficult to define either the tasks, functions, or rank in the wage hierarchy of this type of worker. The profession does not have a fixed label, and twenty years of diploma courses have not really changed anything. The training of these animateurs is most often conducted on the job. Their training does not automatically lead to a formal qualification, indeed the obtaining of such a qualification is not the norm. This is perhaps because the diploma is awarded at the end of a rather lengthy course (with a high drop out rate) but also because the diploma is not absolutely necessary for the exercise of this profession. It is therefore with much greater difficulty than in other professions (such as social work) that the socio-cultural sector has managed to institutionalise its own area of work.

A great number of jobs in the socio-cultural sector have retained a strongly militant flavour. In most cases, training on the job seems to be preferred to formal diploma courses by employees, and because of this, the profession, which is now thirty years old, has been left by the state largely to its own devices (Poujol, 1989). Approximately 50,000 people work in this sphere, and if ancillary jobs are added, it is estimated that the professional branch of socio-cultural animation in 1986 accounted for 350,000 jobs (Jeunesse et Sports, 1990).

The French government, which has not been particularly keen on involvement in leisure as such, has been confronted by problems relating to the use of spare time by some elements of the population. In particular, the state has had to confront the serious risk of social problems as a result of social tensions in the suburbs of some cities. The authorities have sought to find solutions to the problems of embittered youth, who are unemployed, with time on their hands and little to do, and they have turned towards non-profit associations and their professional representatives, social workers and in particular social animateurs. In most cases it is quite a challenge to work out a training programme for young people in need, particularly since they are located in areas of serious unemployment. Animateurs have had to innovate in situations for which they have not been prepared. Nevertheless, experience has shown that they sometimes succeed where education professionals in particular have failed. The authorities are perfectly aware of the gaps in the training and qualification of animateurs, the curriculum having been developed at a time when social problems experienced by client groups had not been so gravely serious. Thus, if there is a sector where new elements of policy (mainly but not exclusively concerning leisure) have had to be applied, it is work with young people facing employment difficulties. Several ministerial departments have been concerned with aspects of this area, but inter-ministerial communication has always provided significant difficulties in French administration. In principle, a new *Ministere de la Ville* should be co-ordinating the efforts of several départements and those of local groups who will be the first to benefit from them.

Contrary to the position taken by *Jeunesse et Sports*, the Ministry of Culture, has only belatedly taken an interest in the problems of professional education. First it had to battle against the hold that the *Académie des Beaux Arts* had on the professional education of architects. The reforms in the field of architecture worried the Academy, but the profession of architect falls under the aegis of *l'Ordre des Architectes* (Architects Guild) and since 1978 oversight of the teaching of architecture has not been a responsibility of the Ministry of Culture. The Ministry in the late 1970s and early 1980s, turned its attention to the teaching of music, and the needs of students and teachers in the Music Colleges or Conservatoires. Since 1987, the development of artistic education has been given special priority by the ministry which devotes 10 per cent of its budget to vocational education. Special targets are the new 'professions of sound and image' as well as circus and puppet theatre, which had previously been neglected.

In the field of sport, almost all professional education is regulated by law. In 1972, a 'Brevet d'Etat' offering three diplomas was created, with each of these three diplomas corresponds to three levels of professional competence.

Thus, if we take into account the 350,000 jobs in the animation sector, a sector which is partly in the hands of public authorities, it is estimated that 2 million jobs have been generated by leisure activities. Of these 200,000 are in the sports field, 700,000 in the cultural sector and 800,000 in the world of tourism.

Significance of Cultural Industries and Leisure

Augustin Girard, the head of the Department of Surveys and Prospects of the Ministry of Culture, was the first to underline the essential role played by the cultural industries in cultural production and broadcasting. Indeed, European commentators have claimed that the report presented to UNESCO by Girard in 1972 helped to increase the awareness in other European countries of this issue (Council of Europe, 1988). In France the public authorities have intervened several times to give support to cinema production and distribution, and more recently, to support publishing. By fixing the price of books, the state sought not so much to advantage readers, but to protect the book shops and the small publishers confronted with competition from major retailers.

In the area of media policy it was the Socialist government which put an end to state monopoly of television by privatising one of the major channels (TF1) and by authorising the creation of new private ones. This has resulted in the rapid multiplication of television channels and a formidable growth in the volume of television broadcasting, which rose from under 15,000 hours in 1983 to nearly

45,000 in 1988. The idea was to aim for a strong public sector spurred by private competition, but by 1991, the audio-visual public sector had, like the government, retreated in 'a state of shock'.

> All this resulted in frenetic competition, causing an
> upheaval on the French audio-visual scene. The private
> companies have been drawing on the incessant growth of
> advertising funds, imposing their commercial logic which in
> turn translates into a despairing uniformity in programmes;
> screens are invaded by American and Japanese products -
> very often violent and aggressive, and games where money
> is the only glorified prize value. This being the case, there
> are hardly any signs of an economic equilibrium, given that
> some private channels have been accumulating operational
> deficits and the public sector has also suffered set backs
> with its audience being whittled away.
>
> (Report by the Government to Parliament, 1989)

Today the Ministry of Culture has extended its area of activity into the field of communications and it exercises control over both public and private television, a feature specific to the French system. Since 1974, an annual *cahier de charges* (a statute book of rules and terms of reference) has been imposed on the broadcasting companies for radio and television. Thus a law of 30 September 1986 requires that :

> a register of rules fixed by decree, defines the obligations
> of every one of the national broadcasting companies and
> especially of those which are linked to educational, cultural
> and social vocations.
>
> (Council of Europe, 1988)

These provisions mainly concern the advertising and broadcasting of cinema productions. Moreover a committee of experts appointed by the government was charged with making sure that a minimum programme time be reserved for productions in French, and that a minimum of programme space be devoted to cultural, educational, and consumer rights programmes. This control by outside bodies is of limited effect, since television companies are very adept at circumventing the rule book. The cultural and educational programmes have only a small audience and as such do not attract advertisers, thus these are the programmes most under threat.

Finally legislation on the development of sponsorship was enacted in order to improve the access of the cultural industry to the resources of private enterprise, through various fiscal measures. It is significant that this new legislation has had little impact on the financing of the cultural industries. Sponsorship is far from playing the enviable role it does in Anglo-Saxon countries. Moreover, where sponsorship has been made available, its pattern has mirrored, rather than compensated for, the decisions made by the cultural administration with regard to financial support from the public purse (Fumaroli, 1991).

It is obvious that the state alone cannot determine the nature of leisure provision: it needs partners. The non-profit private sector is naturally sympathetic to the policies of state subsidy, and the commercial sector has also shown an interest in leisure as an area of investment. This was the case for both the cinema and publishing sectors, and it is also true of the sports sector, which represented 1 per cent of the GDP in 1988 and 2 per cent of household consumption.

Leisure expenditure has grown in France in volume and importance, a fact which has begun to interest economists. There certainly is a market for leisure, a market for leisure goods to which cultural and leisure industries can respond, and a market whose future appears even more promising than that of the service sector generally. On one hand there are areas where the profit margin could be large, but where there is considerable international competition (as with hotels and tourism), and on the other, there are many more individualised services which seem likely to create jobs in the areas of 'health care' and 'social services', which generate lower profit margins but are less prey to international competition.

Decentralisation and Leisure Policies

One and a half centuries of French republicanism has undoubtedly given Paris the edge over the 'provinces' in terms of cultural leadership, particularly in relation to theatre, museums, and literary productions. Ever since the 1950s efforts have been made to remedy the situation. The first decentralising initiative concerning art was aimed at the theatre, when *Centres Dramatiques Nationaux* (National Theatre Centres) were established in the provinces. There are 28 of these today of which six are for young people. This is certainly a step forward in comparison with the era when the only theatrical companies to tour the provinces were Parisian ones. It is still the case that most new media productions are launched in Paris. Even if an influential regional press exists, it is not through regional press exposure that provincial companies gain recognition for cultural productions. Nor is regional television of real significance in this respect. With regard to private theatres, most of which are located in Paris, central government played a key role in the 1960s by sharing funding between the various groups promoting centralism in the private sector.

In the 1960s, immediately after the creation of the Ministry for Cultural Affairs, the *Maisons de la Culture* became a crucial means of decentralisation. For the first time *local* government became involved in cultural action projects. Even if the financial turnover of these expensive facilities was not particularly high, there is no doubt that an impetus was given to most towns, which, from then on, were to develop their own cultural policies and plans, a process accelerated by the requirements of the 1982 legislation on decentralisation. As a result centrally controlled cultural facilities went into severe decline. In February 1991, announcing the closure of the Maison de la Culture in Nevers, *Le Monde* ran the headline : 'La Ruine des Maisons Malraux':

> Created in 1962, the structure was progressively put in place with 50 per cent of the financing from the (central) state, 38 per cent from the municipality and 12 per cent from the Département's General Committee. The Maison de la Culture, had a great deal of success in the seventies, in spite of endless budget deficits and heavy overheads; the establishment employed more than 50 people. .... In Nevers, as in most other cities, the structure as a communicative nerve centre never really caught on between on one hand, local groups .... with plenty of funds, but never quite independent in the decision making process, and on the other hand, cultural professionals appointed by the Ministry at the centre, with a great deal more financial and artistic liberty.

There was no better way of expressing the institutional malaise of the *Maisons de la Culture* of which by 1991 only 10 remained of the 100 that Malraux sought to develop all over the country.

Established much earlier, the *Maisons des Jeunes* (youth centres) did not owe their existence to a central government initiative. The earliest of these associations were formed and partially united within a 'movement', that of the *Maisons des Jeunes et de la Culture* created during the Liberation period by a Socialist and protestant Député, André Philip, who was interested in institutions which would bring young people together, irrespective of their political and religious affiliations. The movement progressed and received strong backing after 1958, from the High Commission for Youth and Sport. In 1969, the same department disbanded the *Fédération Française des Maisons des Jeunes et de la Culture* (FFMJC) which was held to be too close to the Communist Party and also to be poorly managed. A new movement, the UNIREG (*Union Régionale des Maisons des Jeunes et de la Culture*), then made its appearance as an offshoot from a split with the FFMJC. Yet another movement, the FONJEP (*Fonds de la Jeunesse et de l'Education Populaire*), originally founded to finance the management of the above two competing groups, continues to survive, representing an interesting formula of co-management between public authorities, associations, and professional animateurs.

The principal protagonists and financiers of the *Maisons des Jeunes et de la Culture* have nevertheless always been local groups and associations. The latter often adopted the formula of the Youth Centres without actually being affiliated to a socio-political movement. These Youth Centres were typical of the establishments abandoned by the state, under the framework of the law on decentralisation. In principle these Centres were intended for youth, but for reasons of convenience, or for economic management on the part of local groups, they became centres for all, but with women in a clear majority.

Another effect of decentralisation for this type of cultural facility has been that they suffer from political instability. When municipalities change their political colours following a local election, the relationship between a youth centre and its municipality often undergoes a corresponding change, swinging from centrally delegated management to that of a local association, and vice-versa, with no permanent management arrangements as there had been under the old centralised system. Centralisation did have some advantages in this respect.

According to European experts, it is in the field of music that progress in decentralisation has been most apparent. France was very late to enter the musical domain in terms of state support, and the situation, as the administrator under Malraux was to discover, was deplorable. Marcel Landowski thus conceived a 10 year plan which was followed fairly closely.

> From 1975 to 1986 the number of approved and subsidised
> music schools rose from 40 to 145, the number of national
> music schools from 39 to 96, and the number of national
> conservatoires in the regions from 21 to 31. The state
> contributes to the running costs of all these establishments.
> The number of musical students has increased considerably
> in all musical areas, as has the practice of music by amateurs
> .... [however] .... The major increase in the means devoted
> to decentralising music .... has not altered the privileged
> status of Paris in this field, quite the contrary.
> (Council of Europe, 1988)

With regard to public reading, France was well behind its neighbours and the English model of state support for libraries was much admired. Britain spent as much on libraries as France did on theatre. According to UNESCO statistics, in France there were only 1,026 libraries as against 2,295 in Sweden, 13,763 in the Federal Republic of Germany, and 13,597 in the United Kingdom. The per capita figure for public libraries was ten times higher in Denmark, six times higher in Sweden and The Netherlands and seven times higher in the United Kingdom. However, the situation has improved over the last fifteen years. The experts conclude that:

> In fact library space has doubled staff has tripled and a
> great number of books added to the collections. At the
> same time the number of users and the number of books
> loaned have more than doubled. In order to encourage the
> supply of books in communes without municipal libraries,
> in each of 100 Départements there are central lending
> libraries, using mobile library vehicles.
> (Council of Europe, 1988)

Special emphasis was given, in state support for sport, to high performance sports (Comte, Luthi, and Zananiri, 1990). France, the birthplace of Pierre de Coubertin, hosted the 1992 Winter Olympics and public authorities sought not only to encourage, but also to control sports organisations. A 1984 law redefined the institutional framework of sport in France. The Ministry of Youth and Sport was to support the training and the promotion of top performance athletes, and the training of sports teachers and sports executives in six national schools. The National Olympic and Sports Committee was to manage sports activities by taking responsibility for the sports federations and other sports groups.

In France, in 1984, there were more than 150,000 sports associations with 12 million members and 1 million volunteer workers. Indeed the voluntary sector in sport is experiencing considerable growth and the figures for the 1990s are likely to be much higher. The Secretary of State for Youth and Sport is responsible for competitive sport, but also has a watching brief in respect of recreational participation in sport. The government insists on the use of professionally qualified staff, though the state approved Sports Federations manage their own respective sectors. Some categories of sporting activity are not under the responsibility of non-profit associations, but are the prerogative of private enterprise as is the case of ten-pin bowling and squash. A network of laws relating to the development of physical education and sport provides a policy framework for French sport, and this legislative framework lends itself to developing sports participation as well as to the promotion of the sports élite. It is indeed in the field of sports that one can most readily identify a national policy for leisure activities. Prior to the 1982 legislation on decentralisation, the central state, by agreement with local groups, planned national priorities for sport and managed them by means of special budgets. Since 1982, the central state has allocated annually a global sum for facilities to local and regional governments, which have been free to manage the funds as they choose. In this framework, the regions play a role in conceiving and co-ordinating policy, while the départements and the communes execute policy.

The sports world, however, is not immune from political storms:

Political currents, directly or indirectly, play a predominant role in the framework of important sports events. In the local world, even at the most elementary level of sports activity, a subtle game is being played, between associations and their organisers on the one hand, and their political representatives on the other. Local sports activities which necessitate increased financial support, go into a 'strategic period' of negotiation and 'contractualisation' of fund allocation, and, if necessary, involve the population of the commune in the bargaining process. Problems linked to the allocation of subsidies, free use of halls and stadiums, to the professional recruitment of athletes to municipal jobs etc., frequently arise. Debates confronting the parties for and against the 'municipalisation' of sports do not often mean very much. They take place around issues such as whether subsidies should be direct or indirect, whether the insignia of a club should incorporate the adjective 'municipal' etc. Despite such debate, the role and influence in sport of municipalities, whether controlled by the right or the left, is certainly on the increase. Subsidies allocated to sports associations, availability and usage of facilities provided by the commune, policies concerning the organisation of, and provision for, sport reinforce the dominant role played by local groups, the commune and the General Committee (of the départements) in particular.

(Callède, 1987)

In the domain of leisure activity for children the state exercises considerable control, most notably in relation to the organisation of holiday centres and day leisure centres without residential facilities (*Centres de Loisir Sans Hebergement*) (Comte *et al.*, 1990). These latter centres play a social role which goes far beyond that of planning suitable activities, since they also take care of children outside school hours. It is mostly thanks to this type of institution that many French women have been able to take up paid employment outside the home more easily than some of their European counterparts. According to the State Secretariat for Youth and Sport, a census at the end of the 1990s showed that more than 38,000 leisure centres were frequented by 3 million children between the ages of 6 and 14. Their numbers seem likely to increase in the years to come. sixty per cent of the *Centres de Loisir Sans Hebergement* are run by voluntary associations with 40 per cent run by municipal authorities. The state has instituted formal examinations awarding vocational qualifications for the professionals who run these establishments as well as for the voluntary workers who provide children's activities. The finance is provided jointly by the state (through the Caisse d'Allocations Familiales) and by the local groups, but families also contribute up to a quarter of the finance, generally in proportion to their ability to pay.

Less affected by decentralisation, and abandoned by the public authorities, the *Centres des Vacances* have not followed the same pattern. The French tend to go away on vacation more often and also take their children with them. Thus the holiday centres are being used much less frequently than was the case ten years ago, apart from camps for adolescents. Nearly a million children spend a part of their holidays there. Besides the associations and municipalities, there are the *Comités d'Entreprises* (work committees) which organise this sort of vacation and are required to follow the same rules, in particular those concerning the use of professionally qualified staff. All the camps organised by youth movements come under the same legislation, particularly those concerning safety for children. The scouting movement has adapted to these rules as best it could, but the camps in general have lost their appeal even though it is in this institutional framework that camps for young people have been most successful in the past.

Policies for Towns

Every town has a policy for leisure and culture in one form or another. This policy varies according to the awareness of the electorate of the issues and the resources of the communes, and hence according to the social composition of the town. Moreover, policy commitments are largely those inherited from previous administrations. Revenue costs for leisure and culture vary according to whether significant funds are used for the management of local cultural heritage. Castles, monuments, and museums are funded as aspects of cultural heritage; while the following facilities also attract cultural funding - cultural centres, youth centres, social centres, theatres, stadiums, swimming pools, libraries. Indeed, 'the creation of these cultural avenues is a fundamental act of cultural policy' (Gilbert and Saez, 1982). This is true as much of the Pompidou centre in Paris as it is of the *Salle des Fêtes* (community centre) in a little village in the provinces. It is true of the youth centres, cultural centres and social centres. Almost everywhere public involvement in the construction of building facilities preceded the elaboration of policies. As Augustin Girard (1978) has pointed out 'The first temptation for a Mayor, following election, is to start funding facilities'. This was still true even in the early 1990s. We may condemn the extraordinary waste of some of the land in public ownership which has been turned into leisure parks (e.g. Disneyland, which is not altogether viable in France), or into sports and winter sports facilities (often totally disproportionate to the size of the commune in which they are located). Indeed, the prospect of the Winter Olympics and the construction of hotels for it, have led some communes to the brink of financial disaster.

In the field of sports facilities, tennis has hit a high peak in popularity. 7,862 communes had constructed at least one tennis court between 1980 and 1988. By 1991, one commune in three had an open air tennis court against one in seven, eight years earlier; and 62 per cent of the population was able to participate in this sport, in its own commune.

Several cities are now well known for their cultural and socio-cultural policies. Grenoble, for example, is a city with 400 animateurs. Rennes gained a reputation for innovation by creating a Social and Cultural Bureau, bringing together the voluntary associations to share out the 'global funds' voted in by the municipality; while Le Havre gained its reputation after giving birth, almost by chance, to the first Maison de la Culture (Poujol, 1989). The three cities have very varied political histories. Grenoble innovated through its associations, appealing to the inhabitants of some areas to participate in the formulation of cultural policy. This did not prevent the Socialist-led local government from losing the elections in 1983, when power passed to a centre-right group. In Rennes, a Christian Democrat majority transferred its power to a non-communist left grouping without causing any notable change in cultural policy. In Le Havre, a city with a significant working class population, a Communist group took over from a right wing administration in 1965, and since that date (up to the time of writing), the Communists had presided over management of the cultural and socio-cultural institutions in most of the municipalities within the city. Le Havre, with its share of cultural expenditure protected within the municipal budget, was committed to increasing per capita expenditure between 1978 and 1984, and by the end of the 1980s was very close to Rennes in terms of expenditure levels. Grenoble, however, even exceeded these levels in its expenditure. Thus, these three cities, with very little social and political history in common, are among those (such as Bordeaux and Annecy) which are most noted for the level of their investment in cultural policy. The case of these three cities illustrates the claim made by Augustin Girard, that the link between political control and cultural policy programmes is difficult to establish.

> When we try to find out if the cultural policy of a city
> changes according to the political shades of its municipality,
> to its political leanings, or according to whether or not it is a
> university town, and whether it is tourist oriented or not, or
> whether it is in the hinterland of a metropolis or not; it is
> indeed curious that we find no clues to help link a certain
> cultural policy to a certain political trend, so that we cannot
> say that there is indeed a typical policy for a suburban area,
> or that there is typical policy for a university town. For the
> purpose of budgetary analysis these distinctions between
> different types of communes cannot be translated into
> figures.

(Girard, 1978)

It would seem that rather than local political complexion, the weight of past history, and the necessary political stability to push projects forward are crucial factors. Equally important is the presence of determined political actors within the municipal framework. The role of the Mayor and that of her / his assistant are of primary importance. As for management choices to be made, these do not appear to correlate with any political phenomena. Both municipalities controlled by the right and communist controlled municipalities are just as likely as socialist authorities to favour the 'municipalisation' of cultural facilities and animateurs, while the management of public cultural facilities by voluntary associations may regularly be found in socialist municipalities. It has been observed, however, that in case of a change in the political control of a municipality, the new group in power is likely to favour the type of management which is exactly the opposite of its predecessor. Thus, in those municipalities with an unstable majority, the professional life of the animateurs, especially that of leisure animateurs, is an uneasy one because of the potential shift in their professional status in the wake of each election. This situation is of particular concern for socio-cultural institutions, such as the *Maison des Jeunes et de la Culture*. Municipal establishments such as libraries and museums, however, enjoy greater stability because although they are staffed by local government personnel (or state civil servants in the case of national museums) there is less variation in the way they are managed.

Cultural Policy and Practice

In 1988, the Ministry of Culture conducted its third survey on the *Cultural Practices of the French (1990)*. In this publication the results of three studies made in 1973, 1981, and 1988, were made available, permitting an evaluation of the development of cultural and leisure practices over a period of fifteen years. The study illustrates, for example, that appreciation of music had diffused throughout all levels of population. It would seem that technological progress in the electronic reproduction of music, and its low price, have triggered off a growth in listening to music (modern as well as classical), far greater than any which might have been stimulated by government music policies. Nevertheless, even in 1988, more than half the French population aged fifteen and over had never been to a single concert, nor to a dance performance, or a play, or even to an amusement park or a painting exhibition. The democratisation of culture, often invoked by Malraux to justify cultural policy, is far from having been achieved. The audience for theatre, music, museums and exhibitions was for the most part better educated than the majority of the population, but, as the level of education of the French rises, so the potential market for such cultural practices seems likely to grow.

Some institutions such as la Comédie Française and l'Opéra of Paris, exist because they contribute directly to French cultural prestige. The Opéra, for example, has seen its budget systematically increased, permitting expansion in personnel, among the orchestra, the singers and the dancers in the ballet, and facilitating the booking of international stars. In 1986, its subsidy represented half of that provided for all the theatres in France. The price of tickets (which are considered to be expensive) is less than one tenth of the real cost price. The new Bastille-Opera is faced with similar problems, but this also is regarded as a question of prestige for France, and therefore as worthy of support.

Apart from the massive increase in listening to music at home or in watching television, the studies indicate that:

> many more French people went out in the evening (and went out far more frequently) in 1988 than in 1973. ....

socialising, and activities outside the family home are
generally on the rise. We must make a note of the fact that
traditional cultural venues and events (plays, concerts), have
benefited much less from this increasing inclination of the
French to go out in the evenings, than, for example,
restaurants or discotheques.

(Ministère de la Culture, 1990)

When introducing the results of the study (either because of
methodological or political reservations) the researchers thought fit to
advise caution, emphasising that

it would be a major mistake to use a survey such as this as a
tool by which to measure the impact of cultural policy.

But further they add in their conclusion that this study is :

a demand for the redefinition of public policies at the dawn
of the twenty first century. These policies sometimes
conceived a quarter of a century ago, modified since, but
only marginally so, often seem inconsistent with new habits
which have evolved faster, moving at the speed of social
transformation itself. Of course cultural policy does not
necessarily have to follow to shades of social change; first
and foremost it has to initiate creativity, and to memorise
and record its own evolution. But it cannot continue to
survive if it lags behind certain current lifestyles.

(Ministère de la Culture, 1990)

Table 2.1 Changing Rates of Participation in Cultural Activities 1967 & 1987-8

	1967	1987-8
Watching television everyday :	51%	82%
Reading a book	32%	31%
Going to theatre at least once a year	18%	21%
Going to a restaurant once a month	10%	25%
Visiting a museum in the past year	10%	32%
Visiting a monument in the past year	30%	41%

source: Ministère de la Culture (1990)

Notwithstanding the understated attitudes of the researchers vis-a-
vis their own ministry, the results from this type of study can be used
to answer (at least tentatively) some questions concerning the

efficiency of some cultural policies. It seems safe to argue, for example, that without a policy in favour of theatre, its audience would have been smaller and without a policy in favour of reading and public libraries the readership would have been smaller still. The results of consecutive studies underline the growth in these and other areas of cultural activity. The figures in Table 2.1 represent activity levels in 1987-1988.

Indeed, assistance given to museums and historical monuments has been justified as having significantly increased public usage. With regard to cinema, the Ministry of Culture has achieved some real success. The state has assisted both film production and the installation of multi-screen cinemas. Moreover, the Ministry of Culture contributed to the costs of the reproduction of films so that cinemas in the provinces might show them at the same time as those in Paris. The Minister, Jack Lang, declared to *Le Monde* on the 9 March 1991 :

> The decline in cinema going has been arrested. Stemmed in
> 1988, it levelled off in 1989, and, for the first time in eight
> years attendance grew in 1990. Another positive indication
> is the recovery of the national cinema market share, from
> 34 per cent to 37 per cent.

This increase in the audience for cinema is not a feature of cultural life of Paris, since cinema attendances have dropped by 2.5 per cent in the capital. The increase in attendances has thus occurred solely in the provinces.

Thus, in spite of the fact that it is impossible to separate 'spontaneous' changes in social behaviour from those due to policies aimed at changing them, we can infer that the action of public authority has overall had some positive effects. The role of the state in conserving the artistic heritage has probably been significant.

Prospects for the Future

In France, perhaps more than in other cultures, the notion of 'work' has always been *the* central standard of reference, with leisure a 'residual' corollary. A state policy worthy of the name had, therefore, to reflect the importance of work, and thus a series of measures were deemed necessary for its organisation and planning. There have been significant worker victories in the struggle to reduce work time, dating back to the introduction of legislation in 1941 relating to the working hours for children and women. In 1936 the 40 hour week was achieved, with more recently, some success in relation to reducing the age of retirement. In the period of Socialist control, from the early 1980s to the 1990s, further reductions in retirement age have not been achieved, though a fifth week of paid leave was obtained. Indeed, many categories of workers have gained even more leisure time. However, French trade unions have not been predominantly motivated by objectives concerning free time and leisure, any more than their English counterparts have.

> In France increasingly employers have tended to take the
> initiative in experimenting with new working time patterns,
> thus moving closer to the British system, but with
> government support in the form of subsidies for schemes
> which lead to job creation. As a result the trade unions have
> been forced to rethink their position, and they have begun
> to show more interest in flexitime and in the development
> of part-time work and job-sharing as a means of reducing
> unemployment.
>
> (Hantrais, 1987)

Today, the value attached to work per se, is not the motivating principle of our Western societies in general, nor of France in particular. If the creation of a Ministry of Free Time failed to put leisure squarely on the policy agenda, it did at least seem possible to make policy statements relating to 'free time'. Thus a report for the Ninth National Plan in 1983 was able to ask:

> Considering that paid employment is in the process of
> losing its raison d'être in an individual's existence and social
> life, where is the new balance between life in work and life
> outside work to be found and fostered ?
>
> (Jeunesse et Sports, 1990)

Free time rose on a weekly average, from 24 hours 16 minutes in 1975 to 28 hours 28 minutes in 1985; whereas work time dropped from 28 hours 7 minutes to 24 hours 44 minutes. We seem to be witnessing what Marcuse termed an 'historic inversion'. However, it is not this aspect of things which is preoccupying policy makers. They are seriously worried about that other form of 'spare time', unemployment, which represents a growing burden to the tax payer.

Unemployment, which affected 2 per cent of the population of working age 25 years ago, now concerns more than 10 per cent. This is due to a decrease in the volume of jobs available, as well as the increase in the number of people (particularly women) wishing to enter the job market. It is also a reflection of the failure of vocational training, to adapt to new systems of production. On the outlook for the year 2000, forecasters predict up to 20 per cent unemployment, with a stable but ageing population, and estimate that there will be a 2:1 ratio, in the year 2010 of economically active to economically inactive persons (Jeunesse et Sports, 1990).

At the start of President Mittérand's tenure, emphasis was placed on the adjustment of working hours, and a better distribution of employment. This policy was disappointing particularly in respect of attempts to reduce working hours and as such it was abandoned. Another problem was that of the deficit in the welfare system, a fact which discouraged the planners from lowering the retirement age for all, since they wished to retain as many economically active members of the population as possible. Finally by adopting the *Revenu Minimum d'Insertion* (a minimum income level), they opted for social provision for the unemployed.

As in all Western countries, the unemployment problem is a major one, and public authorities are under pressure to diminish costs. The employment sector for leisure activities representing 10 per cent of the active population is of considerable importance, and the public sector is therefore turning its attention to this sphere of activities. The state is interested in tourism particularly as it has the potential to earn overseas income.

France is the fourth biggest country for tourism after the United States, Spain, and Italy. In 1987 France welcomed 36.7 million international tourists, a figure which represents 10.1 per cent of the world market. With Europe in perspective the number of international tourists has tended to decrease. Even so forecasts have been optimistic, and the National Council for Tourism has provided for an increase of 50 per cent to 60 per cent of foreign tourists by the year 2000. .....

Without giving up the funding of work relating to public monuments aimed at generating national prestige, France has renounced policies for social and socio-cultural facilities, which had generally been the responsibility of the central state. With its 100,000 sports facilities and 20,000 socio-cultural facilities representing a considerable financial burden on the communes, France is perceived as approaching saturation point. The future seems less likely to incorporate public involvement in social facilities aimed at creating interaction between members of the community, or in facilities meant for the occupation of leisure. It is anticipated that, by the year 2000, almost all public need in this field will be amply satisfied, and that, from then on, the multipurpose community centres and halls will fall into disuse, only to be relegated to use for social action or social service.

(Jeunesse et Sports, 1990)

In the late 1980s and early 1990s violent events in the periphery of large towns and cities, involving young 'delinquents' could well draw the public authorities into contributing to the expenses of the communes, for new facilities designed to occupy these young people in their free time. In 1991 the new Ministre de la Ville announced measures to install sports facilities to 'prevent delinquency'. As Joffre Dumazedier strongly and appropriately emphasised; leisure today is at the core of change in everyday life, it is not just a mere complement to work (Comte, Luthi, and Zananiri, 1990). These remarks have not yet been taken on board by those who govern France in the early

1990s. Perhaps those in charge of committees closer to the local inhabitants understand them better. It continues to be the case that public authorities have other priorities, and the weight of tradition and ideology does not suggest that the French will put a leisure policy per se in place in the immediate future. Paradoxically, however, some policies, with objectives other than those of leisure, have been able to influence the practice of leisure and seem likely to continue to do so.

REFERENCES

Callède, J. P. (1987) *L'esprit sportif*, Bordeaux : Maison des Sciences de l'Homme de l'Aquitaine-Presses Universitaires de Bordeaux.

Comte, F., Luthi, J. J. and Zananiri, G. (1990) *'L'Univers des Loisirs'*, Paris: Letouzey & Ané.

Council of Europe (1988) *La politique culturelle de la France,* Paris: Conseil de l'Europe-Documentation Française.

Dumazedier, J. (1967) *Toward a Society of Leisure,* New-York: Free Press.

Fumaroli, M. (1991) *L'Etat culturel, Essai sur une religion moderne,* Paris: Editions de Fallois.

Gilbert, C. and Saez G. (1982) *L'Etat sans qualités*, Paris: Presses Universitaires de France.

Girard A. (1978) 'Les politiques culturelles communales: une compétence nouvelle', *Les Cahiers de l'Animation,* 20, 1-14.

Hantrais, L. (1987) 'The implications of Comparative Research into Leisure for Social Policy; a Franco-British Example', *Loisir et Société / Society and Leisure,* 10, (2), 323-335.

Jeunesse et Sports (1990) *Le temps et rien d'autre*, Paris: La Documentation Française.

Laurent, J. (1982) *Arts et Pouvoirs en France de 1793 à 1981*, Saint-Etienne: Université de Saint-Etienne, travaux XXXIV.

Ministère de la Culture (1990) *Nouvelle enquête sur les pratiques culturelles des Français en 1989*, Paris: Direction de l'administration générale, Département des études et de la prospective du Ministère de la Culture: La Documentation Française.

Poujol, G. (1980) 'Action culurelle, action socio-culturelle', *Les Cahiers de l'animation,* no. 30, 25-40 Marly-le-Roi.

Poujol, G. (1986) 'La bonne volonté créatrice', *Les Cahiers de l'Animation,* no. 54, 3-22, Marly-le-Roi.

Poujol, G. (1989) *Profession: Animateur,* Toulouse: Editions Privat.

Poujol, G. (1991) *Eléments pour la recherche sur la création du Ministère des Affaires culturelles,* Paris: Rapport au Ministère de la Culture et de la Communication.

Rapport du Gouvernement au Parlement (1989) *L'avenir du secteur audiovisuel public,* Paris : La Documentation Française.

BIBLIOGRAHICAL SUPPLEMENT

Dumazedier, J. (1974) *Sociology of Leisure,* New York-Amsterdam: Elsevier.

Kamphorst, T.J. and Parker, S. (1987) 'Horizons sociologiques/ Sociological Horizons', *Loisir et Société / Society and Leisure,* 10, 2, Quebec, Canada.

Samuel, N. (1984) *Le Temps Libre, un temps social,* Paris: Klincksieck, Les Méridiens.

Samuel, N. (1984) 'The origins of the movement of Free Time in France'. in H.E. Olson (ed.) Actes du Congrés de ELRA *: Leisure Research,* Upsala: Université d'Upsala.

Samuel, N. (1986) 'History and Sociology of Free Time in France'; *International Review of Social Science,* Vol. XXXVIII, 107.

Chapter 3

Leisure Policy in the Netherlands

Hugo van der Poel

Introduction

In the Netherlands, many things are not what they seem at first sight, and social developments are often 'out of tune' with those in neighbouring countries. To start with, people are probably more familiar with the name 'Holland' than 'the Netherlands'. Holland was once the most powerful province of the Republic of the Seven United Provinces - the Netherlands. More than 150 years ago, the province of Holland ceased to exist when it was divided into North and South Holland. At present, the country is neither a republic nor a federation (as the plural 'Netherlands' might suggest) but a constitutional monarchy. Amsterdam is the capital of the country, but the seat of government is in The Hague. Ever since the sixteenth century the Netherlands has been highly urbanised, and today it is one of the most densely populated countries in the world. However the largest city, Amsterdam, has a little less than 700,000 inhabitants, and there are only three other cities with more than 200,000 inhabitants (Rotterdam, The Hague and Utrecht). Despite its population density, the Netherlands is one of the three biggest exporters of agricultural products in the world. Although some of the world's largest multinational industrial conglomerates - Shell, Unilever, Philips, Akzo - have a Dutch background, a relatively small proportion of the population is employed in their industries.

These peculiarities have affected the country's policies in general, and its leisure policies in particular, which in turn have often developed idiosyncratic traits and reinforced some of these 'local' peculiarities. A classic example is the Dutch broadcast system, heavily rooted in religious / political 'pillars', another curious feature of Dutch

41

society (see page 48 below). To be able to grasp some of the
institutionalised complexities of the relationship between local and
central government and their respective leisure policies, it is necessary
to go back to the formative years of what was to become the Dutch
nation-state, that is, the 'Eighty Years War' with Spain, bridging the
sixteenth and seventeenth centuries. In the case of the Netherlands,
developments in this relationship are very much interwoven with
changing international contexts. Insight into this interconnectedness
may help to clarify the preference expressed by Dutch representatives,
ever since the establishment of forms of European integration, for the
development of supranational structures rather than intergovernmental structures, and the Dutch preference for the 'subsidiarity
principle' in the constitution of the relations between state and society.

State, Economy and Culture: the Historical Context of Dutch Leisure Patterns and Policies

The Republic of the Seven United Provinces

Looking closely at the roots of Dutch politics and policies, it is clear
that the Dutch have a long tradition of meetings, of bargaining and
compromising, and of forging and ending coalitions, in both internal
and external relations. It is part of the overall 'burgher' character of
Dutch society, in which the economic interests, the values and the
cultural preferences of the urbanised and relatively well-educated
middle class prevail. The traditional view of the Dutch burgher is that
'he' is interested in a stable and well ordered context that leaves him
free to mind his own business. He dislikes despotism and puts a heavy
emphasis on privacy. Behaviour should not be guided by force, but
by moral standards provided through religion and/or education. In
particular, the Dutch burgher is said to display an almost
schizophrenic double personality, alternating between an idealistic
preacher and a pragmatic merchant.

Politically, the Republic was a loose federation. The 'Stadhouder',
or governor of the provinces, was in the service of the provinces as
captain-general of the army. Although the 'stadhouderschap'
remained in the hands of the Princes of the House of Orange who had
some nomination rights, they never gained enough influence to
constitute a powerful monarchy of their own. The Republic even saw
two long periods with no stadhouder appointed. Because the
stadhouder had little land himself and had no strong nobility to
support him, particularly in the most important provinces of Holland
and Zeeland, he had to rely on the assistance and support of the
provinces and the cities. The 'City Boards' held a pre-eminent place in
Dutch politics. Cities were centres of wealth and contained large
segments of the population. In 1500, about 16 per cent of the
population lived in cities in the northern provinces and 21 per cent in

cities in the southern provinces. In Holland, more than half of the population lived in cities. At that time, the urban population as a whole in Europe represented only 5.6 per cent of the whole population (and a mere 2 per cent in the British Isles). By 1700 the northern provinces had reached an urbanisation rate of 30 per cent, still more than three times as high as in the rest of Europe, including Great Britain (De Vries, 1984; 't Hart, 1989).

Besides the sheer *number* of burghers, it is also important to note their dispersal over a great many cities. Although Amsterdam was the biggest and most powerful city, it never succeeded in gaining full national supremacy, such as that boasted by London and Paris. Whenever it sought to do so, it was immediately confronted with coalitions of the other cities, provinces and the Stadhouder. Because of the lack of a centralising force, each city could develop its own strengths and its own character. Leiden was granted the first Dutch university (in 1575) and had a strong textile industry. The Hague, a village which did not have city rights, developed into the bureaucratic centre - it was chosen as the seat of the 'Staten-Generaal', the governing body of the Republic, to avoid rivalry among the major cities. In naval politics this rivalry led to the formation of no less than five admiralties based in various parts of the country. Utrecht remained a religious and cultural centre and Gouda was the major inland market place. The cities with access to the sea all specialised in different trades. Amsterdam had strong links with the Baltic and Mediterranean states; Middelburg and Rotterdam with France and England, and Hoorn and Enkhuizen concentrated on fisheries and northern trade ('t Hart, 1989).

All these specialisations gave the cities different interests, for instance concerning tax regulations, the relative amount of money going to the army and the navy and whom to declare war or seal peace with. This is important because at one time 58 cities had obtained voting rights in the provinces and thus, indirectly, in the Staten-Generaal. The voting rights were privileges the cities had won during the war against the Spanish, in return for their financial support. Internal politics were thus very much a game of balancing powers between the cities, the provinces, the Staten-Generaal, various other central Colleges and the stadhouder. Once they (or at least most of them) were united in a common cause, they tried to play the same game in their foreign policies; siding with one party against another, paying rebels to keep their enemies busy, and negotiating money for influence. Lacking an authoritarian centre, the unification of all the different interests was often difficult and provisional. For instance, the relatively untrammelled accumulation of merchant capital being the primary source of Dutch prosperity, contradictory effects arose when the rate of capital accumulation was higher when the money was invested abroad than in the Netherlands itself. Due to the relatively volatile nature of merchant capital - compared to the more fixed nature of industrial capital, and the political influence of the more wealthy merchant-families on their city's politics, it often happened that commercial interests prevailed above 'national interests'. Dutch bankers and merchants financed and provided weapons and fleets for enemy states, such as the Portuguese who fought the Dutch West India Company in Brazil, and were heavily involved in both the industrialisation of England and the Independence War in the USA (Kennedy, 1988). This is not to say that the seventeenth century 'state apparatus' did not play an important role in the establishment of the Republic as a mercantile power. Perhaps it is better to say that, given the absence of an absolute ruler with his own political interests, the merchants had a relatively large influence on the state's policies, and could direct it to support their interests, as when the Scheldt to Antwerp Canal was closed off, monopolies to the East and West India Company were granted and military assistance given to these companies (Israel, 1991). In fact, what we see here is a predecessor or non-confessional (non-religious based) form of the 'subsidiarity principle'; the idea that the state has a limited 'raison d'être' and that it should support the plural initiatives of the burghers for matters of public interest rather than stressing the primacy of state intervention.

Writing about Dutch culture in the Golden Age, Schama stresses that this culture was not ...

> the culture of all Dutch men and women, neither was it the property of the very few. It was shared, in large measure, by that very broad stratum of the population between artisans and trading merchants that in England would have been known as 'the middling sort'; in Holland the 'brede middenstand'. It described a world that was predominantly urban, surprisingly literate for its time; one that nourished a market hungry for prints, engraved histories, poems and polemics. It worked and rested in what, by seventeenth century standards, was a remarkably stable society. And it was stable in great measure because it was well fed and, most important of all for this overwhelmingly residential culture, decently housed.
>
> (Schama, 1987, p. 4)

Not surprisingly then, Dutch culture is characterised by the absence of 'grands travaux' and influential Maecenatism and by the relative importance of the performing and 'marketable' arts. While absolutist rulers built castles and patronised playwrights and composers, the Dutch burghers built plain churches and weigh-houses, refined their houses and bought pamphlets, books and paintings (Boekman, 1989, pp. 6-7). They were eager to read news about political and economic events, such as new developments in the war against Spain, that might affect their businesses. At the same time, the translation of the Bible into Dutch and many intense religious disputes proved to be an enormous stimulus for book production.

When Amsterdam became the hub of contemporary trade, it also took over Venice's place as the international news centre (Schneider and Hemels, 1979). Printing of pamphlets, newspapers, maps and books became an important industry. The first newspapers in English and French were printed in Amsterdam, as were the books of scholars like Descartes, who had to deal with censorship in their home countries. Painting, theatre and music were art forms that led to products that could be commodified relatively easily. This early commodification of the arts and the tolerance towards its diversified forms and contents have to be taken against the backdrop of the complicated balance of power in the major cities. Not all burghers were easy going humanists, but groups such as the Calvinist preachers simply never succeeded in gaining overall power. What could not be printed in one city or province, could probably be printed in another as centralised state control was absent. Printing houses took advantage of these differences. Proclamations against books such as the English and Spanish texts that defended anti-Dutch policies were evaded in all manner of ways, when publishers saw a market for these books at home and/or abroad. For instance, it was debatable as to whether 'Lugdunum' was Latin for Leiden or Lyon ? (De Vrankrijker, 1981, p. 165).

Unification and Industrialisation, 1795-1945

The second half of the eighteenth century saw growing political unrest, fed by economic stagnation. In 1781 an anonymous pamphlet 'Aan het volk van Nederland' (To the people of the Netherlands) heavily attacked stadhouder Willem V for gaining too much power and losing the war against the United Kingdom. It indicated the rise of the 'Patriotic Movement' that criticised the old political order for its inertia, short-sighted localism, patronage to the detriment of talented people and non-patriotic behaviour. The Patriots gained in importance and took over the power of the regents in the cities and of the gentry in the more rural areas of the eastern Provinces. Regents, particularly in Holland, who had first supported the Patriots against the stadhouder, withdrew their support and subsequently, in 1787, the 'old political order' succeeded in persuading the Prussian King to intervene and restore them to their former pre-eminence. Further unrest culminated in the 'Bataafse Revolutie' (Batavian Revolution) of 1795, an event which was itself soon overshadowed in the Netherlands by the impact of the Napoleonic wars (Schama, 1977).

The period 1795-1813 is now commonly referred to as the French period, a period which brought political and legal unification, the definite loss of the status of great (colonial) power and the beginning of a reorientation of the economy. In the aftermath of the French period, the Kingdom of the Netherlands was created, containing most parts of present Luxembourg, Belgium and the Netherlands. The British favoured a unitarian state, large and strong enough to contain the French in the north. This was made a precondition for the return of a part of the colonies of the former Republic, which Great Britain had conquered during the Napoleonic wars (Kossman, 1976). Although there was now a clearly designated state, it is probable that a 'Dutch nation', as such, did not exist until the latter half of the century. The partition of the southern Provinces in 1830 and the recognition of Belgium by King Willem I helped to create some national feeling in the northern Netherlands, but it would be decades before cultural-political unity would take shape (Knippenberg and de Pater, 1988).

The Patriots had formulated their critique of the old Republic and its perceived economic decline (the decline was more relative than absolute) in political and moral terms. The real problem, however, was that the Republic, particularly Amsterdam, had lost its use for the expanding world economy, because the staple-market and its many related activities had become obsolete. The staple-market had been the source of the economic supremacy of the Republic for most part of the seventeenth century, making it the first nucleus of the emerging world economy (De Vries, 1984; Wallerstein, 1978). But it was no longer needed, as concrete markets had been replaced by abstract markets, where producers dealt with merchants and retailers with the help of modern communication techniques and more efficient and reliable modes of transportation; production was industrialised and mass consumption had developed (Brugmans, 1961, pp. 66-68). Moreover, the struggle against the increasing naval power of Great Britain and the landward threat of France, the adoption of mercantile policies by these countries and their increasing control over the Channel had drained the Republic of its resources (Kennedy, 1988, pp. 112-114). It would take the Dutch more than a century before they had more or less adjusted themselves to a world dominated by industrial capitalism, in which they could at best play second fiddle. Up until 1870, the nineteenth century was very bleak, with growing poverty, a decreasing middle class and a lack of cultural initiative. This was not so much due to industrialisation, but rather to a *lack* of industrialisation. Industrialisation only took off in 1870, in harbours, as a result of the industrial development of the Ruhr area of Germany (Rotterdam) and the more intensive exploitation of the colonies (Amsterdam). Textile-factories and engineering-works were founded in the rural areas in the eastern and southern parts of the country, which had finally become accessible by railways across the large rivers, and which provided abundant cheap labour.

During the eighteenth century the regency was influenced by Franco-Italian aristocratic tastes. The regents lived a distinguished and respectable way of life, but within the confines of a burgher lifestyle and did not develop a separate elite culture. The more powerful patricians were particularly proud of their burgher ancestry and scorned the aristocratic lifestyle. When the monarchy was established at the beginning of the nineteenth century, some of the Amsterdam patricians turned down the offer to be raised to peerage (De Jong, 1987, p. 178).

The second half of the eighteenth century saw the establishment of various societies, such as the Holland Society for Sciences (1752), the Society for Netherlands Literature (1766) and the Society Felix Meritis, which patronised a concert hall in Amsterdam from 1788 onwards. In 1784 patriotic burghers founded the 'Maatschappij tot 't Nut van het Algemeen' (The Society for Public Welfare), which had as one of its central aims the education of the common people to the status of respectable and responsible citizens. In these burgher initiatives, particularly in those of the Patriots, one can see the first signs of emerging cultural policies. The 1798 Constitution of the Batavian Republic decreed the establishment of several Agencies, among which was an Agency for National Education. In 1806 the first national law on education was accepted. Louis Napoleon (1806-1810), installed by his brother Napoleon as King of the Netherlands, founded the 'Royal Institute for Sciences, Literature and Fine Arts' and made plans for a 'Royal Academy for Fine Arts', which came into being in 1820. After the defeat of Napoleon, the House of Orange continued with some form of royal patronage for the arts, but with growing parliamentary control of state expenditure this increasingly became a private matter for the kings. The liberal cabinets that governed the country during the midst of the century discontinued state expenditure on the arts. In 1851 the Royal Institute was converted into the 'Royal Academy for Sciences', once again leaving concern for the arts as a matter for burgher initiatives (Oosterbaan Martinius, 1990, p. 44).

In 1889 the opening of the Concertgebouw (Concert Hall) was one of the milestones of a new interest in the arts and arts provision. Opposite what is now known as the Museum Square another prestigious building, the Rijksmuseum, had opened its doors a few years earlier, in 1885. Societies and Associations were founded, such as the Wagner Society (1884) and the Rembrandt Association (1883). Boekman, the social-democratic alderman for Education and Arts in pre-war Amsterdam and the first to publish a wide ranging view on arts policy in his doctoral dissertation on the subject, relates the increasing interest in the arts to the economic revival in the last quarter of the nineteenth century (Boekman, 1989). The burghers had more money to spend and there was an increasing 'need for the arts, particularly in the cities' (Smithuijsen, 1988, p. 15). Industrialisation stimulated the industrial arts and arts education via schools and museums. At the same time, the formation of modern nation-states in Europe was at a crucial stage. These (new) nation-states had begun what would prove to be the last round in the imperialist wars in Africa and Asia. In this context, the Dutch were busy restructuring Java and the chain of trading posts on the other isles in the Indonesian archipelago into a proper colony: Dutch East India. The intensification of the links with the colonies not only contributed to the revival of the economy, but also to the revival of a sense of history, of the great heroic past of the 'Golden Age'. What finally triggered the government to become involved in the arts were protests against the selling off of national heritage, particularly the sale of seventeenth century paintings to the United States of America. In 1875, with the appointment of one of these protesters, de Stuers, to a senior post in the Ministry for Internal Affairs, the government started to give some financial support to private enterprises to build a national museum in Amsterdam, which would lead to the creation of what is now the Rijksmuseum, in 1885. As well as providing money and land for a new museum, the city of Amsterdam contributed towards her art collection, donating for example, Rembrandt's Nightwatch (Braat *et al.*, 1985, pp. 10-17). Cities had been involved in the arts for centuries, often in co-operation with private enterprise, but in the nineteenth century they had become very poor, were lacking an interest in culture and even refused to accept art-collections that were left to the cities under the proviso that they would be made accessible to the public (Boekman, 1989). So what was really new was that the government, although grudgingly, became involved, and what we see here is an element of the formation of national identity or collectivity.

In 1918, the sections of Education and of Arts and Sciences were taken out of the Ministry of Internal Affairs to form a new Ministry of Education, Arts and Sciences. New subsidies were introduced for contemporary art forms such as orchestras (1918) and opera (1921), and the 1930s saw the beginning of direct subsidy to artists. However, until the Second World War, the emphasis in national arts policy remained on the preservation of the more prestigious aspects of 'national' culture. Beyond this, it still proved to be very difficult to establish some form of consensus at a national level. The confessional (religious based) political parties, for instance, were able to block national subsidy for theatre until the war. For the most part it was intellectuals in the socialist movement that promoted the distribution of culture amongst the population at large (see Van Dijk, 1990). Boekman, one of these intellectuals, called for greater accessibility of museums (most of them were only open for a couple of hours and fit for use by academics) and a policy directed at teaching the mass of people to enjoy the arts. To him, the arts were still intrinsically good and full of beauty. It would be a matter of time and education, before the labourers would see this and exchange their popular pastimes for the pleasures the arts could bring (Smithuijsen, 1988). After the war these ideas would provide the primary justification for the extension of arts policies.

The effects of pillarisation (the division of socio-political organisation by religious affiliation and class) were particularly felt in the areas of sport and the media (Beckers and Van der Poel, 1990, pp. 70-74). Some authors restrict the concept of pillarisation to religiously motivated organisational complexes, thereby maintaining a clear distinction between pillars and classes (Stuurman, 1983). Others refer to ideologically motivated organisational complexes, thus introducing a 'socialist' and sometimes even 'liberal' pillar alongside the Catholic and Protestant pillars (Righart, 1986). Pillarisation did not replace class distinctions, but was the outcome of attempts to deal with the threats posed by intensifying class divisions and emergent socialism, in a historically 'pluralist' context. 'Pluralism' here refers to the fact that whatever the reasons that kept burghers divided were, these divisions were politically relevant. In the Dutch case, the central state proved not to be strong enough to prevent religious divisions from having political effects.

Pillarisation first took off in those areas where the lower clergy witnessed the impacts of industrialisation and urbanisation: poverty, secularisation, slums and the emergence of socialist organisations. By using the same media (newspapers, radio) and organisational forms (unions, social funds) as the socialists, they tried to prevent further secularisation, to safeguard the position of the church in society and to keep organisational control of the masses. A crucial element of this strategy was to stress the importance of being Catholic or Protestant rather than being a member of the labouring classes. All Catholics or Protestants, whether rich or poor, entrepreneur, shopkeeper or labourer, were to be incorporated in the pillarised institutions. The social and economic elite became interested in these institutions, even managing and funding them once the socialist threat had become apparent - on condition that working class members would temper their claims. Internally therefore, the religious pillars clearly provided instruments for hegemonic control. However, they proved an emancipatory force for Catholic and Calvinist labourers and members of the lower middle class, because the pillarised institutions were still faced with competition from their socialist counterparts. At a national level the pillars, as forms of popular movements, also provided the means for confessional middle and upper class leaders from the eastern and southern parts of the country to gain influence over the liberal regents from Holland. A clear demonstration of the impact of the pillars on national policies is provided by the expansion of moral legislation and the intensification of moral control in the first half of the twentieth century, resulting, amongst other measures, in the Bioscoopwet, a restrictive law on cinema, in 1926 (Van der Burg and Van den Heuvel, 1991).

Although the ideological roots of the pillars date back to the sixteenth and seventeenth century, they started to take their modern organisational form at the turn of this century. They really dominated public life from the so-called 'Pacification' in 1917 until well into the 1960s, but even today their influence is felt in many areas of society. The Pacification was a kind of truce agreed between the confessional pillar elite, the leaders in the socialist movement and the liberal regents, that finally settled several political issues that had been under discussion for some decades. The most important were the introduction of universal suffrage and the provision of equity in denominational and state education. It also smoothed the process of deliberation about the introduction of new labour laws, which, among other things, led to the introduction of the eight hour working day in 1919.

The leaders in the pillars, particularly in the Catholic pillar, wanted the pillar to encompass all aspects of life and cater for everything one might need or want to do, in order to prevent the lower strata, in particular, from coming into contact with people, ideas and habits from outside their own (confessional) circle. There were (and often still are) pillarised newspapers, sports clubs, building societies, social funds, pensioner's homes, broadcast organisations, unions and political parties, besides hundreds of other organisations.

It would take a long time before socialists were allowed to participate in national government, (this did not happen until 1939), but the Socialists were more successful on the local level, where they played an important role in the introduction of public recreational, sport and cultural facilities. In the burgher society they became gradually accepted, but in the form of another pillar. They were granted access, provided they would give up the ideal of a socialist revolution and an active policy of seeking to unite all workers. This posed a dilemma between immediate influence and gaining more power by attracting larger masses, that would never be fully resolved. When in 1926 the Dutch Labour Sport Union was founded, this was disapproved of by the leadership of the Social-Democratic Labour Party. They recognised that pillarisation was a strategy directed at undermining the attractiveness of socialism. By contributing to further fragmentation, it would prove to be even more difficult to reach the pillarised part of the labour class! (Dona, 1981).

One of the most well known and important results of pillarisation was, and is, the Dutch broadcast system. Amateur radio enthusiasts had already been experimenting with the new phenomenon of radio when the Hilversum Radio Broadcast (HDO) started to broadcast programmes on a channel that was supported by the Philips company, in 1919. Philips foresaw the possibility of a mass market for radio equipment and wanted a national broadcast channel to make the idea of buying of a radio set attractive. Very soon, however, the pillars had their own radio clubs and wanted access to the channel. In the spirit of the Pacification, the government, dominated by the confessional parties, decided to give all the pillarised radio clubs more or less equal access to the radio channel. This countered the claim of the confessional radio clubs that the HDO was not a national broadcast, but a 'liberal' broadcast channel. The socialist radio club was formally accepted on an equal basis with the other radio clubs, but had most of the confrontation with the censors that were instituted to control radio broadcasting. The mutual adjustment of the socialist radio club and the censors, i.e. the confessional pillars' leadership, mirrored the gradual adjustment of Dutch society and the socialist movement (van den Heuvel, 1976; Wijfjes, 1988). After the war, when Philips pressed for the introduction of television, access to the television channel would be granted to the already existing radio clubs, which were then converted into broadcast associations catering for both radio and television.

Up until the present day, the pillarisation has proven to be one of the main obstacles to the development of a national leisure policy. Of course, the idea of government intervention in people's leisure has always been quite difficult to accept for the traditionally autonomous burghers. But in addition to this was a real dislike of 'national' policy. The confessional elites, in particular, have been able to preserve their more direct influence in leisure provision via the plethora of boards, advisory councils, committees, representational bodies and so on. When the confessional parties had a firm hold on the government they gradually expanded financial subsidy, but preferred to do it 'on request', leaving the initiative to the societies and clubs. The 1960s brought about changes to this system, but on the whole the 'subsidiarity principle' has proved to be an effective way of depoliticising the topic of leisure provision. The government did not govern, but has made it possible (financially as well) for burghers to govern themselves. Many profited from this system by conforming to the rules of the game. And those who did not were never able to muster sizeable enough influence to change these rules. On the whole, the system was flexible enough to cope with the 'non-burgher' demands directly, taking the sting out of the threat to the policy system as a whole. For instance, when the pillarised broadcast system was challenged by commercial initiatives in the 1960s, a second television channel was introduced and rules were adjusted to allow for non-ideologically motivated broadcast associations. Typically, commercial television had been debated since 1951 - cabinets fell (in 1965) or almost fell (in 1963) on this matter - but the end result in 1969 was a broadcast system, that, despite the fact that it allowed for advertisements and non-ideological broadcast associations, was still non-commercial and dominated by the classic, pillarised broadcast organisations (De Goede, 1990).

Leisure and Leisure Policies in the Post-war Period

The Construction and Reconstruction of the Welfare State

The traditional neutrality between France, Germany and the United Kingdom was violated by Nazi Germany during the Second World War, and after this, the Netherlands developed into a firm protagonist for Western defence alliances (Western European Union, North Atlantic Treaty Organisation) and forms of world-wide and European political and economic integration (United Nations, European Community). The loss of the most important colony (today's Indonesia) in 1949 went together with a second phase of industrialisation, which turned the country into a prosperous welfare state.

The first decade after the war was dominated by austerity, cultural pessimism and the common goal of the post-war reconstruction of the Netherlands. Cinema, radio and voluntary organisations, including sports clubs, tended to be the more conspicuous leisure forms. Most leisure provision was still strongly pillarised. It is remarkable that even just after the war, 'national consciousness' was lower than in most other Western countries, and, quite exceptionally, even lower than 'class consciousness' (Lijphart, 1984, p. 33). Although not explicitly included in the research, no doubt it would also have been lower than 'pillar consciousness'. In fact, the pillarised elite used the example of Nazi Germany to point to what might come from 'nationalism' when not taken in its proper context - one of the most important features of Dutch national character was supposed to be tolerance to pluralism. Again, a lot could be said about the accuracy and background to this, but to the extent that these ideas legitimised a strong position for the pillarised institutions at the expense of the development and execution of clear-cut national cultural and leisure policies, this tolerated pluralism would prove fertile ground for the 'fragmentation of lifestyles' witnessed in the 1980s, once leisure opportunities had broadened, due to economic and technological growth and open borders.

The Netherlands saw an enormous increase in population from 9 million in 1945 to 13 million in 1970, and a high rate of economic growth, leading to rapidly rising wages and government tax income. This all translated into a consumption boom of cars, televisions, refrigerators and package holidays. The rising tax income, together with new sources of government income such as profits from the exploitation of natural gas reserves, were translated into subsidies for housing, an extensive social security system and educational, cultural and recreational facilities. Youth and their preferred activities gained considerable influence in the general image of leisure.

The crises of the 1970s eventually led to a 20 per cent unemployment rate at the beginning of the 1980s and a slowing of the growth rate in public spending. During the 1980s, a relatively moderate 'Thatcherite' regime prevailed. Nevertheless, the equalisation of incomes was reversed during this period. With regard to leisure this led on the one hand to a growing diversity of groups (being unemployed, with less education, welfare-dependent, old and/or immigrant) with few opportunities to develop a rich leisure pattern, due to a lack of resources, facilities, knowledge, mental and physical capabilities and/or time, and on the other hand to a group with increasing opportunities to have several holidays per year, to buy CD players and video recorders, to dine out at least once a week and to enjoy a variety of cultural, recreational and sport facilities. Attempts to introduce shorter working hours aimed at the spreading of work among the *whole* population only partially succeeded, but did inspire thinking about leisure and the development of a 'time-policy' or a 'time-spatial policy'.

Well-being and Post-war Leisure Policies

As the French occupation had done one and half centuries before, the German occupation proved to be important in centralising and intensifying policies in a wide range of issues. The Germans split the Ministry of Education, Arts and Sciences into a Ministry of Edification, Sciences and Cultural Preservation and a Ministry of Public Information and Arts, in the image of Goebbels' 'Reichsministerium für Volksaufklärung und Propaganda'. The Ministry for Public Information and Arts had sections dealing with tourism and recreation, cultural exchanges and all manner of popular recreation. The arts were imputed an important role in edifying the population, granted larger sums of money and included cinema, theatre and dance. Of course this edification was directed solely at the promotion of the Nazi ideology; all other ideologies were repressed (Beckers, 1983, pp. 201-202; Oosterbaan Martinius, 1990, pp. 49-50). The Germans also stimulated the establishment of the Agency for National Planning, that would continue to play an important role in outdoor recreation planning for some decades.

After the war, the Ministry for Education, Arts and Sciences was re-established. The first Minister, the Social Democrat Van der Leeuw, advocated an 'active cultural policy'. Although he rejected the Nazi ideology, in which the state had to play the central role in initiating the organisation of free time, he saw an important task for the state in regulating private enterprise and in the distribution of cultural artefacts and opportunities for artistic expression among the population. He set up a new Directorate Edification outside Schools, which would tackle the problems of youth and leisure. Van der Leeuw was in office for only one year, and his (confessional) successors did not carry out his more ambitious plans. They wanted to return to the politics of the subsidiarity principle. However, they did not stop the process of increasingly higher subsidies on an increasingly broadly defined area of culture, which had been initiated by the Germans. In 1950 a new but small Bureau for Leisure had the explicit objective of promoting the 'sane use of leisure'. The plan to install a Leisure Council almost came to fruition, but failed because of resistance from the confessional pillars. The confessionals feared that the Leisure Council would end up promoting 'national culture' and 'socialist citizenship', threatening the existing pluralist liberties. The focus of resistance was not the *idea* of a council as such - councils were and are the pre-eminent form of pacifying the different interests of the pillars - but their 'procedural', or political aspects, such as whether the members of the council would be chosen as representatives of existing (pillarised) institutions or on the basis of their professional qualities (Beckers, 1983, p. 206 ff).

Until the end of the 1950s the core element of the legitimation of cultural policy remained the idea that 'beauty' and all those other 'good things of life' would edify the lower classes and could work as an antidote to the growing impact of modern amusements and the 'decline in moral standards'. Despite differences, the elites in all the pillars were convinced of the intrinsic qualities of 'culture' and agreed that a lack of money should not prevent people from enjoying it. Social Democrats stressed that a more active policy was needed to reach the labouring classes, but even in the pre-war period Boekman did not really question the burgher concept of 'culture'. Pacification at the top, nonetheless, temporarily stopped the process of erosion at the pillars' bases. Commercialisation of leisure was heavily criticised, but proved to be irresistible. In 1947, when the British entrepreneur, Billy Butlin announced the intention to open holiday camps on the Dutch coast, he evoked huge protests against the 'commercialisation of holiday-making' and was forced to abort his plans. However, in 1954, the Football Association could no longer hold off professionalism in soccer, after the better players had begun to go abroad to play in professional teams and some of the more popular newspapers had made it the subject of a press campaign. The formation of a Directorate Edification outside Schools must be seen as indicative of the strength of concern about the moral standards of post-war youth, who had supposedly learned from the war that breaking the law, stealing and truancy were acceptable. But soon, edification outside schools was down-graded to lower administrative status, and in the 1950s the coming into existence of a separate youth culture (or at least the very beginnings of such a culture, centred around forms of leisure outside the pillarised youth centres and away from the supervision of concerned educationalists) was gradually accepted. Around 1950, a large research project on 'bewildered mass youth' had already attracted much criticism for its moralism, lack of empirical findings and lack of suggestions for applicable guide-lines. Furthermore, the interest in the results, when they were published in 1952-53, was minimal because the general concern for youth had subsided. There was confidence that any remaining problems could be solved through education itself.

Interestingly, the gradual decline in moral concern gave way to an increasingly important role for state-involvement in leisure provision. Compared to the pillarised organisations, the state was considered to be more 'neutral' and concerned with general welfare. An early example of this 'technocratic' state intervention in leisure is a memorandum published in 1953, called 'Sport als vormingsmiddel' ('Sport as a means of edification'). Until then, most 'sports policies' were ad hoc, reactive and restrictive, trying to ensure that sport remained 'decent', and these were in evidence within schools and pillarised voluntary organisations. In the memorandum, the municipalities stated that the traditional pillarised youth organisations seemed to have lost their attractiveness to the young, when compared with the situation in the pre-war period. Even after the pillarised youth organisations had incorporated sports into their activities, it was the independent sports organisations that attracted youth. Being pragmatic about it, they proposed that 'youth sport leaders' be employed by the sports organisations; thus sports organisations could fulfil an important 'edifying function' in the so-called 'third milieu'. Over time, a dialectic of complementary interests evolved between local governments (pillarised) clubs, and people wanting to participate in sport. Most sports clubs became dependent upon local government money. Thus they could be forced to comply with conditions attached to public subsidy. Clubs had to do away with restrictions on membership; anybody who wanted to join a club now had to be accepted. Later clubs were to be asked to try to actively attract members from under-represented groups such as women, the elderly and ethnic minorities. On the other hand, clubs gained access to funds for new and increasingly expensive facilities which they would never have been able to afford solely on the basis of membership fees. When sport was imputed with new values, such as personal expression and social integration, it also became feasible to use sports facilities as a policy instrument to attract investment money and employment. In the 1960s this became an element in regional policies which aimed at shifting industries and services from the overcrowded Randstad area to the outer provinces (Stokvis, 1979; 1989).

These new values attached to sport indicate the general shift towards a more encompassing politics of welfare and well-being in the 1960s and 1970s. The state gradually gained more influence, although the initial organisation of leisure and leisure facilities often remained in the hands of clubs, associations and foundations. Beckers (1985) gives an indication of this growing importance of the state in leisure provision by presenting figures which indicate a rise in government spending from Fl 14.5 million in 1946 to Fl 150.9 million in 1960, Fl 933.6 million in 1970 and Fl 4477 million in 1980. In 1990 this figure rose to Fl 5893 million.

In 1965 a ministerial re-organisation led to the establishment of a Ministry of Culture, Recreation and Social Work (CRM). The subsidiarity principle was taken yet one step further. The government not only had the task of taking care of the preconditions for the creation of welfare, but also of those for the creation of people's well-being and self-development. The emphasis on edification was replaced by an emphasis on cultural democratisation and differentiation, which legitimised the expansion of government concern for leisure pursuits such as sport and outdoor recreation. In government expenditure this becomes clear in the higher proportion spent on outdoor recreation and sports (16.9% in 1950, 54.3% in 1980) compared to culture (82.7% in 1950, 45.7% in 1980), particularly by local government (Beckers, 1983, pp. 289-290; 1985, p. 117). Culture had to be distributed both geographically and socially in order to make it possible for everybody to fill their growing free time with artistic experience. Between 1950 and 1980 the number of subsidised symphony orchestras rose from 7 to 16, theatre companies from 7 to 20 and various other companies (ballet, mime) from 5 to 40 (Oosterbaan Martinius, 1990, p. 51). Money was also made available to promote artistic expression by the people themselves; the amateur practise of the arts became a new item on the arts budget. Art now had to be 'socially relevant', offering opportunities for everybody, including the lower classes, to identify themselves with.

In 1972 the government was asked to do something about the proliferation of its socio-cultural policies. In 1974, a new 'left-confessional' cabinet published the 'Knelpuntennota', a thorough analysis of problematic aspects of the government's socio-cultural policies, and announced an ambitious programme to change the situation. The plans originally incorporated most leisure sectors, with the exception of tourism. It took about ten years, but these initiatives were then effectively smothered by the joint efforts of particular interest groups, opposing civil servants worried about their department, directorate or bureau losing its autonomy, and the shifting power balance between political parties.

Leisure and Supply-side Policies: the Examples of Art and Tourism

With the ministerial re-organisation of 1982, recreation became part of a directorate of the Ministry of Agriculture and Fisheries. The rest of the Ministry of Culture, Recreation and Social Work was merged with the Directorate of Health to create the new Ministry of Well-being, Health and Culture (WVC). Culture was only retained as a significant element of the new ministry after heavy lobbying and protests by the cultural elite when it became known that it was to be neglected.

The break-up of the well-being oriented Ministry of Culture, Recreation and Social Work facilitated the shift of the central legitimation for subsidising the arts from 'well-being' to 'quality'. Although there had always been doubts about the success of the ideal of social distribution of the arts, a new report by the authoritative Social and Cultural Planning Bureau made the inescapable conclusion that the policy directed at social distribution of the arts had largely failed, at the same time that the pressure to cut back government spending had increased quickly. Inspired by Bourdieu, sociologists pointed to the cultural dynamics of processes of distinction, implying that the ideal of cultural distribution was self-defeating. The emphasis has now shifted towards the preservation of a 'flourishing art life' and 'quality'. Quality has to prove itself, both in the assessment of colleagues and in public response. The latter criterion indicates that even in those cases where particular art is assessed positively, subsidy may be withdrawn when, after a period of promotional activity, there is still no sufficient public response. In 1986 the 'Beeldende Kunstenaars Regeling' (BKR), the arrangement for visual artists, was abolished. The BKR was a form of direct subsidies to visual artists that had been expanding ever since the 1930s. It combined social and artistic criteria and the implementation of this arrangement also involved the municipalities and the Ministry of Social Affairs. In its place was developed a new form of subsidy, with a budget of Fl 60 million for project subsidies that have to be applied for by artists. The Council for the Arts then considers these applications. These policies were intended to lead to lower subsidies, and terms like sponsorship and privatisation have been introduced into the vocabulary of arts policy makers. There is increasing pressure to subsidise low income art consumers, instead of art producers. This leaves the idea of social distribution of the arts via low prices intact, but affects the majority of consumers, who can and must pay more realistic prices. It would mean a heavier emphasis on 'consumer sovereignty' without making the arts inaccessible to lower income groups. These proposals are opposed by those who stress that direct subsidy of art production is necessary because there has to be supply before there is something to choose. So far, all these debates have not implied a real attack on the budget for arts policy. In 1990, arts made up 0.23 per cent (Fl 408.7 million) of the total state budget, against 0.2 per cent (Fl 222.2 million) of the state budget in 1980 (Oosterbaan Martinius, 1990, p. 50 and passim).

The history of tourism policy is different from the leisure policy discussed hitherto. Since the 1960s, tourism has become an aspect of economic policy and has more or less ceased to be an element of socio-cultural policy.

In 1989, 71.8 per cent of the Dutch population was away on a holiday of 5 days or longer. The average number of holidays per holiday-maker was 1.66. Of all holidays 57 per cent were spent abroad (SCP, 1990, p. 238). The most popular foreign destinations being France, Germany, Austria and Spain, while interest in long-haul destinations such as Turkey, Kenya, the USA and Indonesia is increasing. The Dutch typically travel by car (70 per cent) and camp (31 per cent), which helps to keep the average amount of money spent on vacations abroad - Fl 1599 per holiday-maker per year in 1985 - lower than anywhere else in the EC (SCP, 1990, p. 243). The total expenditure on the tourist traffic balance has risen from Fl 2.8 billion in 1972 to Fl 13.6 billion in 1989.

In terms of incoming tourism, growth was relatively low in the 1970s. In the period 1973-1980 the growth rate was 1 per cent, compared to 5 per cent for Europe and 6 per cent world-wide. This poor performance, together with the fast growing number of holidays spent abroad by the Dutch, led to an increasing negative effect on the tourist traffic balance: Fl. 0.4 billion in 1972 compared with Fl. 6 billion in 1980 (EZ, 1984, p. 14). In the period 1980-1986 the growth rate increased to 3.4 per cent per year, which was higher than in Europe (2.5 per cent) and the world (3 per cent). The Dutch share of the European tourism market, which had gone down from 5.5 per cent in 1970 to 3.3 per cent in 1980, grew again to 4.3 per cent in 1986 and then stabilised at this level. But although the revenue from tourist traffic rose from Fl 3.8 billion in 1980 to Fl 6.4 billion in 1989, the negative effect on the tourist traffic balance grew from 6 to 7 billion guilders because of increasing expenditure by Dutch tourists abroad (EZ, 1990, pp. 13-14). Neighbouring countries are the main source of incoming tourists. Germany alone caters for about half of all visitors. At the end of the 1980s the numbers of Italian and Spanish visitors were growing fastest. The Germans concentrate at the coast and the lakes, most other visitors come for short stays to Amsterdam from where they take tours to other cultural and historic places of interest and the tulip fields. Whereas domestic tourists tend to stay in chalets (33 per cent), tents (15 per cent) and caravans or trailer tents (32 per cent), most foreign tourists stay in hotels. In 1985, the number of foreigners staying in hotels reached 3.4 million, 1 million of whom were visitors on business (Williams and Shaw, 1988, p. 219). This last figure is an indication of the relative importance of conference tourism in the Netherlands. The Dutch share of the world conference market, as registered by the 'Union of International Associations' in Brussels, rose from 2.7 per cent in 1982 to 4 per cent in 1988. With 68 of these conferences, Amsterdam lies fourteenth on the list of conference venue cities. Expenditure related to conferences was estimated at Fl 600 million in 1988 (EZ, 1990, p. 71).

The policies of all the ministries affect tourism in one way or another, but the Ministry of Economic Affairs (EZ) is directly responsible. Until the late 1970s, explanatory statements to the yearly budget of EZ provided the main source of written information about national tourism policy, with the exception of 1956 and 1962, when the ministry provided more extended memoranda on tourism. In 1978, debating the 1979 budget, parliament asked for a new memorandum, given the rapidly deteriorating tourist traffic balance. In 1979, the ministry's section dealing with tourism policy was promoted to a higher status and published the 'Nota Toeristisch Beleid' (Memorandum on Tourism Policy). The national budget for tourism policy was doubled to almost Fl 50 million per year (Van Doorn *et al.*, 1981). Tourism policy was further intensified after the publication of the second 'Nota Toeristisch Beleid', in 1985. In 1989, the budget was increased to Fl 66 million per year. In 1990 the Ministry published the 'Nota Ondernemen in Toerisme. Het toeristisch beleid voor de jaren negentig' (Venturing in Tourism. Tourism policy for the nineties) and raised the budget to Fl 75 million per annum. Thus, over the last ten years tourism policy has expanded, grown more complex and gained in depth. The ministry - traditionally a stronghold of entrepreneurial interests - sometimes seems to be a bit insecure about the growing involvement of the government in this sector. In the latest memorandum heavy emphasis was placed on the growth of tourist-recreational expenditure and employment over the 1980s. About 9 to 10 per cent of all firms in the market sector and 6 per cent of the working population (230,000 people) are wholly or partly dependent on the more than Fl 31 billion spent on tourism and recreation (EZ, 1990, pp. 16-18). It is also stressed that other countries have higher budgets for their tourism policies, and that these budgets are growing faster (EZ, 1990, pp. 22-23). In reference to the evaluation of tourism policies in the period 1985-1989, it is said that the tourist business community itself wants more government intervention, instead of a 'retreating government' (EZ, 1990, p. 27). Notwithstanding all this pressure to intensify its policies, the ministry emphasises that it will continue its favourable policy towards the tourist business environment but act 'reservedly'. It will not - as is done in some competing countries - invest in tourist firms directly, subsidise wages or grant the sector specific tax advantages (EZ, 1990, p. 57). Hence, the implications of the ministry's 'favourable policy' are unclear.

The memorandum says that tourism policy in the 1990s is aimed at both the Dutch consumers and the Dutch suppliers. However, the main thrust of the attention paid to consumers is to identify 'threats and opportunities' for Dutch tourism firms and to try to keep as much of the money spent by Dutch tourists within the Dutch economy. A passing remark is made on the elderly, the unemployed, etc. who are have a growing amount of free time (EZ, 1990, p. 77), but there is no sign of a policy to confront this. Terms like 'social tourism', 'deprivation' and 'inequality' do not surface in the memorandum; even in its attention to consumer interests the tourism policy appears to be wholly supply oriented (see also Van Doorn *et al.*, 1981). In this supply orientation, the ministry distinguishes four themes: professionalisation; reinforcement of co-operation between various governments; consumer organisations and the business community; a growing interest in the environment; and the prioritising of certain product-market combinations. The Ministry proposes to concentrate tourist development around four fields, in which the Netherlands would have a relative advantage over competing neighbouring countries. These are 'The Netherlands - Waterland'; the coastal area; cultural-historical tourism; and city tourism in the main cities. The policy instruments are grouped in six main policy areas: integration and international co-operation; management improvement; protection of consumer interests; recreational tourist infrastructure, promotion; and research and statistics.

In terms of finance (Fl 75 million per year in total) the most important instruments in Dutch tourism policy are promotion and improvement of infrastructure. The money for promotion is divided between the two organisations that were established in 1969, after the break-up of the 'ANVV-old-style' (Algemene Nederlands Vereningen van VVVs): the 'ANVV-new-style' and the Netherlands Bureau for Tourism. The 'ANVV-new-style' is the umbrella organisation for the more than 400 local, regional and provincial tourist information bureaux, the VVVs (Vereniging voor Vreemdelingen Verkeer) that exist around the country. The ANVV was founded in 1915 as a federation of the existing VVV's . During the years that followed, the ANVV expanded and started to include other (commercial) organisations which expressed an interest in incoming tourists. It ended up operating as the national tourist organisation, but at the same time the associational structure of the ANVV hampered its development because of the diverse interests of its members. In 1969 the ANVV was reorganised and became the protector of the interests of the VVVs (Kosters, 1981). To this aim the ANVV is subsidised with Fl 750,000 per year. The promotion of the Netherlands, both abroad and internally, became the task of the Netherlands Bureau for Tourism (NBT). The NBT is an autonomous, private law organisation that operates for both the government and the business community. General tasks, such as 'Holland-Promotion', strategic market research and market development are mainly paid for by the government. Promotional services, such as (combined) advertising campaigns, workshops, sales-missions, presentations at exhibitions, etc. are mostly paid for by the participating companies. The government subsidy for the NBT is Fl 38.5 million per year. The money for tourist infrastructure (Fl 16.5 million) is spent on roads, car parks, boulevards, promenades, jetties and so on. It is meant to improve the quality and accessibility of tourist destinations, but it remains public infrastructure. The money is not used for direct subsidy to private enterprise, although the way the money is spent will be decided in close co-operation with local government and the business community.

The increasing importance of tourism and cultural policies are counterbalanced by the decline of sport and recreation policies. Here it is important to bear in mind that since the 1960s and 1970s a lot of sports and recreational facilities have been built and that the rate of population growth has declined sharply. It would be assumed that if there is less need to erect new facilities in the sphere of sports and outdoor-recreation, it should also be the case for cultural facilities. However, this is not so. Since 1980 the government's net spending on recreation and sport, compared to culture, has fallen again from 54.3 to 40 per cent. Whereas the state spends about the same amount of money on recreation and sport as it did in 1980, the net spending on culture (for example libraries, amateur arts, museums, music schools, heritage, etc.) has increased from about 2 billion to almost 3.5 billion guilders. Also, substantively, some of the merit good arguments for subsidising sports and recreational facilities seem to have lost their attraction. The municipalities in particular still spend a lot of money on sports facilities and organisations (Fl 905 million), because these facilities are well defended by sports clubs, popular with voters and supposed to be important in creating a favourable business environment. However, the Fl 36 million spent by the government can be better regarded as a token of interest, rather than as expressing a real concern with increasing leisure opportunities for disadvantaged groups or one of the other formerly important policy goals. In the sphere of outdoor recreation, a recently published memorandum, 'Kiezen voor recreatie' ('Making a choice for recreation') should really be read as 'Making a choice for tourism'. It fits with an already existing trend to attune subsidies for outdoor recreation infrastructure and tourist infrastructure. The money available for investments in outdoor recreation facilities has been continually decreasing since the early 1980s and many expect that with the formation of a new cabinet after the next elections (in 1994), the political responsibility for outdoor recreation and tourism will come under the same authority, probably that of the Ministry of Economic Affairs.

Some Recent Trends and Preliminary Conclusions

The Dutch are rather home-loving in their recreational activities and boast, together with the Danes and Germans, the highest expenditure on leisure pursuits of all EC citizens. They rank highest in home consumption of alcohol and supermarkets provide a dazzling variety of crisps to go with it. Also, a comparatively large amount of money is invested in hardware for home entertainment such as television sets, CD players and video recorders. In 1983 there were 450 television sets per 1000 inhabitants, a number only exceeded by Great Britain (479), but well above the 375 in France, 360 in the FRG, 303 in Belgium, 258 in Spain and 243 in Italy. For 1991, it was estimated that 60 to 70 per cent of households had a CD player at their disposal. The amount of time spent with audio-visual media rose from 12.3 hours in 1975 to 13.4 hours in 1985. The high penetration of television coincides with as high a penetration of newspapers and as large a number of book titles released every year as elsewhere in Western Europe. In Denmark, Germany, Great Britain and the Netherlands more than 80 per cent of the population read a newspaper regularly, compared to 50 per cent or less (all figures for 1981) in France, Italy and Spain (SCP, 1990, pp. 241-245).

The preservation of 'national heritage' has been quite successful, including artefacts that have been collected in the former colonies. The number of museums has almost doubled since the end of the 1960s - to 633 in 1988 - and the number of visitors has more than doubled to 1.35 visits per year per person (SCP, 1990, p. 236; CBS, 1990, p. 65). The emphasis on 'quality' - relating in many cases to art forms and performers that have proved themselves nationally, and preferably internationally - seems to fit quite well with a more general trend towards concern about 'corporate image', 'national identity' and 'city marketing'. Arts are used to attract attention, to 'show-off', to distribute an air of respectability and/or social concern, by local and national government as well as private companies. In a way this brings us back to the beginning of substantial national intervention in the arts in the last quarter of the nineteenth century, when the government began to support private and local initiatives. The well-educated seem to agree with this. Old and new opera houses and music halls are doing well, supporting prestigious projects.

The abolition of the BKR was of course the subject of protest, but for the most part only by the art world itself. The general public either did not seem to care much, or supported the abolition. Spending money on paintings that 'nobody would want, even for free' did not fit well into the general atmosphere of 'no nonsense' that pervaded the 1980s.

With regard to the aim of social distribution of the arts it has become quite obvious that 'the labouring classes' do not visit concerts and museums. So far, research has been inconclusive in discovering why this is so and what this means in a society with a decreasing number of labourers. Indications are that money is of relatively little importance in explaining their absence, but hitherto these findings have hardly led to other pricing policies. Familiarity with the art form and the 'proper' way to 'interpret' it, seem to be more important factors in cultural participation (Oosterbaan Martinius, 1990, pp. 74-78). If so, this would mean that policies would have to focus more sharply on the ways in which people can acquire this familiarity. Traditionally, the opportunities to develop this kind of policy have been limited. Art should be treated either as a commodity that has to be sold to a public that only needs a little help to discover what its own cultural needs are, or as a core element of the socialisation of the young. In both cases however, the general feeling is that the state can only be allowed to play a subsidiary role; the initiative should be left to private companies or to the family and schools.

Important forms of physical activity today include walking, cycling, (aerobic) dancing, martial arts, and jogging. Water sports are particularly popular forms of recreational sport. Swimming is the physical activity most frequently engaged in. On weekends when the weather is warm - say above 25 degrees Celsius - hoards of people can be found at swimming pools, on North Sea beaches and the shores of the lakes, busy surfing, sailing, swimming, sun-bathing and teaching their children how to build dykes and sand-castles. On winter weekends they skate on canals, lakes, ponds, moats and ditches. Although in general the attractiveness of team sports seems to be declining, about a million Dutch are still members of soccer clubs, and hockey is gaining in popularity.

In 1989, one hundred years after the Concertgebouw was opened, tens of thousands watched and listened to the outdoor performance of the Royal Concertgebouw Orchestra at the 'Uitmarkt' (the 'Going Out' Fair) in the Museum Square in Amsterdam. The Uitmarkt signals the start of the 'cultural season' in August each year. It epitomises some of the continuities and changes that take place in culture and leisure provision and policy. Culture is quite literally 'marketed'; the Uitmarkt displays a great variety of specialised cultural forms and attracts large numbers of people who are *presumably* interested in art. We say 'presumably', because the Uitmarkt has become a social event in itself, not only boasting performances and rehearsals by theatre companies, poets, dance groups and orchestras, but also places where you can have a drink or something to eat, watch people and enjoy the mood. At least for this weekend, arts are, once again, part of urban street life. The Uitmarkt brings together spectacle and culture, 'vorming' (edification, formation) and 'vermaak' (amusement). It expresses the enormous number of differences and the specialisation in cultural supply that matches the 'fragmentation of lifestyles' and 'individualisation' of the public.

Whilst the population at large seems to be able to amuse itself perfectly well, a growing unrest among the cultural elite is apparent. Not only sport and recreation, but also media and arts policy is gradually moving towards the tourism policy model, with a greater emphasis on 'consumer sovereignty' and a government that restricts itself to being favourable towards private enterprise (Van der Poel, 1987). The unrest is also becoming apparent in the debate about the chances for survival of Dutch culture within integrating Europe. There is a diversity of opinions, ranging from doubts as to whether such a thing as 'Dutch culture' exists, to demands for a cultural paragraph in the Treaty on European Union to safeguard the autonomy of national government with respect to culture. It is also proposed to establish a quasi-independent body for the promotion of Dutch culture abroad, somewhat comparable to the German Goethe Institute and the British Council. Behind these debates are political and economic developments that call into question the position of the Netherlands within Europe. The situation, to a certain extent, resembles the situation at the end of the eighteenth century, when the Netherlands had lost its place as a pivotal staple market in the world economy. Now, there are serious doubts as to whether firms in the south-east will be strong enough to survive as autonomous companies and not be turned into assembly units within larger international conglomerates. For the rest of the country, the economy hinges on agriculture and Europe's largest harbour, Rotterdam. However, environmental considerations and EC policies set ever more strict limits on the expansion of the agricultural sector, and the distributional importance of Rotterdam is threatened by the opening of the borders in the EC. Politically, the country's position is undermined by the emerging directorate of France, Germany and Great Britain within the EC. It is likely that these developments will reinforce the search for, and expression of, a Dutch national identity, an issue which has not been debated as fiercely since the 1930s. Experience from the past, however, warns us not to expect too much from this new urge for a national cultural policy. Meetings and conferences will be held, committees installed and memoranda written, all concluding that everyone has a different opinion about what Dutch culture really is, and that *all* views must be respected, because *that*, when it comes down to it, is the essence of national identity. Or perhaps it will simply fail because nobody will have enough power to be able to convince the others. In the meantime, most people will do what they always have done. They enjoy the fact that they live in a country where they can take their pick of all the world's cultural products: American cinema, French wine, British pop music, Russian ballet, German television, Indonesian restaurants and Dutch novels.

The Future for an Integrated Leisure Policy

A policy textbook would say that the challenges for leisure policy in the 1990s are to be found in the gaps between policy objectives and the extent to which these objectives are realised, now and/or in the foreseeable future. However, by now it will be clear that there is no overall leisure policy in the Netherlands; only policies concerned with various leisure sectors, such as the media, tourism and sport. A detailed treatment of the challenges for each of these sectors runs the risk of being redundant, given what has already been said. Therefore, attention will be focused on the opportunities for an integrated leisure policy. Figure 3.1 is an impression of how leisure policy making is embedded in the administrative structure of the Netherlands.

The experiences encountered in earlier attempts to establish an integrated leisure policy - which all failed (see Beckers, 1983, and Van der Poel, 1987) - would indicate that it is highly unlikely that the policy system will be able to transform itself in such a radical way, if not more or less coerced by 'outside' forces. Short-term profits and the pre-occupation with the procedures which safeguard one's position in the game of checks and balances always conflict with pro-active and long-term strategic policies. Substantial long-term investment, be it in machinery and brand names or infrastructure and national identity, presupposes either centralised forms of decision making or lengthy discussion to convince and compromise with at least a majority of involved parties. The likelihood of the emergence of an integrated leisure policy therefore hinges upon (a) the identification of outside forces that seriously threaten the existing system of leisure policy making, (b) the simultaneous formulation of policy objectives and the development of policy instruments that promise to be successful in countering these threats and (c) the availability of a catalyst that makes the necessity of this policy shift convincing for those who have to decide on it.

Whatever the leisure policy objectives are, they will need to be concerned with changing the conditions for the development of leisure patterns in order to favour those patterns which match the policy objectives. Ideally, this means that the 'outside forces' we have to identify must be forces that have a bearing on the constitution of leisure. However, this line of thinking is already one step too far ahead; it presupposes the existence of an entity that is interested in and knows about the ways in which leisure is produced and reproduced and continuously scans the context in which leisure develops.

Figure 3.1 Dutch Leisure Policy System	
National level	Leisure Sector(s)
Ministry of Agriculture,	Outdoor recreation
Nature Conservation & Fisheries	(Nature conservation)
Ministry of Well-being, Health & Culture	Media Sport Culture
Ministry of Economic Affairs	Tourism
Provincial level	
12 Provinces	Tourist recreational Development Plans
	Sports Council
	Socio-Cultural Councils
Inter-municipal level	
About 60 outdoor recreation boards	Outdoor recreation
Municipal level	
About 650 municipalities	All sectors, but particularly important in the sport and cultural sectors

At this stage we have to start with the threats to the existing policy system itself. Only if these threats are acknowledged as being serious threats can policy makers become interested in adjusting the existing system. Politically, a main threat would seem to be the impact of the European Community (EC) on national policy making. After decades of debate, it was EC regulations and directives that finally got the move towards a post-pillarised media policy going. Another threat is posed by the increasing pressure on the government to cut back on expenses. Economically, it would seem that we are moving towards a post-scarcity situation with respect to many leisure provisions, which results in less need for government regulation. When a situation of competition replaces a situation of monopoly, for instance with regard to the radio and television channels, this has an impact on the need to control and subsidise the supply of leisure facilities. Culturally, the scientific underpinning of the legitimacy of existing policies is weakening. Social scientists relativise cultural hierarchies, pointing to processes of conspicuous consumption, civilisation, disciplinarity and distinction and declare the failure of the project of cultural distribution. This raises the question as to why the government should go on spending money on manifestations of a particular culture that are mainly of interest to relatively well-to-do citizens.

These structural changes threaten the power and legitimacy of the present policy system, but they are not likely to lead to a coherent leisure policy. If there is to be any change at all, what is most likely is a further segmentation of leisure policy. The EC will add a new governmental layer to the system and the movement towards a post-scarcity situation will further enhance the shift of leisure policies from well-being oriented ministries to supply-side oriented ministries. Existing and new councils will continue to help legitimise government regulations and spending on leisure facilities by compromising the various parties involved and keeping the issues (art, recreation and so on) off the parliamentary agenda. The more it is stressed that the government cannot decide for its citizens what they should pursue in their leisure, the more existing departments and sections will stress other objectives, such as health, sustaining democratic rights of expression and free speech, improvement of business environments and so on to legitimise their existence. The irony of this development is that stressing the liberties and equality of people's leisure preferences weakens any policy aimed at contributing to people's well-being, which at least has the promise of combining the various leisure policies, and reinforces tendencies to subsume leisure policy objectives under a variety of other policy objectives. Outdoor recreation facilities are then developed not to increase opportunities for leisure per se, but because they contribute to the improvement of the (tourist) business environment or are another reason to turn a certain area into a natural park.

Developments in leisure will continue to have time-spatial consequences that might sooner or later urge the government to do something. One of the most conspicuous problems at the moment is leisure mobility and its environmental impacts, one of which is the deterioration of the quality of recreational facilities. Again, it is highly unlikely that these consequences will lead to a coherent leisure policy. The problems become manifest at different times and places, and with varying intensity, and will be dealt with by various parts of the existing state apparatus. When the tourism balance of payments showed rapidly increasing deficits, the Ministry of Economic Affairs intensified its tourist policy. Similarly, the Ministries of Transport,

Justice, Physical Planning and Finance will all be involved in trying to contain leisure mobility; by increasing taxes, introducing regulations or adjusting the existing infrastructure, probably in a non-coherent way.

Admittedly, these policies aimed at time-spatial consequences may not be very successful. They are reactive and not proactive, as that would mean direct intervention in the conditions of those forms of leisure behaviour that had these consequences. That brings us back to the level of structural forces influencing the leisure policies just discussed. The dispersed and fragmented character of time-spatial problems encountered in and through leisure does not help by calling into existence pressure groups, comparable to labour organisations. Many groups, clubs, foundations and movements react to problems posed by leisure pursuits, but their interest is never in leisure per se. Thus, if the Green Movement reacts to leisure mobility, it is to defend the interests of nature by proposing to curtail mobility for recreational purposes.

In conclusion, it is possible to identify outside forces that threaten present leisure policies, but that at the same time it is difficult to think of a reason why this should point to the development of a new integrated leisure policy. With the dwindling impact of well-being oriented objectives, the most likely development is towards further dispersal of leisure policies over various departments and government layers and the subsuming of leisure policy objectives under other policy objectives. An alternative scenario that involves the generation of a coherent leisure policy, although improbable, is dependent on the availability of a catalyst, which would be able to connect threats and opportunities for the various leisure sectors, with the design of an attractive set of uniting objectives, thus presenting a better alternative for the survival of these sectors than the first scenario would seem to provide. Entertaining the possibility that such a catalyst may appear, is a matter of taking agency seriously.

REFERENCES

Beckers, Th.A.M. (1983) *Planning voor vrijheid. Een historisch-sociologische studie van de overheidsinterventie in recreatie en vrijetijd.* Wageningen: Pudoc.

Beckers, Th.A.M. (1985) 'Planning for Freedom. Ideology and state intervention in Dutch leisure and recreation', in *The Netherlands Journal of Sociology*, 21 (2), 110-125.

Beckers, Th.A.M. and van der Poel, H. (1990) *Vrijetijd tussen vorming en vermaak. Een inleiding tot de studie van de vrijetijd*, Leiden/Antwerpen: Stenfert Kroese.

Boekman, E. (1989) *Overheid en kunst in Nederland*, Utrecht: Bijleveld. (First edition 1939).

Braat, J. *et al.* (1985) *Honderd Jaar Rijksmuseum, 1885-1985*, Weesp: Van Holkema en Warendorf/Unieboek.

Browne, D.R. (1989) *Comparing Broadcast Systems. The Experiences of Six Industrialised Countries*, Ames, IA: Iowa State University Press.

Brugmans, I.J. (1961) *Paardenkracht en Mensenmacht. Sociaal-economische geschiedenis van Nederland, 1795-1940*, 's-Gravenhage: Martinus Nijhoff.

Burg, J. van der and Heuvel, J.H.J. van den (1991) *Film en overheidsbeleid. Van censuur naar zelfregulering.* 's-Gravenhage: SDU.

Centraal Bureau voor de Statistiek (1990) *Jaarboek toerisme en vrijetijdsbesteding*, 's-Gravenhage: SDU/CBS-publicaties.

Dijk, J. van (1990) *Het socialisme spant zijn gouden net over de wereld. Het kunst- en cultuurbeleid van de SDAP*, Amsterdam: UvA.

Dona, H. (1981) *Sport en socialisme. De geschiedenis van de Nederlandse Arbeiderssportbond 1926-1941*, Amsterdam: Van Gennep.

Doorn, J.A.A. van (1989) *Rede en Macht. Een inleiding tot beleidswetenschappelijk inzicht*, 's-Gravenhage: VUGA.

Doorn, J.W.M. van, Kosters, M.J. and Meulemeester, K. de (1981) *Toeristisch beleid in de lage landen. Inleiding en evaluerend overzicht*, 's-Gravenhage: Vuga.

Goede, P. de (1990) 'Commerciale omroep en de val van het kabinet-Marijnen in 1965', in *Jaarboek Mediageschiedenis 2*, Amsterdam: Stichting Mediageschiedenis/SDU, pp. 187-216.

Hart, M. 't (1989) 'Cities and statemaking in the Dutch Republic, 1580-1680', in *Theory and Society,* 18, 663-687.

Heuvel, H. van den (1976) *Nationaal of verzuild. De strijd om het Nederlandse omroepbestel in de periode 1923-1947*, Baarn: Ambo.

Israel, J.I. (1991) *Dutch Primacy in World trade, 1585-1740*, Oxford: Clarendon Press.

Jong, J. de (1987) *Een deftig bestaan. Het dagelijks leven van regenten in de 17de en 18de eeuw*, Utrecht/Antwerpen: Kosmos.

Karsten, L. (1989) *De achturendag. Arbeidstijdverkorting in historisch perspectief, 1817-1919*, Groningen: RUG.

Kennedy, P. (1988) *The Rise and Fall of the Great Powers. Economic Change and Military Conflict from 1500 to 2000*, London: Fontana.

Knippenberg, H. and Pater, B. de (1988) *De eenwording van Nederland. Schaalvergroting en integratie sinds 1800*, Nijmegen: SUN.

Kossman, E.H. (1976) *De Lage Landen, 1780-1940. Anderhalve eeuw Nederland en België*, Amsterdam/Brussel: Elsevier.

Kosters, M.J. (1981) *Focus op toerisme. Inleiding op het toeristisch gebeuren.* Den Haag: VUGA.

Lijphart, A. (1968/1984) *Verzuiling, pacificatie en kentering in de Nederlandse politiek*, Amsterdam: De Bussy.

Ministerie van Economische Zaken (EZ) (1984) *Nota Toeristisch Beleid 1985 t/m 1989*, Den Haag: Ministerie van Economische Zaken.

Ministerie van Economische Zaken (EZ) (1990) *Ondernemen in toerisme. Het toeristisch beleid voor de jaren negentig*, 's-Gravenhage: SDU.

Oosterbaan Martinius, W. (1990) *Schoonheid, Welzijn, Kwaliteit. Kunstbeleid en verantwoording na 1945*, 's-Gravenhage: Gary Schwartz/SDU.

Poel, H. van der (1987) 'Zwischen Politik und Okonomie - Interventionen im Freizeitbereich', in *Freizeitpadagogik* 9, (3-4), 159-168.

Righart, H. (1986) *De katholieke zuil in Europa. Het ontstaan van verzuiling onder katholieken in Oostenrijk, Zwitserland, Belgie en Nederland*, Meppel: Boom.

Schama, S. (1977) *Patriots and Liberators. Revolution in the Netherlands, 1780-1813*, New York: A.A. Knopf.

Schama, S. (1987) *The Embarrassment of Riches. An Interpretation of Dutch Culture in the Golden Age*, New York: A.A. Knopf.

Schneider, M. and Hemels, J. (1979) *De Nederlandse krant 1618-1978. Van 'nieuwstydinghe' tot dagblad*, Baarn: Het Wereldvenster.

Smithuijsen, C.B. (1988) 'Boekman en Kassies over cultuurspreiding' in H. van Dulken *et al.* (eds) *In ons diaconale land. Opstellen over cultuurspreiding. Voor Jan Kassies*, Amsterdam, Boekmanstichting/Van Gennep, 13-26.

Sociaal en Cultureel Planbureau (SCP) (1990) *Sociaal en Cultureel Rapport 1990*, Rijswijk/Den Haag: SCP/VUGA.

Stokvis, R. (1979) *Strijd over sport. Organisatorische en ideologische ontwikkelingen*, Deventer: Van Loghum Slaterus.

Stokvis, R. (1989) *De sportwereld. Een sociologische inleiding*, Alphen aan den Rijn/Brussel: Samsom.

Stuurman, S. (1983) *Verzuiling, kapitalisme en patriarchaat*, Nijmegen: SUN.

Vrankrijker, A.C.J. de (1981) *Mensen, leven en werken in de Gouden Eeuw*, 's-Gravenhage: Martinus Nijhoff.

Vries, J. de (1984) *European Urbanisation, 1500-1800*, London: Methuen.

Vries, J. de (1984a) 'The decline and rise of the Dutch economy, 1675-1900' in *Research in Economic History, Suppl 3 : Technique, Spirit and Form in the Making of the Modern Economics. Essays in Honor of William N. Parker*, 149-189.

Wallerstein, I. (1978) *Europese wereld-economie in de zestiende eeuw. Het moderne wereld-systeem*, Nieuwkoop: Heureka.

Wetenschappelijke Raad voor het Regeringsbeleid (WRR) (1989) *Cultuur zonder grenzen*, 's-Gravenhage: Staatsuitgeverij.

Wijfjes, H. (1988) *Radio onder restrictie. Overheidsbemoeiing met radioprogramma's 1919-1941*, Amsterdam: IISG.

Williams, A.M. and Shaw, G. (eds) (1988) *Tourism and Economic Development. Western European Experiences*, London and New York: Belhaven Press.

Chapter 4

Leisure Policy in Sweden

Hans-Erik Olson

Introduction

Free Time, 'Fritid', and the Concept of Leisure

Before undertaking any discussion of leisure policy in Sweden, it is necessary to have some understanding of how the concept of leisure is used and understood in Swedish. The common translation of the English word 'leisure' in Swedish is 'fritid', which more strictly means 'free time'. In the English language 'free time' and 'leisure' are not synonymous. Leisure is a special form of 'free time', which has connotations of the positive, qualitative aspects of free time. When 'fritid' is used in Swedish, what is understood is a time period which is free, at least in comparison with other time periods, especially with time spent at work. However, the qualitative dimension of leisure is seldom acknowledged in a formal way. 'Fritid' is understood both negatively, as 'just killing time', and positively as 'doing something valuable for one's own satisfaction'.

The problems associated with the definition of the word 'fritid' underlie the difficulty of defining an explicit and coherent leisure policy in Sweden. Sometimes 'fritid' is identified as outdoor recreation, plus sport plus tourism, and sometimes simply sport, or outdoor recreation, or hobbies are referred to as leisure. Any theorising of the 'leisure' phenomenon cannot employ a simple operational definition, so some kind of analytical account is necessary.

The Development of Leisure in Sweden

The Royal Swedish Academy has noted that the first time the word 'fritid' was used in a written text was in 1784. At that time the word was understood as 'the time during which one is free from a periodical disease, especially *ague*'(Svenska Akademiens Ordbok, 1926). Defining leisure in this way has nothing to do with the modern understanding of the word. A more clearly analytical approach to the phenomenon of leisure is required. Even if one does define the concept of leisure as a time quantity (e.g. as a time comparatively free from economic, physiological and social constraints) one should recognise that leisure is not simply a product of the industrial revolution. It could be argued that people have always had leisure, even in the stone age (Olson, 1983). The industrial revolution simply served to throw the concept of leisure into stark relief. However, moving from the general phenomenon of 'leisure' to 'leisure policy', it is evident that the politics of leisure were born during the industrial revolution. When the factory siren blew, the nature of time changed from work time to leisure time. Leisure time began to be seen as a social 'problem'.

The industrial revolution came rather late to Sweden. Until 1900, Sweden was industrially underdeveloped. Between 1860 and 1900 about 1 million Swedes emigrated to North America in search of a better standard of living. During the late nineteenth century the situation gradually changed. From 1880 to 1915 the industrial revolution took root in Sweden (Fridholm *et al.* 1976). During this period many well-known Swedish industrial companies such as ASEA (Brown Boveri), Atlas Copco, and Ericsson were established and developed rapidly. ASEA, for example in 1891 employed only 70 workers, but by 1907 this figure had risen to 2,300 (Gärlund, 1942).

Urbanisation went hand in hand with industrialisation. People moved from agricultural work in the countryside to industrial work in cities. Urbanisation initially developed in the form of small towns, and subsequently larger cities such as Stockholm, Gothenburg, Malmö and Norrköping began to expand. Between 1885 and 1915 the total number of inhabitants in Swedish cities doubled. However, Sweden was still primarily an agricultural country and the majority of people lived in rural settings. It was only in 1957 that the urban population first exceeded 50 per cent, a century later than was the case in Great Britain (Historisk Statistik för Sverige, 1969). The third factor in the rise of leisure as a political phenomenon was the class conflict produced by industrialisation and urbanisation. The Swedish middle class grew in political importance from the beginning of the nineteenth century. In 1889 the working class formed its own political party - the Social Democrats - and in 1898 working class trade unionism was born.

These structural changes influenced both the political and ideological spheres in Sweden. The changes were also important for the development of leisure policy (or, to be more precise, some leisure policies) in Sweden. If one were to point to a specific starting date for leisure politics and policy, it would be 1 May, 1890. On that day, the Swedish working class took to the streets, together with comrades around the industrialising world, in the very first May-day demonstrations. The most important political demand both in Stockholm and elsewhere, was for 'eight hours work, eight hours sleep, eight hours leisure'. The right to leisure was defined as being as important as work and sleep. The political claim for eight hours leisure was made in order to shorten the time spent in work, but eight hours leisure was seen as important to human beings for their cultural growth and for the purposes of recuperation.

While leisure was put on the political agenda in 1890, this new political initiative was separated thereafter into different elements, or types of demand, for youth services, sport, outdoor recreation or tourism. This chapter will therefore explore the ways in which leisure politics and policy have developed in Sweden with particular reference to these subdivisions of leisure policy.

Popular Movements

During the decades just before and just after the turn of the century, a range of popular movements emerged in Sweden. The first voluntary associations were established in the middle of the nineteenth century, with a second wave during the 1870s and the 1880s. The first of the popular movements was associated with the development of the free church. To understand this it is first necessary to be aware that Sweden had (and indeed retains) a state church of Lutheran origin. All Swedish citizens were deemed to belong to the traditional church whether they wished to or not. The Swedish Church was also, until the middle of the twentieth Century a conservative institution, which served the establishment. The free church movement represented a reaction against this conservative apparatus. In the middle of the nineteenth century, mainly due to foreign influences, Sweden witnessed the development of congregations of Baptists, Methodists and some 'indigenous' Swedish free churches, while, in 1900, the Salvation Army and the Pentecostal revival were founded.

The second significant popular movement to emerge in this period was the temperance movement. The Swedish International Order of Good Templars, the key organisation in the temperance movement in Sweden, was founded in 1897. This movement campaigned against the widespread abuse of alcohol which was a key feature of Swedish folk culture. The third significant popular movement was the Swedish labour movement. In 1846, the first trade union was formed by printers, but it was not until 1881 that a socialist labour movement could be said to have developed. In 1889 the Social Democratic Party was formed by 72 local associations of which 54 were trade unions (Bäckström, 1971).

The main objective for each of these popular movements was to evoke change in society. The free church movement sought to convert people to a Christian way of life and thereby to create a Christian society. The temperance movement wanted to build a sober society, free from the many problems brought by intoxicating beverages. The labour movement wanted to establish influence and power for the working class. Since each of these movements sought some form of radical change, it was important for them to maintain their independence from state influence. A second characteristics which the popular movements had in common, was that they drew their membership largely from among the upper working, and lower middle classes. They were led predominantly by skilled workers, who were most interested in ideological questions and problems. (Lundquist, 1974, 1977).

Popular movements came to play an important political role in Sweden, particularly in their fight for democratisation. Universal suffrage was their most significant political demand and this was achieved in 1921. When the popular movements were established during the late nineteenth century, no distinctions were made between adults and youth in terms of membership. One reason for this was that many of the leading figures in the establishment of these movements were themselves young, often in their twenties. However, after the turn of the century, the organisations initiated special 'youth associations', formally independent of the 'mother organisation' but with strong connections, in personnel and in terms of ideological and financial links. However, this formal separation of youth signalled the beginnings of the struggle to socialise youth into appropriate adult roles.

The popular movements brought about a further social distinction, between those who were connected with, or active in, the associations and those who were not. Within the popular movements the active members were building up a new type of respectability, with a set of values and norms similar to, but not identical with those of the middle class. One of these values was the *instrumental* orientation to both leisure and work. For the respectable working class, even leisure time ought to be used in a rational way.

Outside the respectable working classes associated with popular movements were the 'rough working class', those who were more interested in *expressive* leisure activities like singing, drinking and fighting, rather than taking part in responsible political and religious activities (Allardt, 1970; Hobsbawn, 1971; Ambjörnsson, 1988). This separation became crucial, especially for leisure policy. During the first half of the nineteenth century, as the movements grew politically strong, they started to argue for stronger state intervention in leisure and for support of their own instrumental lifestyle.

The Struggle over Youth Leisure

The Legal Foundations of State Intervention

As we have seen, industrialisation and urbanisation created new class conflicts; industrial capital and the middle class on one side, and the working class on the other. The aspect of the conflicts which is of interest here was the clash of values between the different class groups. The new urban, industrial workers brought with them their traditional, agricultural, folk culture which incorporated periods of idleness, drinking bouts, and the use of open spaces for leisure activities. In addition the rural proletarian groups traditionally held more liberal views on sexual relations. This proletarian lifestyle, which had dominated village life, had rarely attracted middle class attention or disapproval. However, as urbanisation brought this behaviour into the midst of the urban middle class, a confrontation ensued, particularly during the late nineteenth century. For many members of the bourgeoisie, the words 'ruffian' and 'worker' became synonymous (Löfgren, 1983). They were ignorant of the fact that the working class in their party and trade union organisations were constructing a respectability of their own. For the bourgeoisie and the establishment, the socialist working class movement represented a threat.

During the latter part of nineteenth century tensions intensified as the middle class began to build up its own identity in order to distinguish itself both from the old nobility and from the new proletariat. This liberal ethic was built around the three watchwords: 'temperance, industriousness and thrift' (Pauli, 1906). To these was added a negative attitude towards all functions of the body, especially those with sexual connotations. Thus, the notion of a refined and cultivated liberal middle class developed (Frykman and Löfgren, 1981). The middle classes were quite sure that their norms and values were beneficial not only for themselves, but for the population as a whole. From 1867 onwards, the elevation of popular mores and values became the moral and cultural goal of the middle class. During the nineteenth century as the middle class grew in political strength, this aim was turned into political practice by the Parliament.

The elementary school, introduced by the Liberals in 1842, represented one of the most important tools in the socialisation of working-class children into bourgeois values and norms. The taming of working class leisure was to become a further vehicle for the inculcation of appropriate values. In 1896 an eminent elementary school teacher and a Liberal member of the Parliament, Fridtjuv Berg, proposed a motion suggesting more guidelines for the upbringing for morally neglected children. He spoke of the 'serious danger which threatened our social order because of moral deprivation experienced by some parts of the younger generation'. It was necessary for a state commission to investigate this problem he claimed (Riksdagen, 1896). In 1900 the Royal Commission presented its findings which pointed to the structural changes which had taken place in Sweden during the preceding decades. It highlighted the limited resources to assist working class parents in bringing up their children, and the state was forced to intervene.

However, the Commission did not just comment on parental practices, it also noted the ideological conflict between employees and employers. The question was raised as to whether any education could be effective if youngsters lived in families, which expressed 'contempt for divine and social order'. The Commission concluded that such an upbringing would mean that young people would 'lose their sensitivity to religious influences, defy school rules and have less respect for the authority of the state' (Tvängsuppfostringskommittén, 1990). The Royal Commission thus involved itself directly in this conflict of values, which was in effect a class conflict, and took the side of bourgeois society against the working class.

The Commission's work resulted in a new 'law against deprivation', passed by Parliament in 1902, which gave the State the right to take a child from her/his parents and to send her/him to a reform school. The law also gave permission to communities to establish a new local government body, the *Child Care Authority*. It was thought that this would be needed, especially in industrial cities (Riksdagen, 1902). This decision demonstrated the view that socialisation and child care problems could no longer be solved by the traditional agencies of the family, the church and the school. A new body was required, which could, if necessary, give government total responsibility for the education and upbringing of any child up to the age of 15. As a result leisure came to the attention of local government officials, who belonged in general to the middle classes and represented the establishment views. Middle class state professionals thus received a new instrument with which to control the leisure behaviour of working class youth.

The Child Care Authority, introduced in the 1902 legislation, was a reflection of a new departure in state intervention, social work. The nature and functions of social work are complex, but it is interesting to note that this new form of state intervention was first introduced to help to resolve what were seen as problems of inadequate social education. During the first decades of the twentieth century this form of state intervention grew in popularity. New organisations and new magazines were founded to stimulate and develop this new area of professional activity. Social work was something other than education. Two agencies of government were engaged in the socialisation of young people, though operating with different goals and methods. This distinction is important, because leisure policy for young people was developed as an aspect of social work rather than education.

In the period 1900 to 1925 a range of new laws were passed by the Swedish Parliament in the field of social work. In 1924, the 1902 law expired and was replaced by a new *Child Care Law*. From 1926 all communities were required to establish a Child Care Authority.

They were also forced by the law to 'promote the welfare of youth', a formulation which was used, at least in Stockholm, to legitimate the development of a system of control over young people's leisure. The legal foundation for profound state intervention in the leisure of young people had been established by this social welfare legislation.

Youth Clubs

In parallel with the establishment of child care legislation by the state, there were related developments in civil society. In 1887 the first 'Arbetsstuga' (Home for Worktraining) was started in Stockholm by private initiative. These homes arranged after school activities for poor working-class children between 7 and 12 years of age. Their objectives were a combination of giving the children education in some practical handicrafts, fostering good behaviour, and keeping them off the streets. Implicit in the programmes of the 'arbetsstugor' was the idea that leisure activities could prevent anti-social, criminal behaviour (Hierta-Retzius, 1887), an assumption which was to become very important for the future development of leisure policy for young people.

Just after the turn of the century, the first youth clubs were opened. These were mainly directed towards working class boys but later on, to girls as well. The inspiration for the establishing of these clubs came mainly from youth work abroad, the British Settlement movement being especially important. In 1912 the first Swedish settlement was established in Stockholm - *Birkagarden* - and was followed by others, with the founding of the National Federation of Swedish Settlements in 1927. The Settlements were not at first intended to be a part of the youth work movement. Indeed, Birkagarden started as a missionary station in a typical working class area - Birkastaden - in Stockholm. The objective was to bring Christianity to its anti-religious working-class inhabitants. Some other settlements were secular organisations, but all settlements were oriented towards adult education and social fellowship during leisure time. However, most settlements found that those groups which had most leisure time were young. They therefore incorporated clubs for young people into their programmes (Olson, 1982).

One of the founders of Birkagarden, Ebba Pauli, a famous Swedish social worker, noted that there was a difference between those working class youth who went to the youth associations and those who were playing in the streets. The former had a good vocational education, which the latter lacked. The youth clubs were, according to Pauli, aimed mainly at attracting the second group, those who were not members of the youth associations (Pauli, 1921). Her observation was consistent with the findings of later research but she was not the only actor during those years to draw this conclusion. There always seems to have been a special segment of youth, which has not been interested in the instrumental 'rational' activities of the youth associations, but which may be attracted by the recreational activities of youth clubs.

This assumption remains central to the rationale of local governments developing youth clubs even today.

The youth clubs of the early twentieth century were, however, not founded simply in order to bring fun to working class youngsters. All had more developed objectives. Some were started in order to prevent the socialist movement from establishing a greater influence on working class youth. Others were more directly concerned with instilling a new ethic, based on refined and cultivated bourgeois values, in 'rough' working class youth. None of the clubs was established by the working class movement itself, which instead organised activities within its own associations for young people.

Thus two different types of objectives were evident in the provision for youth. The youth clubs were organised by upper or middle class people for working class young people. The objective was to gain closer *control* over how the youngsters used their leisure time. The youth associations within the popular movements, on the other hand, were mainly (but not totally) organised by the youth and for the youth of the same social strata. Their objective was to stimulate the *autonomy* of young people. I would contend that this conflict between control and autonomy still prevails in Swedish leisure policy, at least in respect of young people.

Local Government and Youth Clubs

Within the first two decades of the century all of the private youth clubs closed, with the exception of those established by the settlement movement. The other clubs were not founded upon a set of paternalistic values, which inevitably undermined the enthusiasm of their clients. In most cases the enthusiasm of the original leaders was not sustained, and inevitably when the leader resigned, the clubs were closed. However, the need to teach the working class street 'hooligans' the 'right' way to use leisure was as great as ever. When private solutions to the problem expired, pressure was placed on local government to provide a solution. The first local government youth club in Sweden was founded in Gothenburg in 1936. The settlement in Gothenburg was a model for this club; the aim, the structure and the personnel, were taken from the settlement (Olson, 1982). A number of authorities followed a similar strategy. However, commentary here will focus on the development of youth policy in the capital of Sweden, Stockholm, since this is the best researched example.

At the end of the 1920s the Child Care Authority in Stockholm considered the social situation in some newly-built housing areas for low paid working class families with many children. The Authority had noted that many gangs formed by youths became involved in 'shop-lifting, mischief, vandalism and sexual misconduct'. It was becoming necessary to teach the youth 'the right way to use their leisure' (Barnavärdsnämnden, 1928). During the winter of 1939/40 the Authority opened a number of youth clubs in these areas.

The aim of these clubs was to exert a better controlling 'influence' over youths between the ages of 14 and 16. Neither the Authority nor the youth associations had been successful in exerting this influence. Instead the youth had caused 'anxiety' to the Authority, which hoped that the clubs would be the solution to the delinquency problem (Barnavärdsnämnden, 1939). From this point on, leisure definitely became part of the policy agenda in the city of Stockholm, not in order to raise the quality of life for working class youth, but as a solution to a social problem.

State Subsidies to Youth Associations

The other side of Swedish leisure policy, concerns policies directed towards 'respectable' youth. This normally took the form of subsidies both from central state and local government to the youth associations of the popular movements. At the central state level, the first decision to provide subsidy on a regular basis, was taken by Parliament in 1908. That year one association in the temperance movement received 2000 SEK to give lectures to students about the dangers of alcohol abuse. The following year other youth associations in the temperance movement also received state subsidies. In 1913 the Swedish Sports Federation, and in 1920 the Agricultural Youth Association, also both received regular subsidies.

Before 1954 little consideration was given in Parliament to giving youth associations in general state subsidies on a regular basis. At the local government level, the situation was different. In 1927 the Child Care Authority in Stockholm decided to give 2000 SEK to two youth associations. The argument was that the Board wanted the organisations to do 'valuable work in the field in preventive youth care'. This new item in the local government budget was termed 'Measures to promote the welfare of the youth', a formulation borrowed from the 1924 legislation on child care (Stockholms stadsfullmäktige, 1927).

The Child Care Law was here used as a legal foundation to bring even the youth associations into a system to consolidate the stability of Swedish society, despite the fact that the main objective of the popular movements which founded these associations was to change society. Thus, as was the case with state subsidy for youth clubs, support for youth associations was not seen as a goal in itself, but as a vehicle for reinforcing social stability.

Almost annually, from the late 1920s to the early 1940s, a political debate took place in the Swedish Parliament about the deleterious impact of modern dance on young people. Christian members of both the bourgeois and Social Democratic parties formed a moral conservative block in order to try to oppose the spread of 'dance fury' among the young. Up until 1939 this group sought different political means by which to control young people's opportunities for dancing. However, in 1939 the tactic was changed. Instead of seeking to suppress by law the 'evils' of dance, the moral conservatives sought to promote positive alternatives. One of the features of the youth world which was viewed most positively was their associations. Youth associations in general, even those for social democratic youth, were now seen as respectable. (Only the Nazis and the communists were viewed negatively.) The political conclusion was that support for positive organisations was a means of promoting appropriate behaviour even among the rougher elements of working class youth. Parliament decided to ask for a Royal Commission to investigate the situation among youth and to establish how it might be improved (Riksdagen, 1939).

During the early 1940s, the moral conservatives were more active than before. The youth situation was deemed to be deteriorating, with not only the dance craze spreading, but criminality and the incidence of illegitimacy growing. The evidence does not bear this out, but the moral conservatives were convinced by the impressionistic picture drawn by clergymen, Christian-oriented teachers, social workers, doctors and others. The moral conservatives main objective was to oppose the Social Democrats, especially their more radical views on sexual questions.

As a product of the long debate over the 'youth problem', youth centres, youth-leaders, youth councils and youth exhibitions, all were established with state funding during the 1940s. Throughout the country, all those concerned with youth were trying to show the public how respectable young people in their associations were using their leisure time with dignity. From 1944 to 1951, with the youth debate as a background, the Royal Commission for Youth Care published proposals for different types of state subsidies for leisure activities of the young. It is interesting to note that the Commission made the same distinction as Ebba Pauli, 1921. It noted a difference between the instrumentally-oriented youth who were likely to join the youth associations, and the expressive-oriented youth, who might use the youth clubs and youth centres. The Commission proposed state subsidies for both (SOU, 1944, p. 31; SOU, 1947, p. 12).

The Social Democratic government showed little real interest in these proposals. During the early years of the 1950s, however, a new threat to the youth was identified in the form of alcohol. Another State Commission revealed in 1952 that almost 70 per cent of those young people charged by the police with being drunk, were not members of any youth association. The Commission thus drew the very dubious conclusion that young people might be saved from alcoholism by joining a youth association. Once again the main problem was viewed as that of 'rootless working class youth' (SOU 1952, p. 53). This argument proved effective and in 1954 the government proposed a new type of state subsidy for so-called 'leisure groups". The youth associations received money for every group meeting which was organised according to the rules decided by government. It is interesting to note that these subsidies did not go to the associations' regular ideological activities, but only to meetings which were designed to be of interest to the 'expressive oriented youth', who were generally not members of the associations (Riksdagen, 1954). In 1954 the state took a different view from that underpinning the original legislation of 1902. The establishment of a Child Care Department was no longer seen to be sufficient. What was needed was a new local government agency incorporating the work of the youth associations.

The Development of Youth Leisure Policy after 1955

The history of the development of youth leisure policy in the period up to 1955 is relatively well researched (Olson, 1991a). Information relating to the period since that date, however, is rather more sketchy. The development of policy up to 1955 has been stressed because both the form and the arguments presented during this period are still relevant to contemporary leisure policy. Initially, youth centres in Sweden were predominantly established by local authority Child Care Departments, which were designed to deal with youth from a social welfare rather than a leisure perspective. The centres were intended to solve the social problems associated with problem groups among working class youth. This was clearly stated in a research report published by the City Council of Stockholm in 1954. The main objective of the centres were that they should contribute to social stability and prevent the formation of youth gangs and other anti-social tendencies. They were especially important in those housing areas where many young people experienced 'difficulties in social adjustment' and were prone to anti-social behaviour (Ungdom och fritid, 1954). This was the principal objective, even though more leisure-oriented goals were also evident in these forms of provision.

During the 1960s and early 1970s almost all communities in Sweden established local authority departments for leisure and recreation. The youth centres were transferred from the Child Care Authorities, (which during the same period were incorporated into new and more broad-based Social Welfare Authorities) to the new Recreation departments. At the same time the 'youth centres' were renamed 'leisure centres'. All of these changes were administrative rather than changes in philosophy or policy content. Some efforts were made to convert the former youth centres into real leisure centres serving all age groups, but this policy was never successfully implemented and 'leisure centres' around the country remain largely age-segregated 'youth centres' in all but name.

The youth work orientation is also still very important. During the 1980s there were youth riots both in Malmö and in Stockholm and as a result, the youth centres in both cities received more money. It was hoped that these facilities would help to keep troublesome youth off the streets. The same rationale had of course been presented some 80 years earlier. In 1989 one of Sweden's best known leisure researchers, Ulf Blomdahl, argued that youth centres should concentrate their work on marginal youth, those most susceptible to lifestyles incorporating drug abuse and criminality (Blomdahl and Claeson, 1989). This was a plea for a return to the old, youth work orientation of social control.

During the 1970s and 1980s there was debate over the possibility of democratising the management of youth centres. Users, it was argued, should be able to make decisions about the management of the centres, and this itself would provide 'training' in democratic practices. However, little has been achieved in this area. Admittedly there were legal problems associated with implementing this policy, but those problems could have been overcome if the political will to develop this policy had been present. A democratic structure for these centres would have had to be based on the notion of autonomy for young people, which would require a radical review of the ideological and political objectives of these centres.

In respect of subsidies to youth associations, the policy changed very little in the period from the 1950s to the 1980s. Support for 'leisure groups' initiated in 1954 was broadened to incorporate support for the 'local activities' of the youth associations in 1974, and during the 1960s Parliament decided to grant aid to the central administrations of the youth associations. By the beginning of the 1990s some 70 associations were receiving such support via 'Statens ungdomsråd' (The State Youth Council).

In 1954 state support for leisure groups was intended to support activities provided by the associations for young people who were not members of the associations themselves. However, the organisations bent the rules so that in effect state support was used to fund many of their regular activities. In 1974 a commission from the State Youth Council proposed a policy change in respect of the objectives for state subsidies. The associations were now seen to be supporting leisure activities which were viewed as intrinsically positive and valuable. The extrinsic rationale of modifying the social behaviour of young people was no longer seen by the state as relevant (Statens ungdomsråd, 1974).

The success of youth interest groups in obtaining state support illustrates the effects of a general political change in Swedish politics after the Second World War. Associations in civil society had become more politically powerful. Where there was a possibility of obtaining money from central or local government, youth interest groups acted in concert. Both right and left, religious and atheist groups orchestrated pressure in order to maximise the funding possibilities. However, certain youth groups and youth agencies remained a substantial concern for government. In 1987 the state established a new subsidy for special projects which was aimed at the 'non-joiners', those young people who have chosen to be independent of, or have been expelled from, the youth associations.

At the local government level it is more difficult to generalise about the situation in respect of youth and leisure. It would seem that many local government politicians still hope that youth associations will act as bulwarks against different types of anti-social leisure behaviour. These politicians are ignorant of, or ignore, the fact that there is no empirical evidence to support any link between leisure opportunity and a reduction in anti-social behaviour (Coalter, 1989; Sarnecki, 1983).

Sport and Policy

The Introduction of British Sport to Sweden

Swedes have a long tradition of involvement in sport, but during the late nineteenth century, the emphasis changed from 'folk cultural sport' to the 'British' system of competitive sport. With the arrival of track and field athletics, football, rowing and many other kinds of sports, traditional Swedish games went into decline. However, one uniquely Swedish sport which did not die was 'Ling-gymnastics'. This type of gymnastics was essentially non-competitive, and required no apparatus. The system was invented by Per-Henrik Ling (1776-1839) in the early nineteenth century to enhance people's health. In 1813 Ling also opened the Gymnastiska Centralinstitutet (Central Institute for Gymnastics) in Stockholm in order to educate teachers in gymnastics. Other types of traditional Swedish sports like skiing, swimming and skating came under the influence of British sport and during the late nineteenth century, rules for competition were devised. This was the general background to the establishment of Sveriges Riksidrottsförbund (Swedish Sport Federation) in 1903, which still is the principal organisation for competitive sports in Sweden and a very important actor in sport and leisure politics.

At the beginning of the twentieth century the Swedish sport movement was headed by key establishment figures, with the Crown Prince at its head (Lindroth, 1974). However, some sports, especially football, became popular among the growing urban working classes. In the new class-based society the sport movement played a double role. At the top level, it is quite clear that it was treated by the establishment as an instrument to promote social order. Many working class leaders also looked with suspicion on the new sports movement and warned members of the working class not to join. On the other hand at lower levels, sport became an area of freedom for the working class. Here workers could play an important role as both sports participants and administrators. There was some evidence, even among the middle class of a suspicion towards sport. In the norms governing behaviour of the 'refined and cultivated middle class person', ecstatic, overt emotional display was forbidden, and also secretions from the body like sweat were frowned upon. Sport was therefore condemned by conservative and nationalistic groups for being 'un-Swedish'.

State Subsidies for Sport

British sport introduced many new conflicts in Sweden. During its first ten years the Swedish Sports Federation was very eager to receive state subsidies. However, the first proposals for state subsidy of sport, though supported by the government were successfully opposed by the Parliament. In 1913 the situation changed. The year before, the 1912 Olympic Games had been held in Stockholm. Sweden had been successful and was top of the unofficial medal table. Even those who criticised sport for promoting improper values, began to acknowledge positive aspects of sport. As we have already seen, the situation among working class youth frightened many bourgeois politicians in the early part of the century. In 1903, a Liberal MP argued that sport was

> an effective agent to keep the youth away from disastrous
> pleasures and amusements and to prevent a great many
> moral threats.
>
> (Riksdagen, 1903)

As time went by, the youth argument became more important. In 1913 when the Liberal Government proposed its successful bill to the Parliament, the Minister of Education and Church, Fridtjuv Berg, pointed to the potential of sport in the moral education of young people. Many Conservative and Liberal MPs underlined the positive effects of sport both in respect of youth and of the working class more generally.

The Social Democrats were, however, divided on this issue. The chairman of the party, Hjalmar Branting, supported state subsidy of sport. He regarded positively the fact that sport had become very popular among working class youth. However, other leading Social Democrats, and also a number of Liberals, stressed the negative characteristics of sport. Boxing and wrestling were cited as unlikely to promote positive values, while tendencies towards 'professionalism' and the use of drugs (strychnine) were also viewed negatively. Furthermore, sport was also a relatively classless movement and could, it was argued, receive money from the wealthier sectors of society. Thus the debate about the socially positive and negative impacts of sport, which still rages today was evident in those early political struggles. Nevertheless, the first regular subsidy was voted by Parliament when it decided to give 100,000 SEK to the Sport Federation and another association to build sports arenas and organise competitions in 1913 (Riksdagen, 1913). In 1913 proponents of state subsidy were able to argue that only by exerting pressure through subsidy could the state hope to avert the negative aspects of sport. Thus state subsidies were governed by rules designed to clean up the sports movement. Another important phenomenon was the political astuteness shown by the leaders of the Swedish Sports Federation before and during the Parliamentary session, when they were very active in lobbying for states subsides. Almost every MP received material which stressed the importance of sports for the people and for the nation. Ever since 1913 the sports movement has been very effective in obtaining funds form central state and local government.

Ling-Gymnastics and the Debate about Competitive Sport

As we have noted Ling-gymnastics was a Swedish form of non-competitive sport. Competitive sport was viewed as 'British', and most upper and middle class Swedes were at that time oriented towards German rather than British culture. Between 1913 and the beginning of the Second World War there was a debate in Parliament, virtually annually, on how much money should be given to *Svenska Gymnastikförbundet* (Swedish Association for Gymnastics) and to the Swedish Sports Federation (SSF). Even though the Association for Gymnastics was a member of SSF, it received its state subsidy from a special source within the budget. This gave those MPs who opposed competitive sport, the opportunity to manifest that opposition by giving more money to the non-competitive Association for Gymnastics. For some years the Association received almost as much money as all the other sports in the Swedish Sports Federation put together.

Boxing, an Example of the Negative Impact of Some Sports

In 1921 the visit of the French boxer Georges Carpentier to Stockholm caused much unrest. Both the visit itself and the general topic of boxing raised considerable criticism in the press and in Parliament. The critics of modern sport now had a good opportunity to argue their case. Boxing was just one example among many of the excesses of modern sport. There was a clamour to 'clean up' the sports movement. Per-Albin Hansson (who some years later became the leader of the Social Democratic Party) argued for greater state 'control over the whole sports movement'. The Government proposed a subvention of 200,000 SEK to the Swedish Sports Federation but Parliament cut this to 90,000 SEK, with 40,000 of that total to go the 'ideologically sound' activity of Ling gymnastics (Riksdagen, 1921).

The controversy surrounding boxing returned after the Second World War. This time the campaign was led by members of the Liberal Party. Boxing, it was argued, did not promote better physical and mental health, which was one important justification for state support to sport. The campaign focused upon the central issue of whether Parliament should have the right to decide which types of sport should be supported. Although many MPs felt that the state should specify which sports were worthy of support, others, including the leaders of the Social Democratic Party, argued that it should not. This latter group pointed out that the Swedish Sports Federation was a voluntary body and insisted that neither the Government nor Parliament should intervene in its work. Funding of sport by the government should therefore be 'at arm's length', without specification in detail of how monies were to be spent. In 1958 those who opposed support for boxing lost a parliamentary vote by 160 votes to 185 (Riksdagen, 1958). The principle that the state should not intervene in the workings of the Swedish Sports Federation was thus finally established.

Competitive Sport or Outdoor Recreation

During the late 1930s Ling-gymnastics declined in popularity. After the Second World War the Association of Gymnastics imported competitive gymnastics from Germany and the association become similar to all the others within the Swedish Sports Federation.

The popularity of outdoor recreation spread in Sweden, and in 1939 a special foundation to promote outdoor recreation was established by Parliament. The Outdoor Recreation Foundation was after the Second World War sometimes used as a vehicle through which to express opposition to competitive sport. However, both the Government and the Parliament continued to express support for sporting competition, and as spectator sport became very popular in the post-war period, few politicians could be expected to find the courage to demand an end to increasing state subsidy of sport. Another type of conflict between outdoor recreation and competitive sport developed during the 1950s. In 1955 'Skid och friluftsfrämjandet' (the Swedish Association for the Promotion of Skiing and Outdoor Recreation), left the Swedish Sport Federation. The 'Friluftsfrämjandet', as it is known as today, was not involved in competitions and found itself out of place within the Swedish Sports Federation. The same was true of 'Svenska Korporationsidrottsförbundet' (the Swedish Industrial Sport Association), founded in the early 1940s, which was also not a member of the Swedish Sports Federation.

These exceptions caused problems for the state, which wanted some unity and order within its sports policy, and now had to establish how to distribute state subsidies to three associations. The founding of a special state agency to stand above all three associations was proposed by a state commission in 1958, but this was rejected by the powerful Swedish Sports Federation which wanted the other two associations to be subsumed within its own membership. The solution, adopted in 1969, was that the Swedish Sports Federation should be asked to act as a neutral state agency and distribute the subsidies in an even-handed manner to the other two associations, without reference to the fact that they were not amongst its own members.

In 1970, despite protests from the two associations, Parliament decided on this solution which has continued to be problematic ever since. A number of MPs have put down motions to liberate the non-members of the SSF, which now has incorporated associations for other activities (including cycling, fishing, boating, and horse riding).

All of these associations have little connection with competitive or élite sport, which is the main concern of the Swedish Sports Federation and its member organisations.

Changing Figureheads: from Crown Prince to Politicians, and from Politicians to Businessmen

When the sports movement was founded around 1900 it was led by officers and other representatives of the upper class. The Crown Prince, (later to become King Gustaf VI), was one of the leading figures in the Swedish Sports Federation. Sport at that time was identified with the establishment and employed as a tool to promote nationalism. After the Second World War the situation changed and the sports movement was democratised. This change was a product of two major factors. First, as we have already seen, competitive sport became popular among Swedes from across the whole of the social spectrum. Secondly, the state's concern with welfare grew after the war, and the question was raised of how the benefits of sport would be made available to the people if the state did not provide money for competitive sport .

Two outcomes emerged. In Parliament an unofficial 'sports lobby' was formed, consisting of members from different parties, to counter those who were either opposed to subsidy or were simply neutral. It is interesting to see which groups were involved; the Communists in particular, during the 1950s supported almost every proposal for state subsidies which came from the Swedish Sports Federation. The second result was that many politicians (particularly those involved in the lobby) were elected to the boards of the Swedish Sports Federation and its member organisations. During the 1960s, for example, Olof Palme, before he became the Prime Minister, was Chairman of the Swedish Canoeing Association

Businessmen, particularly in the post-war period, had shown interest in leading sports federations or sport clubs, but that interest increased during the 1970s. During this decade more money was attracted into competitive sport. Many sports clubs grew and were handling huge sums. In order to deal most effectively with the money, businessmen and bank directors were asked to sit on the boards of sports clubs and associations. Politicians were coming to be seen as less important for the sports movement. This tendency was strengthened during the 1980s when the new Liberals gained electoral success. The major source of funds for sport was no longer, in the early 1990s, the public sector, but private sector investment and sponsorship and income from television.

Commercialisation of Sport

In 1945 the Swedish Track and Field association disqualified Gunder Hägg, Arne Andersson and some 10 other runners, who were accused of receiving money for competing during the War. In the cases of

Hägg and Andersson the amount of money was considerable, but for most of the rest it represented relatively small sums, spread out over five years. In 1963 the middle-distance runner Dan Waern, was subject to a similar ban. By the 1990s professionalism was no longer to be regarded as a serious problem. Drug abuse had replaced it as the key problem in sport.

The breakthrough for commercialised sport came in Sweden in the late 1970s. It had already taken root a decade earlier. In the 1960s even Parliament openly discussed how elite sport should be supported by the state. In 1978 the Sports Federation published a report on commercialisation in élite sport, concluding that it should not be regarded as a threat to the sports movement, but rather as a crucial opportunity since it was a major source of revenue. This report opened the door for major investments in sport. Sponsorship became popular, not only for the big clubs playing in the first division of national leagues, but also for the small clubs in rural settings. During the 1980s this developed further and is a major factor in sports funding in the 1990s.

Sport as a 'Popular Movement'

Today both politicians and representatives of the sports movement argue that sport is the biggest and the most important popular movement in Sweden, but the validity of this argument must be questioned. The sports movement is a complex movement. Any analysis should start with a review of the dominant organisation, the Swedish Sports Federation. An important characteristic of a popular movement is - or at least was - that it organised the lower strata of society. At its inception this was not true of the Swedish Sports Federation. Another criterion is that a popular movement should act independently of the state. The Swedish Sports Federation has, however, never been an independent body. Since 1913 the state has exercised firm control over the subsidies the Swedish Sports Federation has received, placing restrictions and conditions on its grant, having a representative from government on its board, and appointing an auditor.

Virtually, then, from its outset, the Swedish Sports Federation has operated only in a quasi-autonomous manner. In 1970 the government representation on the board of the Federation was doubled. The argument was that they served to ensure that no injustices should occur in the financial allocation to those organisations who received their state subsidies via the Swedish Sports Federation but were not themselves members of the Federation. Thus one must conclude that the Swedish Sports Federation does not constitute a popular movement.

Leaving aside the Federation itself, a defining feature of popular movements is that they incorporate some element of critique of society and seek to change it in some way. Modern competitive sport is dominated, however, by economic concerns. The very ethos of competitive sport, striving to win at all costs, reinforces rather than challenges values in a capitalist system. However, sport involves more than competitive sport, it incorporates activities such as outdoor recreation and jogging which may done for intrinsic satisfactions. Most organisations, for example, working to promote outdoor recreation and social, or community-oriented sport, belong to the leisure sector. Their primary aims are not simply sporting victory, but the use of sport as a tool to achieve leisure policy goals related to personal and/or community development. Sport is thus a two-sided phenomenon, sometimes reinforcing, sometimes challenging mainstream values.

Tourism and Recreation Policies

Two Views on Tourism

Up to the early part of the twentieth century, the Swedish population was predominantly rural. They lived close to nature and the need or economic potential for outdoor recreation or tourism provision was small. The industrialisation of Sweden slowly started to change this situation. In 1885 *Svenska Turistföreningen* (STF) - The Swedish Tourist Association - was founded by academics, mainly natural scientists, connected with the University of Uppsala. Their objective was to develop travelling in Sweden, in part by making it easier. Another objective was to spread information about Sweden, especially about the mountain areas in the north-western part of the country.

The STF reflected two significant movements of the time. The first sought relief from the negative aspects of industrialisation. The second was a patriotic movement in which the STF played an important part. 'Know your own country' became the watchword of the association. Education, and bringing up people to a better understanding of the grandeur of nature to be found in Sweden were two important objectives (STF, 1985; Ödman *et al.*, 1982). Tourism was at that time hardly regarded as an economic concern. Tourism was seen as a leisure activity performed for one's own recreation and education.

In 1887 Victor Balck, the father of modern Swedish sport, published a book on different types of sports with a chapter describing 'Tourism and sport', which in fact related to mountain walking (Balck, 1887). Promotion of walks in the mountains was also the primary activity of the STF up to the 1920s. The Federation created mountain tracks and built small cottages for overnight stays, maintaining responsibility for these activities up to the middle of the 1970s when another state agency 'Statens Naturvärdsverk' (the National Environmental Protection Board) took over.

In 1889, the Parliament decided to give the STF 3,000 SEK in order to support the Federation's activities in the mountainous regions. It was an isolated subsidy and the STF had to wait until the 1940s before it would receive more money from the state.

The origins of state interest in tourism were very much in tourist activity as leisure activity, but fairly quickly it became clear that tourism was also an activity which could generate money. In 1902 some Swedish railway and steamship companies, hotels, and restaurants, and others founded 'Turistrafikförbundet' (The Tourist Travel Association). This branch organisation was mainly aimed at promoting foreign tourism into Sweden, and the state was engaged through its railway company, though the activities of the Association were not supported financially by Parliament.

At the beginning of the twentieth century two different 'camps' in tourism policy emerged. One was based on an idealistic and non-profit view of the benefits of tourism. This was promoted by the STF, which had as its major concern, the tourist and her/his personal experience. The second group treated tourism as a source of potential profit, and this was the line adopted by the Tourist Travel Association. This is important for an understanding of the history of tourism and recreation policy in Sweden.

At the turn of the century another conflict developed in this policy field. On the one hand, increased industrialisation led to greater demand for electric power and land, while on the other, the number of tourists and their demand for access to undeveloped countryside were also growing. The latter became possible as the railroads were extended to the northern part of Sweden. A third party in this policy field was that of the environmentalists.

In 1909 in order to save nature from industrial exploitation, the Parliament, inspired by the example of American Yellowstone Park, decided to establish national parks (Ödman, *et al.*, 1982). Some of the parks were designated for conservation purposes, and some in order to preserve land for outdoor recreation. This legislation has since been developed and modified, but the basic support for recreation and conservation is still evident. A very important step for the future had been taken. Another important step was taken by the Parliament in 1934 when the Tourist Travel Association received 110,000 SEK to promote tourism from abroad. Since that date, broken only by the Second World War, the state annually provided financial support for the Swedish tourism industry.

Social Tourism in Sweden

During the 1920s the notion of the 'normal working-day' was introduced in most European countries. The demands of the first May-day demonstrations in 1890 thus became a political reality in most developed countries. Following the growth of leisure time, the concept of 'social tourism' emerged in the 1930s and spread throughout the continent. After the economic depression in the early years of the decade, prosperity began to grow. The labour movement began a struggle for paid holidays, and the first *semesterlagen* (holiday law) was subsequently passed by the Swedish Parliament in 1938, guaranteeing two weeks' holiday to all employees.

Also during the 1930s, outdoor recreation became popular, and young people, usually with bicycles and tents, went out into the countryside. In 1933, in order to promote lowland tourism in the southern part of Sweden, the Swedish Tourist Association began to open 'vandrarhem' (Youth Hostels). These were initially aimed at youth, but very soon they became oriented also to families. The only restriction imposed was that guests should arrive by cycle or by foot, not by car. In 1937 the labour movement took the initiative to establish, Folkrörelsernas Rese - och Semesterorganisation (RESO, The People's Travel and Holiday Association). Its aim was to organise cheap travel with a social and cultural purpose for the members of some popular movements (Olson, 1991c).

In considering outdoor recreation in Sweden, the Swedish concept of 'everyman's right' (sic) should be taken into account. This 'right' is not a law, but a custom, which goes back to the middle ages. The right means that anyone can walk in the forests as long as s/he does not hinder agricultural work or disturb other people living in these areas. Anyone also has the right to pick flowers, berries and mushrooms, except when they are rare. People also have the right to camp for one night without seeking the permission of the landowner. There are some prohibitions: it is forbidden, for example, to pick nuts or break trees or take plants or flowers home, and fishing and hunting without the permission of the landowner is prohibited. 'Everyman's right' makes no distinction between Swedes and foreigners, though this has been discussed in recent debates about Sweden's application to the European Community (Ahlström, 1982; Westerlund, 1991).

This debate is, however, not new. During the 1930s landowners began to consider how they could stop the urban industrial population, who had little knowledge of the countryside environment, from invading the countryside. In 1936 Social Democrats placed a motion before Parliament seeking to ensure that open land was saved for outdoor recreation purposes, especially for urban, industrial workers. The MPs urged the government to investigate the possible policy measures to achieve this (Riksdagen, 1936). This parliamentary motion is important in tourist and recreation politics in Sweden, because for the first time social arguments were used to justify a policy in this field. This theme was later to become a point of conflict and political struggle.

The Government reacted positively to the motion and a Royal Commission, the first one in this field, was formed to study the problem. The committee presented two important proposals. First, they asked for a state foundation to be established to channel funding for investment in outdoor recreation facilities, such as tracks or footpaths, cottages, playgrounds, camp sites and so on. Secondly, they proposed a 'beach law' enforcing access to beaches for the public, though this was not enacted in legislation until 1952 (SOU, 1940, p. 12). In 1939 such a foundation was established and funded by Parliament. This foundation existed up to the middle of the 1960s and some parts of it are still in existence. A special state agency, 'Statens fritidsnämnd' (State Committee for Leisure), was established in order to handle the proposals for money. At that time 'leisure' was understood to refer solely to 'outdoor recreation'.

Tourism and Recreation Combined in Social Policy

In 1967 the government founded the Swedish Environmental Protection Board. This board was given responsibility for outdoor recreation, both planning and allocation of state subsidies, and also, after 1975, took over from the Swedish Tourism Federation, the responsibility for trails in mountain areas. During these decades the Swedish Tourist Travel Association was concentrating on marketing Sweden abroad as a tourist destination, rather than promoting domestic tourism.

In 1975 this situation changed. Through two bills the government sought to connect the two areas. It first proposed that the Swedish Tourist Travel Association should be wound up. Instead, 'Sveriges Turistråd' (The Swedish Tourist Board) was to be established. The new Board, with a greater governmental responsibility, would not just market Sweden abroad, but would also help the Swedish tourist industry to be more efficient in stimulating the demand for domestic tourism. The bill had a clear economic orientation. Under the second bill a new state agency, *'Rekreationsberedningen'*, was set up whose objective was to plan areas in the countryside and facilitate countryside recreation for all, overcoming social and economic barriers to participation. The 'social goals' of government for tourism and recreation policy were now explicitly stated in the legislation (Riksdagen, 1975).

In 1976 Sweden elected its first bourgeois government since 1936, with a coalition of three parties sharing political power. The Social Democrats went into opposition. However the coalition could not operate effectively, and during the following six years Sweden had four different governments. Even policy in the field of tourism and recreation was affected by this political instability, as the Social Democrats, supported by the Communists, were able to insist on the primacy of 'social goals' over 'economic goals'.

In 1982 the Social Democrats regained power and in 1984 they made a surprising change in their goals for this policy area. In a proposal to Parliament they reversed their previous policy stance and argued that economic goals should take priority over social goals. This shocked many Social Democrat MPs who refused to accept the new objectives set out in this proposal. They rebelled against their own government and together with the Communists and the Centre party they rewrote the policy objectives to be consistent with previous policy priorities. The Social Democratic government was, however, supported by a parliamentary minority consisting of Conservatives and Liberals (Riksdagen, 1984).

Interest groups concerned with tourism and recreation as areas of economic activity started to use this proposal as a base for action, despite its rejection by Parliament. The principal actor among these interest groups was the Swedish Tourist Board, which was given greater powers to act on behalf of government. The Swedish National Environmental Protection Board lost most of its influence in this field, and the 1975 Drafting Committee for Recreation was totally abolished and its personnel and money moved to the Tourist Board. During the following years the Tourist Board almost totally neglected social goals. The Social Democrat Minister for Agriculture, who was also responsible for tourism, showed no interest in intervening, and though Parliament formally questioned this change in policy in 1988, there was no serious response.

In December 1989, *'Riksrevisionsverket'* , a politically important State agency, published a report in which it took a clear stance supporting the government's position of 1984. The Social Democrat MPs reacted once again and used their own research unit to promote counter proposals, which were released a year later. In a further report, 'Riksdagsrevisorerna' (the Parliamentary Auditors) criticised both the Swedish Tourist Board and the Government for failing to have implemented the 1984 decision of Parliament.

The Government was thus pressed from two sides; from the tourism industry, arguing for more state subsidies to market their products, both abroad and in Sweden; and from the majority in Parliament which supported other policy priorities. In this difficult situation the Government decided in January 1991 to launch a further investigation. The results of that investigation were presented in June 1991. Its recommendations were clear. The social goals of leisure and recreation policy were to be delegated to local government. The central state would however, continue to try to expand the numbers and expenditure of foreign tourists in Sweden. It was recommended that this should be the sole goal of the Swedish Tourist Board, and that even its work in marketing tourist attractions to the domestic market should be abandoned.

At the time of writing it was not yet clear how the new bourgeois government, elected in September 1991, will react in this policy area, but the political history of tourism and recreation policy clearly shows the conflict between two totally different standpoints, and the conflict seems likely to continue.

Leisure Policy in Sweden: Some Concluding Remarks

Leisure Policy and the Central State

It is sometimes proposed that youth work, sport and tourism policy are all simply aspects of leisure policy. However, reference to a unified field of leisure policy is misleading. The emphasis in youth work swings between the control of youth and autonomy for young people, between social policy and leisure policy. Sports policy incorporates a concern for both élite sport and mass sport, between economic policy and leisure policy. Tourism policy oscillates between economic policy and social policy, between supporting the tourist industry's quest for profits and facilitating the tourist's search for inexpensive outdoor recreation.

Thus incorporating youth work, sport and tourism in a single policy field is not feasible. Each encompasses a wider sphere of human life than simply leisure. Figure 4.1 illustrates this point.

In Sweden there are, at least in practice, policies for sport and for tourism. A policy for youth work is being developed, but a coherent policy for leisure is lacking. At central government level many ministries are working within different sub-fields of leisure. Among the most important are the Ministry for Civil Affairs (youth and popular movements), the Ministry of Education (support for culture, adult education and mass media), the Ministry of Industry (tourism), and the Ministry of Housing (sport).

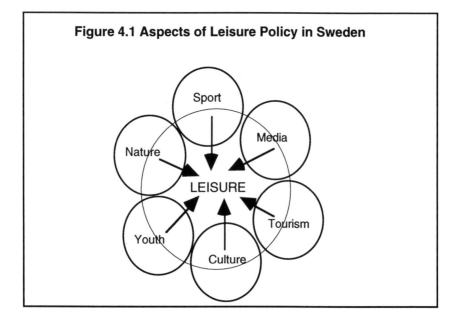

Figure 4.1 Aspects of Leisure Policy in Sweden

Below the level of ministries are a number of state agencies, or organisations which function as state agencies, which implement the policies decided by government. The Swedish Sports Federation, The Swedish Tourist Board, The State Youth Council, The National Environmental Protection Board and The Board for Social Affairs, are all agencies with different approaches to leisure, but which clearly do not consider leisure as their sole, or even primary, objective.

Leisure and Local Government

At the local government level the situation is different. In the 1940s there were attempts in the city of Stockholm and other big cities to form special leisure and recreation departments with a comprehensive approach to leisure activities. That proposal was, in Stockholm, opposed by the five departments with responsibility for different aspects of leisure. The strongest opposition came from the Child Care Authority which, at the beginning of the 1950s stated that youth centres should be working as an instrument of social policy in order to prevent anti-social tendencies among youth. The establishment of a Leisure Department with a 'recreation purpose' would, it was argued, undermine this work.

In the city of Norrköping events took another turn. In 1956 a special Leisure and Recreation Department was established, the first in Sweden. Behind that decision lay a concern to develop a coherent leisure policy, and this model became popular during the 1950s and 1960s. In the early 1970s the Swedish Union of Local Government published a recommendation that communes should establish a special Department of Leisure and Recreation and another for Culture. This recommendation came in a period when many small communities were being merged to form larger units. (In 1960 there were around 2000 communities but by 1975 these had been reduced to 280.) By the middle of the 1980s almost all Swedish local authorities had such leisure departments. However, during the 1980s 'decentralisation' became popular in politics. Many larger local authorities (for example Gothenburg), began to dismantle their central service departments. Political issues, it was argued should be decided locally by the communities affected. New political bodies were set up, to deal with all policy questions as far as possible at neighbourhood level. The city-wide departments were closed, or restructured to allow more local decision-making.

By the later 1980s it was recognised that decentralisation had fostered neither greater participation nor democracy. Instead the power of professionals, developed in local government service departments, seemed to have increased. The process of decentralisation faded in the late 1980s to be replaced by a new market-oriented philosophy in the early 1990s. Influenced by the private sector, the terminology of the 'customer' was borrowed by the public sector (replacing the liberal welfare emphasis on the 'client'). One such set of 'customers' was children. This group, it was argued, should not be the concern of three or four different local government departments organising different types of activities, but should be catered for by a single unified department or organisation. Thus, some local authorities have built up new 'Children and Youth Departments' taking responsibility for schools, kindergartens, afternoon leisure homes and youth centres. It is planned to amalgamate the rest of the Leisure and Recreation Department with the old Culture Departments into new 'Leisure and Culture Departments'. On 1 July 1991 this change took place at central level, at the Swedish Union of Local Government. After the general election of September 1991 it was anticipated that most local authorities would follow suit.

The Absence of a Leisure Profession

The account of leisure policy in this chapter may give the impression of a professionalised Swedish public leisure sector at local government level, but this would be misleading. In the literature on professionalism the following criteria are often promoted as the basis on which professions are constructed:

(a) having a systematic body of theory;
(b) professional authority based on specialised professional preparation;
(c) sanction of the community enforced through admission standards for the field;
(d) a regulative code of ethics;
(e) a professional culture based on professional organisations, shared values, and traditions.

(Kraus, 1984)

It is revealing to undertake an analysis of the Swedish situation employing these criteria.

A systematic body of theory

There is no systematic body of theory at all in the Swedish leisure sector. The sector is oriented, not towards the theoretical but towards the practical. There is virtually no public debate over the goals and the future of the sector, and what debate there is local, largely oral, and 'practical' in orientation. Such debate could not constitute the theoretical base for the development of a professional body of knowledge. Some communities have produced policy platforms for their Leisure and Recreation Departments, but most of these platforms are very simplistic, though there are some exceptions.

Professional authority based on specialised professional preparation

There is no specialised professional preparation focusing on leisure in Sweden. At the university level there is education and research about sport and tourism but not relating specifically to leisure. During the 1970s some universities began higher education study in the field of leisure, but they were forced by the Government and Parliament in 1979 to close these courses down, and the resources were transferred to the Folk High Schools to educate 'leisure leaders'. This education is the only one which comes close to professional preparation for the leisure sector, but the education is primarily practical. Its aim is to educate people to work practically with the community during its leisure time.

Sanction of the community enforced through admission standards for the field

The public leisure sector has a sanction from the community, otherwise it would be impossible to use taxpayers money to finance the sector. But on the other hand we can discuss which standards are underpinning the sanctions. I suggest, this issue is not very well researched and that the Popular Movements, especially the Sport Movement, play a major role in the formulation of these standards of entry to the field. Leisure policy deals to a very large degree with two things: the construction of facilities, which is especially important and expensive for the sport movement; and subsidies to the popular movements, especially youth and educational associations, both subsidy for development of their own facilities, and subsidy for their activities. Very little is given to the public, who are not active in these popular movements or voluntary associations (and that includes the great majority of the Swedish population). Thus although there is a public sanction for the work, of leisure professionals' entry to such work is largely controlled by special interest groups in sport, youth, tourism or environment.

A regulative code of ethics

Where they exist, different sets of ethics may be said to apply to different sub-fields of leisure policy. They are perhaps made most apparent in the field of youth work, in terms of guidelines for working with young people.

A professional culture based on professional organisations, shared values and traditions

It is difficult to identify any coherent professional culture in the public leisure sector. There are, in fact, two organisations representing those who work in the leisure field in Sweden. 'Föreningen Sveriges Fritidschefer' (FSF, The Swedish Association of Chief Leisure Managers) organises the most senior managers in leisure departments at local government. 'Kommunala fritidstjänstemäns Riksförbund' (KFR, The National Association of Leisure Officials) organises the middle management strata, leisure leaders and other groups in the lower part of the hierarchy. The FSF's main interest lies in

8 *Leisure Policies in Europe*

administrative questions and broader political issues which concern the communities. The KFR has until now been interested in more practical issues, especially relating to the management of youth centres.

Outside the public sector, popular movements and other voluntary associations of different kinds exist. They work mostly in isolation from any professional bodies. Thus, in Sweden a forum for discussing common issues of mutual interest for the whole leisure sector, public and private, simply does not exist. In Sweden concern with leisure is viewed as something practical. A theoretical or philosophical debate on leisure and leisure policy has not developed. As a result the need for political debate, academic research, or theoretically informed professional preparation has simply not been considered.

REFERENCES

Ahlström, I. (1982) *Allemansrätt och friluftsvett*, Liber: Uddevalla.

Allardt, E. (1970) *Samhällsstruktur och sociala spänningar*, Almqvist and Wiksell: Tammerfors.

Ambjörnsson, R. (1988) *Den skötsamme arbetaren*, Carlssons: Malmö.

Bäckström, K. (1971) *Arbetarrörelsen i Sverige, del I*, Raben and Sjögren: Stockholm.

Balck, V. (ed.) (1887) *Illustrerad idrottsbok Handledning i olika grenar af idrott och lekar*, Fritzes Hofbokhandel: Stockholm.

Barnavärdsnämnden i Stockholm, protokoll och handlingar 1926-1955 (unpublished).

Blomdahl, U. and Claeson, A. (1989) *Fritidsgården - dess besökare och framtid*, Fritid Stockholm: Stockholm.

Coalter, F. (1989) *Sport and anti-social behaviour: A Literature Review*, Centre for Leisure Research: Edinburgh.

Fridholm, M., Isacsson, M., and Magnusson, L. (1976) *Industrialismens rötter*, Prisma: Lund.

Frykman, J. and Löfgren, O. (1981) *Den kultiverade Människan*, Liber: Stockholm.

Gärlund, T. (1942) *Industrialismens sambälle*, Tiden: Stockholm (dissertation with English Summary).

Hellspong, M. (1982) *Boxningssporten i Sverige. En studie i idrottens kulturmiljö*, Nordiska muséet: Uddevalla (dissertation with English summary).

Hierta-Retzius, A. (1887) *Arbetsstugor för bard*, Nordiska bokhandeln: Stockholm.

Historisk Statistik för Sverige (1969) Del 1, Befolkningen 1720-1963, Stockholm.

Hobsbawn, E. (1971) *Labouring Men*, Weidenfield and Nicholson: London.

Johansson, H. (1952) *Folkrörelsernas och det demokratiska statsskicket i Sverige*, Gleerups: Lund (dissertation with English summary).

Kraus, R. (1984) *Recreation and Leisure in Modern Society*, Free Press: Glenview.

Lindroth, J. (1974) *Idrottens väg till folkrörelse*, Uppsala (dissertation with English summary).

Lundquist, S. (1974) *Politik, nykterhet och reformer. En studie i folkrörelsernas politiska verksamhet 1900-1920*. Studia Historica Upsaliensia 53, Uppsala (English summary).

Lundquist, S. (1977) *Folkrörelserna i det svenska samhället 1850-1920*, Sober, Stockholm (English summary).

Löfgren, O. (1983) 'Klassperspektiv pä ordentlighetens kulturella organisation', *Kaos och ordning*, Umeä universitet.

Ödman, E. Bucht, E., and Nordström, M. (1982) *Vildmarken och välfärden. Om naturksyddslagstitningens tillkomst*, Stockholm: Liber.

Olson, H. (1982) *Frän hemgärd till ungdomsgärd. En studie av den svenska hemgärdsrörelsens historia*, RSFH: Stockholm.

Olson, H. (1983) 'Leisure and Ideological Control', *Leisure Research*. Proceedings from a Workshop meeting in Växjö, Sweden, 13-15 May 1983.

Olson, H. (1987a) 'Staten och de fria organisationerna' (unpublished manuscript).

Olson, H. (1987b) *Staten, turismen och rekreationen*, Stockholm universitet, Stockholm.

Olson, H. (1989) "Fritiden saknar professionalism", *Fritid i Sverige* 1989:5.

Olson, H. (1990) *Frän socialvärdskvacksalveri till elitidrott. Fritidsförvaltning i* Stockholm universitet: Stockholm.

Olson, H. (1991a) *Staten och ungdomens fritid. Kontroll eller autonomi?* Lund (English summary).

Olson, H. (1991b) 'Staten, idrotten och friluftslivet' (unpublished manuscript).

Olson, H. (1991c) 'De sociala mälen? Alternativ till turistindustrins konventionella visdom' (unpublished manuscript).

Pauli, E. (1906) *Fattigvärd och folkuppfostran*, Centralförbund för Socialt Arbete: Stockholm.

Pauli, E. (1921) *Vära barns moraliska uppfostran*, Nordiska bokhandeln: Stockholm.

Pälbrant, R. (1977) *Arbetarrörelsen och idrotten 1919-1939*, Studia Historica Upsaliensia 91 (Deutsches Zusammenfass).

Riksdagen (various dates) Riksdagen protocoll 1896-1955 (Official Proceedings of the Swedish Parliament): Stockholm.

Sarnecki, J. (1983) *Fritid och brottslighet*, BRA/Allmänna förlaget: Stockholm.

Statens Ungdomsräd (1974) *Statligt stöd till ungdomsorganisationernas centrala verksamhet*, Allmänna förlaget: Stockholm.

Stockholms stadsfullmäktige, protokoll och handlingar 1900-1955, Stockholm: Stockhoms stadsfullmäktige.

SOU (Sveriges Offentliga Utredningar) (1940) *Betänkande och förslag ang, inrättande av fritidsreservat för städernas och de tättbebyggda samhällenas befolkning*, Ungdomsvärdskommittén, Allmänna förlaget: Stockholm.

SOU (Sveriges Offentliga Utredningar) (1944) *Stöd ät ungdomens föreningsliv*, Ungdomsvärdskommittén, Allmänna förlaget: Stockholm.

SOU (Sveriges Offentliga Utredningar) (1947) *Ungdomens fritidsverksamhet*. Ungdomsvärdskommittén, Allmänna förlaget: Stockholm.

SOU (Sveriges Offentliga Utredningar) (1952) *Principbetänkande*. 1944 ärs Nykterhetskommitté, Allmänna förlaget: Stockholm.

STF (1985) *STF 100 är Arsskrift 1986*, Svenska Turistföreningen: Uppsala.

Svenska Akademiens Ordbok (1926) Band 8, Svenska Akadamien: Lund.

Tvängsuppfostringskommittén (1900) *Betänkande och förslag avgivna av den av Kungl. Maj:t den 16 oktober 1896 tillsatta kommittén för utredning av frägan om ätgärder för beredande av lämpling uppfostran dels ät minderäriga förbrytare, dels ock ät vanartade och i sedligt avseende försummade barn*, Del II, Allmänna förlaget.

Ungdom och fritid (1954) Stockholms stadskollegium, Bihang nr 53.

Westerlund, S. (1991) *EGs miljöregler ur svenskt perspektiv*, Svenska Naturskyddsföreningen: Stockholm.

Chapter 5

Leisure Policy in Britain

Ian Henry and Peter Bramham

This chapter will focus on the development of contemporary leisure policy in the British context. However in order to understand the nature of the present configuration of structures and policies it is necessary to locate them within the historical context of the evolution of the British state and its institutional framework. The chapter will therefore adopt the following pattern; the first section will seek simply to describe the organisational framework for the development and implementation of state policies in leisure. The second section will articulate the changing nature of the state's involvement in leisure over the period since the beginning of the major phase of industrialisation in Britain. The third section will focus on key changes in the policy context over the period since the end of the Second World War, but in particular from the beginning of the 1970s. The final section will characterise the policy changes identified in the 1980s and 1990s, as a structural shift in the nature of the state's role in leisure policy.

The Structure of the Leisure Policy System

Until relatively recently, the nature of the leisure policy system in Britain has been one of fragmented governmental organisation at central government level. However, even with the advent of the new Ministry for National Heritage, which united government concerns for the arts, sport and tourism within a single ministry, there were still separate ministries dealing with countryside and water-based recreation, the inner city and local government, and education based provision for leisure. In addition to its ministries, government has established many quasi-governmental organisations (quangos) to administer or even initiate aspects of leisure policy. The principal leisure quangos are the Sports Council, the Arts Council, and the Countryside Commission. The British Tourist Authority, the English

Tourist Board, the British Waterways Board, the National Rivers Authority and the Forestry Commission are also quasi-independent bodies with significant leisure responsibilities. Figure 5.1 illustrates the structure of the relationship between the principal leisure bodies. In the late 1970s Travis and Veal's (1979) account of the structure of leisure policy and provision in the public sector revealed a highly fragmented organisational framework, an 'organisational pluralism', which Travis and Veal used to support their implicitly pluralist analysis of the system. Given that since that time Britain has been ruled by a Conservative government with the professed aim of 'rolling back the state', to streamline and reduce the machinery of intervention, perhaps the most remarkable aspect of the contemporary system is the slightly less fragmented but nevertheless wide-ranging framework of governmental organisations in leisure. Indeed leisure investment by the state has actually grew over the first decade of Conservative government as Table 5.2 illustrates.

However, though central government and national quangos may be influential policy bodies in respect of leisure, it is at the local government level that the major provision of leisure facilities and services is made. Here leisure policy operates in a relatively unified framework, with a range of forms of recreation provision not only falling under a single tier of government, but also often within the remit of a single department of the local authority. The range of public expenditures by local government, itemised in Table 5.1, is indicative of the relatively comprehensive leisure policy responsibilities of this tier of government.

Table 5.1 Local Government Revenue Expenditure on Leisure 1989/90 for England and Wales

	% Total Leisure	£ Millions Revenue Expenditure
Indoor Sport	31.7	373.8
Outdoor Sport	37.7	444.6
Theatres / Entertainment	6.8	80.2
Art Galleries	6.9	81.4
Arts Grants	4.2	49.5
Country Parks	3.5	41.2
Tourism	3.2	37.7
Other	5.9	69.6

(Source: CIPFA, 1990)

There is no regional tier of government in the UK (except in Scotland) and regional coordination is therefore monitored in

Table 5.2 Public Sector Leisure Expenditure in Britain 1972/3 - 1989/90

Year	Local Govt. Revenue Estimates for Leisure[1]	Sports Council[2]	Arts Council[2]	Countryside Commission.[2]	Retail Price Index[3]
1972/3		3.6	13.7		
1973/4		5.0	17.1		
1974/5		6.6	21.3		21.7
1975/6		8.3	28.9		18.9
1976/7	373.0	10.0	37.2		17.4
1977/8	452.5	11.5	41.7		7.9
1978/9	523.5	15.0	51.8		10.1
1979/80	633.7	15.7	61.5		21.6
1980/81	732.8	19.3	70.5		12.0
1981/2	832.3	21.0	80.4		9.4
1982/3	881.5	28.0	90.8	11.1	4.0
1983/4	964.9	27.1	94.6	12.5	5.2
1984/5	1000.1	28.6	101.9	12.8	6.9
1985/6	1062.8	30.1	106.0	15.2	3.0
1986/7	1044.5	37.3[4]	135.6[4]	17.8[4]	3.3
1987/8	1188.6	37.1	138.4	22.6	4.2
1988/9	1178.4	38.8	150.0	21.1	3.9
1989/90	NA[5]	41.9	155.5	22.2	8.0

1 Source: C.I.P.F.A. Annual Leisure Revenue Estimates for England and Wales only

2 Source: Government Expenditure Plans White Papers

3 Source: Department of Employment Gazette

4 Abnormal financial year - GLC and Met Counties abolished

5 Estimates for total expenditure not provided by CIPFA because of low response rate by local authorities.

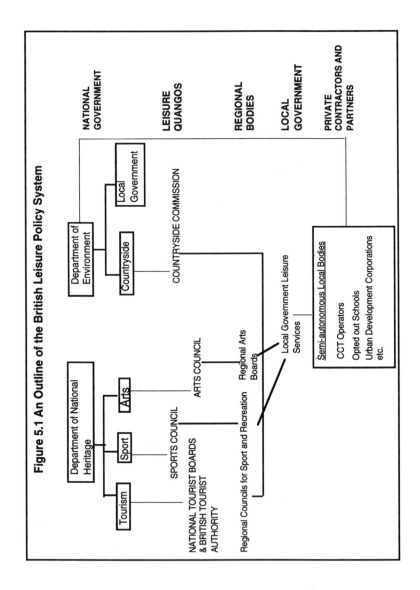

Figure 5.1 An Outline of the British Leisure Policy System

NATIONAL GOVERNMENT

LEISURE QUANGOS

REGIONAL BODIES

LOCAL GOVERNMENT

PRIVATE CONTRACTORS AND PARTNERS

Department of Environment

Countryside

Local Government

COUNTRYSIDE COMMISSION

Department of National Heritage

Tourism

Sport

Arts

NATIONAL TOURIST BOARDS & BRITISH TOURIST AUTHORITY

SPORTS COUNCIL

ARTS COUNCIL

Regional Councils for Sport and Recreation

Regional Arts Boards

Local Government Leisure Services

Semi-autonomous Local Bodies

CCT Operators
Opted out Schools
Urban Development Corporations
etc.

England and Wales by Regional Councils for Sport and Recreation which incorporate representatives of local governments within the region, of the Sports Council and Regional tourist boards, the Countryside Commission, the British Waterways Board and other minor bodies with leisure-relevant interests. These Regional Councils are charged with producing Regional Recreation Strategies, which are strategic assessments of regional demand, evaluations of existing provision, and statements of priorities. The concept of regional recreation strategies and Regional Councils for Sport and Recreation were introduced by the 1975 White Paper *Sport and Recreation* (DOE, 1975), and two sets of strategy documents have been produced by most regions since that date.

The Historical Development of the Role of the State in Leisure Policy

The state's interest in intervention in leisure is most clearly associated with periods of high social and political tension. Perhaps the most obvious intervention by the pre-industrial state took the form of the *Kings Book of Sports* (1618, reissued by Charles I in 1633), a defence by the monarchy of peasant rights to popular recreations on the Sabbath. For some this represented the use of 'sport' as a tool for cementing the interests of the peasantry and the aristocracy in opposition to a 'middle' class, puritan merchant minority which had begun to challenge the dominance of the landed class (Hill, 1964). For others it represented the inevitable consequence of the emergence of a new dynamic individualism which was undermining the organic solidarity of an agriculturally based system of production (Brailsford, 1969). Similarly contrasting explanations of the role of the state in the period of accelerating industrialisation and urbanisation are evident with neo-marxist historians seeking to explain the emerging popular culture by reference to shifting class interests, while liberal historians have located explanations of emerging cultural patterns on the changing social context and the available resources (technological and economic) which became available in the process of urban industrialisation to the new urban working classes.

If Britain's bloodless revolution of 1688-9 can be characterised as a 'bourgeois' revolution, this is not in the sense of there having been a class-conscious bourgeoisie, seeking actively to dismantle the structures of feudalism. Rather that the net result of the revolution was to install a set of political structures which would facilitate the development of capitalism and its attendant social relations (Mooers, 1991). James II had sought to use his feudal powers to pack his administration with low born catholics as a bulwark against the powers of Parliament (Doyle, 1978). His replacement by William of Orange at the invitation of Parliament and the subsequent financing of William's war against the French by virtue of credit raised by Parliament, effectively pre-empted any further use of quasi-feudal powers on the part of the monarchy (leading William to complain that as monarch his power was more tightly circumscribed than as Stadtholder in the Netherlands). However, although the political structures for the development of capitalism might have been fostered by Britain's 'bourgeois' revolution, the social, economic, technological and cultural conditions were to develop in a set of separate, but related, trajectories.

The notion of a bourgeois class is one which is derived from that of 'urban dwellers' who are neither members of the nobility nor artisans working with their hands. This broad social categorisation incorporated a wide range of occupational types including fairly wealthy merchants and relatively poor master craftsmen, and clearly the social category predates the development of industrial capitalism most closely associated with the development of the industrial bourgeoisie. Nevertheless, although such a group could be identified before the period of major industrial growth, its size and its wealth grew significantly in seventeenth and eighteenth century Britain. Perkins (1969) for example, estimates that the bourgeoisie accounted for 9% of the population in England in 1688, and 20% of the nation's wealth, while these proportions had grown to 15% and 40% respectively by 1803. Thus the changing social structure reflected the growing proportion and economic importance of those whose wealth and earning capacities were not directly linked to land ownership.

The religious identity of the developing bourgeois class was to be identified in the eighteenth century with groups of dissenters. In the early part of the century there were an estimated 300,000 Presbyterians, Baptists, Congregationalists, and Quakers and although their numbers declined throughout the century, their exclusion from public life (they were allowed access to municipal offices in 1727 but did not acquire civil equality until 1828) meant that this group was more susceptible to the development of private enterprise, and more receptive of new ideas (Doyle, 1978). The point Doyle is making is not simply a weak version of Weber's protestant ethic thesis, but rather that oppositional tendencies in religious practice tended to be associated with bourgeois groups. In Ireland for example, the merchant class were drawn predominantly from the Presbyterian and the Catholic communities.

In the sense that the Enlightenment represents a calling into question of the old order, a healthy scepticism concerning accepted practices, it is associated with a bourgeois world view (Hasard, 1973). The rejection of tradition as the basis of beliefs about the social as well as the natural world is consistent with the political position of an emergent group. It is therefore unsurprising that the new modes of thinking should take root in, and provide technological advances for, the bourgeois group of proto-industrialists. Advances in science, of which the most impressive were Newton's laws, provided a model for empirical analysis of physical phenomena, and were to be followed by technological innovations (such as those of Hargreaves, Arkwright and

Crompton) which facilitated the move of industry from home-based to factory-based production. The intellectual tradition of the Enlightenment also fostered a particular view of the social world, and in this respect few social treatises were as significant for the emergent bourgeoisie as the writings on economics of Adam Smith.

Nevertheless, Enlightenment thinking should not be regarded as counter cultural, since it was embraced also by members of the establishment, the landed aristocracy. Indeed one of the most striking features of this period of social restructuring was the relatively peaceful accommodation of the new industrial bourgeois by the landed classes in Britain. To some extent this is explained by the potential for the growing returns from agriculture as the effects of enclosure, technological advances, and economies of scale were realised. Although this barred a classic route for the growing trading and industrial middle classes to join the establishment by land purchase (land became too valuable), it also signalled a lack of serious economic rivalry.

Smith's book *The Wealth of Nations*, first published in 1776, was enormously successful, running to eight editions before the turn of the century. Smith's work is important, not simply in that it represents the new world view, the 'appliance of science' to the social world, but also because it promotes the ideology of the emerging industrial middle class. Smith's economics is important also as the first comprehensive statement of libertarian economics, and, given the rise of the New Right in contemporary Britain and its harking back to nineteenth century values, it is more than simply an historical curiosity. The implications of the world view encapsulated in New Right programmes clearly relate to those of Smith's free market philosophy, in that a role for the state in social and economic policy, including leisure policy, is contingent on these ideas.

The argument promoted in *The Wealth of Nations*, rejects the rationalist tradition of the philosophy of Descartes, Locke and Hobbes. Smith wished to employ historical, empirical analysis to support or to test his economic thesis, in a way analogous to method in the natural sciences. Just as Arkwright, Crompton and Hargreaves had provided the physical technology to promote wealth generation in manufacturing, so Smith provided the intellectual technology to deal with problems in the social environment. Empiricist method was essentially bourgeois epistemology, since it relied on analysis and testing by the individual rather than on the received wisdom of tradition.

Smith rejected mercantilist economics which guided government policy in seventeenth and eighteenth century Europe. The old economics regarded land as the source of wealth and saw the overall level of wealth as relatively static. Any growth in the wealth of a single nation therefore had to be achieved by a similar decline in the wealth of at least one other. The policy implications of this way of looking at the world, protectionism and tariff barriers, were the normal instrument of economic policy. Smith however, argued for viewing labour rather than land as the source of wealth, and since numbers in the work force and labour productivity could be increased, so growth in wealth was possible, without an associated decline in the wealth of another party. Indeed protectionism was to be avoided, since this deflated trade, discouraged labour productivity, and suppressed economic growth. Smith did not simply oppose barriers to international trade, he also advocated the sweeping away of internal barriers to economic growth, arguing that the state should not provide protection for labour from the effects of a free market. A domestic and international market free from the frictions of protectionism, would generate economic growth which ultimately would be beneficial to all. Clearly this commodification of labour, treating labour markets as analogous to trade in goods, devalued and dehumanised labour, and provided an intellectual legitimation for the negative impacts of free market capitalism.

The early nineteenth century British state, influenced by free market philosophy, introduced the 1834 Poor Law Amendment Act which effectively reduced relief for those without employment. In the amended system the relief payments and working and living conditions of the work house were so austere that only the utterly destitute would willingly submit themselves to this regime. Work house earnings were to be set well below the minimum wage for those working in the open market so that the work house could not be regarded as a friction, forcing up wage levels by competing with low wage employers.

The history of the state's role in leisure in 19th century Britain is normally characterised as falling into three distinct phases. The first is a period of *suppression of popular recreations* ; the second is a period associated with the *promotion of acceptable forms of leisure*, most notably in the form of the rational recreation movement. The third phase may be characterised as one in which attempts to foster acceptable leisure were overtaken by the *success of commercial investment* in meeting the demand for recreation. The nature of these phases has been contested in debates in the literature, predominantly between liberal / pluralist historian and neo-marxists, though the periodisation employed is common to both. Feminist historians have, in addition, challenged the failure of these two schools of thought to theorise the role of leisure in the reproduction of patriarchy.

It is ironic that, in a period in which Smith's economics provided a rationale for a non-interventionist state, the state should become involved in considerable prohibition or control of leisure forms, as it did in the period c. 1780 - c. 1840. However it seems clear that the attack on the system of poor relief represented in the Poor Law Amendment Act 1834, was insufficient to guarantee self discipline on the part of the working class. The process of urbanisation itself, with large numbers gravitating towards urban centres, at a time when political insurrection in France and the United States was fresh in the minds of the authorities, lent urgency to the wish to control public gatherings. Wakes, fairs, boxing matches, animal baiting, and even public executions, were occasions for potentially volatile groups to gather. In addition the rationalisation of tasks and mechanisation in factory production meant that the discipline of the urban work force was an industrial priority, while the density of the urban environment did not lend itself easily to the rowdiness of traditional rural pursuits which had been practised in more spacious settings. Despite the non-interventionist philosophy of the time in economic terms, it is hardly surprising that the state should seek to control popular recreations, either centrally, through parliamentary legislation, or locally through the actions of the local magistracy.

The Society for the Suppression of Vice, which was revived in 1802, attempted to suppress unnecessary fairs (those which were not hiring fairs or not predominantly used for commerce), and also pressed for the preservation of the Sabbath from non-religious activity. In 1803-4 678 prosecutions were brought for breaking of the Sabbath of which 623 resulted in convictions (Harrison, 1967). In 1787 the Royal Proclamation for the Encouragement of Piety and Virtue made licensing of alehouses stricter and campaigning by the Temperance Movement encouraged the magistracy to enforce sanctions.

Although suppression of wakes, fairs, sale of alcohol, and public recreation on a Sunday, involved predominantly control of working class activities by a middle class magistracy, the Sabbatarian and Temperance Movements did incorporate some 'respectable' working class membership. However, perhaps the most obviously class related attempt at control involved the suppression of animal blood sports through the Suppression of Blood Sports Act 1833, which sought to ban animal baiting, throwing at cocks, dog-fighting and related activities which were essentially the preserve of the working classes without prohibiting or limiting shooting and fox hunting on the part of the middle class.

Concern with prohibition and control is described by neo-marxist analysts (Bailey, 1987; Cunningham, 1980; Hargreaves, 1986; Malcolmson, 1973) as an attempt at the establishment of class domination, while liberal pluralist historians (Golby and Purdue,1984; Walvin, 1978) explain this legislation as a functional response by legislators to the transfer of 'inappropriate' attitudes, values and behaviour from rural to urban environments. Feminist historians (whether liberal, marxist, radical or socialist) have highlighted the failure of these two dominant perspectives to identify and explain the increasing separation of public and private spheres which was accelerated by the replacement of home-based by factory production. If control of working class male behaviour in public was achieved in this period by legislation, that of working class women (Alexander, 1990) and of middle class women (Hall, 1990) was achieved predominantly in private by the exercise of patriarchal power within the household.

Despite attempts at control through suppression, evident in the early part of the century, it seems clear that this had proved relatively ineffective (Cunningham, 1980; Golby and Purdue, 1984). Thus the state's role in mid-century changed from one of suppressing popular recreations to one of promoting alternative, acceptable recreational forms. Given the fact that Britain's population had doubled between 1801 and 1851 and that by the latter date the majority of that population lived in towns, it is hardly surprising that the imposition of controls should have a limited effect. Certainly some change had occurred, but this was insufficient to assuage the concerns of middle class and temperance reformers, evangelicals, political radicals and industrialists, all of whom sought to promote new forms of respectable behaviour.

Thus the failure of suppression, together with a growing confidence in the political stability of the new urban industrial working class (confirmed by the failure of Chartist agitation for social and political change in the 1840s), and also a growing recognition of the dangerous social and physical implications of unfettered industrial capitalism, served to reinforce the attempts by reformers to foster alternative and wholesome leisure pursuits. The use of the term 'rational recreation', indicates something of the influence of Enlightenment thinking which underpined reforming zeal, with its implicit fear of the unbridled nature of sensual, rather than intellectual, pleasures.

Church groups, temperance reformers, and some working class organisations such as Mechanics Institutes sought to provide alternative pleasures to compete with baser attractions. The first railway day trip, was organised by the entrepreneur and temperance reformer Thomas Cook, to take 3000 children from Leicester to Loughborough in July 1841 to avoid the evils of race day in Leicester.

Thus, the state began in the mid-nineteenth century to adopt a more positive role in promoting social reform. The philosophy of laisser faire was undermined by a series of Factories Acts aimed at protecting initially children, and subsequently women and male workers in particular industries, from exploitation in the form of long hours and dangerous conditions. In the mid-century period (c. 1840 - c. 1870) the state also sought to foster, or complement the work of middle class philanthropists in promoting appropriate leisure forms. The Museums Act 1845, and the Libraries Act 1850, promoted intellectual pursuits. Following the Select Committee on Public Walks in 1833, the purchase of land for public parks from public subscription, by private benefactors, and (in London) by government greatly increased the open space available in cities, while the Public Baths and Washhouses Act 1846 and the Recreation Grounds Act

1852, reflected a concern to provide for the physical recreational needs of the working classes.

The promotion of rational recreation by the state and middle class philanthropists was not, however, simply a matter of the imposition of the values of one class upon another. The working class membership of the temperance movement and of evangelical groups, together with the efforts of mechanics institutes, trades unions and the cooperative movement, represented a considerable push towards respectable leisure on the part of certain sections of the working class itself. However, where middle class philanthropy failed to obtain working class support, forms of provision either withered from underuse, or were subsequently the subject of struggles for control. Thus, 'alcohol-free pubs' promoted by temperance reformers failed to take off and were abandoned, while the Working Men's Club movement ousted from its national executive the middle class founder member, the Reverend Henry Solley, who advocated temperance in the Clubs (Bailey, 1987). Mechanics institutes set up to provide an education in science were by the 1840s in Yorkshire running educational classes for only a small proportion of its membership, the remainder enjoying leisure classes and activities under its aegis (Golby and Purdue, 1984).

The codified sports and games, in particular football and rugby, developed in public schools and promoted by the 'muscular Christian' movement as a means of promoting discipline through sport, were a site of struggle between different factions. In the case of rugby, a dispute between the sport's governing body and clubs in the north of England with predominantly working class membership over payment for time lost at work while playing, resulted in the break away organisation, the Rugby League being formed (Dunning and Sheard, 1976). Similarly in association football there was a schism between the predominantly northern clubs which formed the Football League and the establishment body, the Football Association. The Amateur Athletics Association sought to ban manual workers and artisans on the grounds that they might enjoy an advantage by virtue of the training effect of their physical jobs, though this ruling was rescinded in the 1860s (Bailey, 1987).

However, the reshaping of popular recreation which had been the object of policies of suppression in the earlier part of the century, and of policies of substitution by the state, and middle (and working) class reformers in mid-century, was ironically to be accomplished, not by these strategies, but by the attractions of commercial recreation, acting in response to increasing discretionary time and income, improved technology for production and transport, and the economies of scale which a mass urban leisure market provided. The enfranchisement of urban and rural male adults in 1867 and 1884 respectively, signalled the acceptance of the 'responsibility' of the working class, and perhaps also a sense of freedom on the part of the authorities from the need to control the non-work time and activities of that class. The availability of relatively cheap mass transport in the form of the railway, the development of large public stadia for mass sporting events, of large scale music halls,and subsequently cinemas, the sales of mass produced recreational equipment, and, with the invention of the radio, the arrival of mass broadcasting, all contributed and/or testified to the emergence of a mass market for leisure.

Not all commentators recognised this as a positive feature. Social commentators from the right (e.g. Matthew Arnold) and the left (cf. Waters, 1990) bemoaned the quality of experience represented in mass popular culture. Indeed, as Waters points out, municipal socialists sought to either combat it, or to harness popular recreation for other purposes (as in suggestions that the local state should municipalise pubs), but these ideas failed to come to fruition, though many municipal authorities spent considerable sums on 'improving' forms of recreation.

The process of commercialisation of leisure which had begun in the nineteenth century continued to gather momentum in the first half of the twentieth, as the prerequisite conditions of expanding demand, discretionary time and income continued to grow. Even in the period most commonly associated with the depression, between the world wars, wages grew in real terms by 18% between 1920 and 1938 (Howkins and Lowerson, 1979), while paid holidays for manual workers grew to be the norm by the late 1930s. Associated with this growing market was the establishment of oligopolistic structures in some of the leisure sectors of industry, most notably that of brewing and the cinema (Jones, 1986).

The voluntary sector also grew in importance with the establishment of national voluntary organisations such as the National Trust, the National Playing Fields Association (NPFA), the Central Council for Physical recreation and Training, and the Labour-linked organisation, the British Workers Sports Federation. These organisations acted as pressure groups, stimulating government response in terms of legislation, and increased provision of leisure opportunities. The Forestry Commission, set up in 1919, became the first governmental organisation with a mandatory responsibility (rather than simply permissive powers) to provide for recreation (Travis and Veal, 1979). The NPFA, with its powerful patron, the Duke of York, promoted a greatly increased provision of recreation grounds. Swimming provision grew steadily in the inter-war years as municipal authorities responded to a demand for such provision from sporting interests. Even the mass trespasses, largely orchestrated by the working class British Workers Sports Federation, and the more middle class local rambling clubs, were successful in provoking a policy response from government in the form of the Access to the Mountains Act 1939 (although this proved to be an ineffectual piece of legislation).

The potentially most significant governmental initiative, however, in state intervention in leisure between the wars, was the Physical

Recreation and Training Act 1937, which established the National Fitness Campaign, and an associated National Advisory Council, with Government earmarking £2 million for grant aid. Up to the 2nd World War, when the Council was suspended £1.47 million was allocated with £442,000 spent on swimming baths, £287,000 on clubs, £333,000 on other recreation centres, £337,000 on playing fields with sundry other sums for youth hostels, camping, coaching and leadership and other facilities (Jones, 1986). The inspiration for the Act was not however one of recognition of the intrinsic importance of recreation per se, but rather a response to concerns relating to the dangers of unemployment, particularly for the young, fear of the use of leisure by fascist youth movements in ways analogous to the Hitler Youth movement and the Italian dopolovoro (de Grazia, 1981), and a concern relating to national fitness with the impending threat of war. A further anxiety was Britain's decline in international sport which had been underlined in her poor performance at the Berlin Olympics of 1936 (Evans, 1974). Thus social cohesion, national security, and national prestige, represented the primary motivations for government intervention, though at least one prominent Labour politician, Aneurin Bevan, spoke out in the parliamentary debate for the state funding of leisure on the grounds of its intrinsic value (McIntosh, 1963).

In the media field the British Broadcasting Corporation was established as a public corporation in 1927, effectively giving state control over broadcasting, since the governors of the Corporation were to be appointed by the government. In fact the state seems to have been reluctant to exercise power overtly in this period, neither exercising sanctions nor seeking to influence programme content. The corporation's first Director General, John Reith, though fiercely independent, was also staunchly conservative in cultural terms. He felt that the corporation had a duty to elevate the tastes of the nation, and sought to introduce the highest cultural standards. In addition to a diet of serious music and drama, he is even reported to have insisted that news readers, when addressing the nation by radio, should wear formal evening dress.

Leisure Policy in Post-war Britain

The pattern of policy represented by a quasi-independent BBC, and by the National Fitness Campaign, was one of reluctant intervention, justified only by the need to combat the potential dangers of a monopoly in the case of broadcasting, or by the need to achieve urgent social goals, such as the combating of potential social disorder, or of preparations for war etc. Leisure policy in the immediate pre-war period might thus best be characterised as a form of traditional pluralism, with intervention only taking place to alleviate market imperfections or to achieve externalities. This traditional pluralist rationale is one which continued to dominate policy thinking in respect of leisure in the post-war period, even though the Labour

Government of 1945-51 promoted the rapid growth of welfare provision based on analysis of 'needs'.

1945-64 Traditional Pluralism and Leisure Policy

Although in the immediate post-war period, following a surprise, landslide victory by the Labour Party, the new Government spent considerable effort on developing the rights of its citizens to welfare services, leisure did not appear on the welfare agenda. Certainly leisure organisations were promoted in the form of the new Arts Council founded in 1946, and the National Parks established in the 1949 National Parks and Access to the Countryside Act. However, the rationale for these interventions was not solely inspired by the wish to expand the rights of citizens but rather by a concern to preserve the cultural and environmental heritage of the country.

The Arts Council represented the state's first direct intervention in the arts in peacetime. Its predecessor, the Council for Entertainment, Music and the Arts (CEMA) had been established in 1940 with funding from a charitable trust, in order to provide cultural opportunities to sustain wartime morale. The government provided financial support from 1941. During the war CEMA held more than 6000 concerts despite a paucity of facilities, and the organisation successfully demonstrated both that there was significant latent demand for both high and low brow provision, and that, by providing funding for professional artists, standards of performance could be raised.

In the period of immediate post-war reform there was general agreement across the political parties that the arts should be supported, and the Arts Council received its Royal Charter in 1946. The concerns of the Council, however, in contrast to CEMA, were to promote professional rather than amateur art, to limit itself to promotion of high arts, to concentrate on excellence rather than participation, and to involve itself in only very limited direct provision, stimulating provision by others through grant aid. A function of this concern for a focus on excellence was the concentration on arts provision in London, which would generate the critical mass of audience and artists required to achieve and support international quality performance. By the early 1960s the regional offices inherited from CEMA had been closed down and London based companies were able to account for more than half of the Arts Council of Great Britain's budget (Braden, 1978; Clarke, 1980). The concern of the state with this area of leisure was therefore rather less reformist, in the sense of reducing inequalities through state provision, than it was 'conservationist', or even 'paternalist' in attempting to maintain and improve standards of provision in high cultural forms. There was some attempt at the 'democratisation of culture', improving access to the high arts (for some), through subsidy of such cultural forms, but there was little credence given to 'cultural democracy' (allowing groups to promote and foster their own cultural forms).

Similarly, the state was as much concerned with conservation matters and the protection of industrial interests in the countryside as it was with promoting recreation (Shoard, 1980). The National Parks and Access to the Countryside Act 1949 was not designed to achieve wide ranging access for urban populations to countryside. Indeed National Parks were established in isolated areas and a proposal for the establishment of a Park in the Norfolk Broads, relatively near London was turned down. Rather this legislation was concerned with the preservation and management of remote areas of landscape subject to increasing recreational pressures. The Act designated nine National Parks which still remain, with land predominantly (78%) in private hands.

Sport was not one of the areas of activity in which the immediate post-war governments involved themselves, and it was not until the late 1950s that the Wolfenden Committee was set up to report on the vexed question of the state of sport in Britain and the potential role of government. The report of this Committee (Wolfenden, 1960) did advocate the establishment of a 'Sports Advisory Council' but the justification it produced, and indeed the reasons for establishing the Committee in the first place, were not based on a realisation of the *intrinsic* value of sport, and the rights of individuals to opportunities in this field. Rather the rationale for state involvement was founded on *extrinsic* factors, such as Britain's failing reputation in international sporting competition, and, on the domestic scene, a concern with the emergence of new youth sub-cultures (particularly the 'Teddy Boy' phenomenon), and the presumed moral qualities inherent in sporting activity which might provide a useful antidote to counter anti-social tendencies on the part of the young.

Although a Minister for Sport was established in 1962 by the Conservative Government, no Sports Council was established until after the return of a Labour Government in 1964. In practice, then, the rationale for state intervention in leisure had not changed significantly from that underpining the Physical Training and Recreation Act 1937. State intervention or subsidy was justified by reference to the extrinsic gains which might be achieved by support for leisure. In the pre-war period the concern with sport had been in part motivated by worries related to unemployed youth and the dangers of alternative uses of recreation by fascist movements intent on attracting the young. In the post-war period, the Wolfenden Report was also in part promoted because of worries about youth, but on this occasion *affluent* youth who were a product of post-war economic growth. The national prestige associated with the sporting performance was also seen as an externality which might justify state investment, though not perhaps direct state involvement in the administration of sport. The rhetoric of the Wolfenden Report suggests a concern with preservation of Britain's sporting heritage, which in some senses parallels the conservationist concerns of arts and countryside policy. This is a form of traditional pluralism because competing interest groups are seen as meeting their own interests through the market or through voluntary associations, and state intervention is only to be justified where externalities accrue or there are market imperfections or disbenefits generated by the operation of the unrestricted, 'free' market. Traditional pluralism is to be contrasted with 'welfare reformism' which far from justifying state involvement on the grounds of some extrinsic gain, promotes the rights of the individual to have access to leisure opportunities for their own sake. Welfare reformism seeks to modify the market in terms of social goods, and it was not until the Labour Governments of 1964-70 and of the mid-1970s that such reformist thinking became evident in government policy.

1964-75 Welfare Reformism

In the development of leisure policy in Britain, the Labour government of Harold Wilson of 1964-70 was highly significant. Not only did this government introduce a Sports Council which adopted the slogan of 'Sport for All', but also it produced White Papers on the arts and on leisure in the countryside which in effect were the first such policy proclamations on leisure since the *Kings Book of Sports* in the seventeenth century. The first of the White Papers *A Policy for the Arts: the First Steps* signalled the concerns of a Labour government to widen the range of the arts which were to be subsidised (though only marginally) but also to decentralise provision so that the population beyond the capital would have access to arts of the highest quality. To this end Regional Arts Associations were to be promoted. The White Paper *Leisure in the Countryside* was also to seek to broaden provision for countryside recreation beyond the limits of the National Parks by replacing the National Parks Commission by the Countryside Commission, a body with a wider remit, and one specifically charged with fostering country park provision in close proximity to Britain's major urban areas.

However, though the two White Papers and the establishment of the Sports Council by Labour brought leisure policy more clearly into the framework of social policy, the measure which most significantly influenced the provision of leisure opportunities through the public sector, ironically, was the reform of local government, which took place in most parts of Britain in 1974, but the process of which had been put in train by the Wilson government of the 1960s. This reform reflected the conviction that larger scale local government units were required to counter some of the serious social problems faced in particular by Britain's cities, and that the liberal welfare professions should provide a powerful presence in these new large scale units, advising on, and influencing, social policy and service delivery. Government had consolidated the areas of youth work and social work in the 1960s, recognising the central importance of these service areas by according professional status. In the 1970s in the new local government units, large scale local government departments were created in many local authorities, to take responsibility for a wide range of local services which had previously been dealt with by a disparate range of departmental structures. Thus sports centres, swimming pools, and parks, often combined in metropolitan areas with cultural services such as libraries and art galleries, came under control of new departments of leisure services with large budgets generating a need for a new kind of liberal welfare professional in leisure services. The mere process of creating new local governments fuelled the provision of leisure facilities because those local councils going out of existence, sought to use up their remaining resources before relinquishing control, and often did so by committing capital expenditure to leisure facilities. In 1972 there were 30 municipal sports centres and 500 indoor swimming pools in England, but this had increased to 350 sports centres and 850 pools by 1978. By the end of the 1970 the various bodies with professional membership in the field of leisure services had amalgamated (with one exception) to form the Institute of Leisure and Amenity Management, a unified body which set about defining an educational framework with professional examinations to control access to the profession.

The clearest statement of the welfare reformist rationale for leisure provision, however, was to come in the form of the White Paper on *Sport and Recreation* issued by the following Labour Government in 1975. (Labour regained power between 1974 and 1979). In the interim the Conservative administration of Edward Heath despite having ideological qualms about the nature of state involvement in sport did not rescind the decision to establish the Sports Council, but instead decided to give it quasi-autonomous status, giving it the same status as the Arts Council. The significance of this is that government, while providing the finance for quangos, in theory at least, did not 'interfere' with the policy of such bodies. However, since the government continued to be the paymaster for the Sports Council, policy autonomy was never clear cut, and accusations that quangos are merely tools of government policy were difficult to deny in the late 1970s and 1980s. The Sports Council at its inception had modified the policy slogan recommended by the Wolfenden Committee from 'recreation for all' to 'sport for all', though its initial strategy was one of focusing predominantly on excellence, rather than participation (Coghlan, 1990). However in the 1975 White Paper, the Labour government placed a much clearer emphasis on universal access, describing recreation as 'one of the community's everyday needs' and as 'part of the general fabric of social services'. The White Paper also continued to assert that externalities, in the form of the reduction of delinquency in urban areas, could be achieved through leisure provision, but the new thrust of 'provision for all as a right', analogous to other welfare rights, was perhaps the defining feature of this document.

The irony of this policy statement is that, just as leisure was being added to the range of services to be accommodated within the welfare state, the country's ability to pay for even existing levels of social provision was being seriously undermined. The oil crisis of the early 1970s when oil prices were quadrupled within a year, the costs of Britain's entry into the European Economic Community, the impact on sterling of the floating of the major currencies, and the structural weaknesses of Britain's ailing industrial economy appeared to reduce the freedom for manoeuvre of governments to spend on new welfare services. Nevertheless public sector investment in leisure continued to grow across the 1970s.

In terms of arts policy the reforms of the earlier Labour White Paper had been minimal, though indicative of a willingness to change the emphasis of spending. The cultural goals represented in Arts Council Policy had been 'democratisation of culture', that is the spread of high culture to a wider audience. The White Paper's concern had been with widening access to established art forms by decentralising provision, and to some extent with widening the range of the established arts. However in the wake of the cultural upheaval of the 1960s which had its clearest expression in the events of 1968, Arts Council policy came under scrutiny from those working within the field, and in particular those working within the community arts movement (Braden, 1978; Kelly, 1984). This movement advocated the adoption of 'cultural democracy' as a central policy goal, arguing that individuals and communities should be encouraged to foster their own cultural forms, rather than being 'educated' to appreciate the traditional, high arts. The welfare right to be stressed was, for this group, not a right to access to established arts, but a right to the resources required to express ones own cultural predilections. The Arts Council responded to this challenge to its historic policy goals by establishing a Community Arts Working Party between 1976 and 1978 and providing some limited funding for community arts experimental schemes. The funding for these projects was only ever marginal (approximately 1.5% of the Arts Council budget) and in 1983 with the publication of its policy review *Glory in the Garden* the Council devolved funding for such projects to the Regional Arts Associations, arguing that they had no place in national policy, and thus defusing a potential clash between high and low arts funding, in times of economic decline.

By the time the economic difficulties of the world recession had taken hold, and the Labour government had attempted to introduce a squeeze on public expenditure following the negotiation of a loan for Britain from the International Monetary Fund in 1976, the welfare state itself, and in particular the role of liberal welfare professionals within it, had been under severe criticism. A series of research reports by the Sports Council (e.g. Gregory, 1977; Grimshaw and Prescott-Clarke, 1978), the Arts Council (e.g. Arts Council, 1974; Hutchinson, 1977) and by independent bodies (e.g. Hillman and Whalley, 1977) illustrated that provision of facilities and opportunities for leisure did not of itself eliminate recreational disadvantage. In terms of sport and active recreation white, male, middle class, car owning young people were over represented among the users of public facilities, while in the subsidised arts, though gender and age profiles were different, in other respects, beneficiaries of public spending were very similar. As the period of severe economic difficulty began in the mid 1970s, the welfare framework was under attack from commentators on the left and the right of the political spectrum. From the left came the criticism that services (including leisure services) failed those most in need, and that this reflected the fact that the liberal welfare professionals, who were drawn from a different social stratum from the recreationally disadvantaged, could not successfully identify or meet their needs (Whannel, 1983). The right argued that public sector professionals were 'budget maximisers', bureaucrats in whose interests it was to expand their own service area regardless of criteria of efficiency and effectiveness, and that the segments actually served by public leisure services would be able to meet its own needs through the market. By the end of the 1970s under the combined weight of the economic recession and the managerialist critiques of right and left, welfare reformism was no longer a guiding principle.

New Economic Realism 1976-84

As we have already noted the public expenditure squeeze which has characterised the period since the mid-1970s was initiated by a Labour government, albeit influenced by the conditions required by the International Monetary Fund for its granting of a loan. In such circumstances, one might have expected leisure expenditure to have fallen disproportionately in the period from the mid-1970s, given that leisure was the last of the services to be added to the welfare framework, and given its assumed status as a luxury when compared to more basic needs such as housing, health and education. However, as Table 5.1 illustrates, despite the public expenditure squeeze, in real terms leisure expenditures generally did not fall universally from the mid 1970s to the mid-1980s. What occurred was not a wholesale reduction of welfare spending, a dismantling of the welfare state, but rather what Gough (1979) terms a restructuring of the welfare framework.

As we have noted, public sector leisure provision continued, even in the 1975 White Paper *Sport and Recreation,* to be justified in part by reference to social control. The White Paper argued that 'By reducing boredom and urban frustration, participation in active recreation contributes to the reduction of hooliganism and delinquency among young people' (Department of Environment, 1975, p.2), and this rationale became even more significant as Britain experienced a wave of urban unrest in the early 1980s. Serious urban disorders in Brixton, Bristol and Toxteth in the early period of Margaret Thatcher's tenure as Prime Minister, tempered any tendency to reduce spending on leisure, or at least on sport and active recreation.

Although there were concerted efforts by the new Conservative government elected in 1979 to control local government expenditure, leisure spending by local authorities continued to increase until the mid 1980s. Even more significantly, since it was directly controlled by central government, spending on leisure in the inner city increased considerably in the form of the Urban Programme (a central government scheme for earmarking sums for deprived urban areas). One of the Thatcher Government's early White Papers announcing public sector financial allocations indicates the exponential growth of this form of funding from £12 million in 1975/6 to £203 million in 1981/2 (Treasury, 1981). Although the proportion of the Urban Programme as a whole spent on leisure is difficult to ascertain, in 1984/5 £84 million was spent on social and community provision (Treasury, 1986), while in 1985/6, the allocation for sport and recreation represented 18-20% for each of the local authorities supported by Urban Programme funding (Treasury, 1987). Thus the Conservative Government might be said to be shifting or restructuring, welfare spending towards social expenses associated with maintaining social integration, and away from social consumption (O'Connor, 1973).

Areas of leisure spending which might not be so readily defended by reference to the appeal to social integration, such as arts expenditure were however more likely to be subject to attack, and the incoming Conservative Government for example, upon taking office, cut the Arts Council's grant by some £1.1 million, despite pre-election pledges to the contrary (Baldry, 1981). In the case of the Countryside Commission also, the government was less than supportive of recreation and conservation interests, in particular where these were in conflict with the requirements of industry (Blunden and Curry, 1985).

State Flexibilisation and Disinvestment 1985-91

The Conservative governments of the 1980s, however, have not merely been concerned to reduce overall the size of the public expenditure budget. They have actively sought to reduce the range of public sector activities and to challenge the bureaucratic dysfunctions of the traditional public sector organisations. The terms 'flexibilisation' and 'disinvestment' represent a series of policy thrusts which may be characterised as falling under five headings:

- the sale of public sector assets;
- the introduction of market competition and market principles into the management of public sector leisure facilities;
- the introduction of a market imperative rather than social or aesthetic goals as the primary criterion for the development of new leisure policy initiatives;
- the sacrificing of accountability for market responsiveness in the management of some public sector bodies;

- and the politicisation of areas of work previously regarded as 'autonomous' (or quasi-autonomous areas of government policy.

In relation to the first of these headings, the major form which sale of public assets has had in relation to the public sector has been the major privatisation projects involving services such as British Telecom, government oil and gas interests, public sector water companies, and so on. In the leisure field such privatisation has been limited to the sale of recreational land formerly under the control of schools which have experienced falling rolls with a general decline in the school population. Some local authorities have, however, sold off sports facilities to private companies when they have been unable to meet the financial costs of running them.

Public sector leisure facilities in Britain have traditionally been managed by public, unusually municipal, employees. Perhaps the most significant policy change in relation to public sector leisure provision in recent years has been legislation to require local governments to open up the management of such facilities to competition from the commercial sector. Contracts to manage all local authority owned sport and recreation facilities had to be drawn up by 1993 and municipal management had to tender a bid for the management of municipal facilities in competition with commercial management companies, if the local authority wished to continue to manage its own facilities. This requirement under the Local Government Act of 1988 is seen as endangering the social welfare approach of local government to management of such facilities since, in order to compete in price terms for the winning of such contracts, public sector employees may be forced to emulate commercial management in pursuing market segments which can afford to pay high prices. The legislation allows local authorities to specify prices to be charged, and even disadvantaged groups to be targeted, but the difficulties of achieving the expenditure reductions required by central government may undermine the policy priorities, even of Labour controlled local authorities. The rationale for the introduction of competition is clearly one of increased efficiency with public bureaucrats either being replaced by commercial operators, or effectively becoming more commercial than those counterparts in order to win contracts. However, the net result of this process may be that the requirements of economic efficiency preclude the social effectiveness of the services provided, and that the egalitarian goals of 'sport for all' give way to slick marketing to generate revenue.

The introduction of competition is obviously related to the replacement of social and aesthetic rationales for leisure and cultural provision by the market imperative. A review of Arts Council annual reports across the 1980s illustrates just how clearly the rationale rehearsed by the Council has slipped from one which relates to aesthetic standards and promotion of access, to one which relates to the economic importance of the arts, and it is hardly surprising therefore that both the Arts and Sports Councils should have commissioned research to evaluate (and highlight) the economic significance of the arts and sport respectively (Myerscough, 1988; Henley Centre, 1986). The economic rhetoric is clearly seen as one which will appeal to government thinking and is echoed in the government's expenditure White Papers. The White Paper for 1988, which comments favourably on the funding of cultural schemes which have 'had a marked and immediate effect on their neighbourhood and have attracted both businesses and customers into the area' (Treasury, 1988, p. 3). The use of sport in economic regeneration is however more difficult to justify as Sheffield found to its cost when it sought to obtain assistance from central government to contribute to the cost of the World Student Games which it hosted in 1991. (However, failure to support this initiative may have more to do with a history of marked antipathy between this particular Labour controlled local authority and Conservative central government, than a simple lack of enthusiasm for the project.)

The social rationale for expenditure on sport and recreation had clearly lost some of its appeal even in relation to inner city areas by the end of the 1980s. The Inner Area Programme (part of the Urban Programme through which central government directly funds local projects) reduced its expenditure on sport and recreation by 41% in cash terms between 1987/8 and 1989/90, with expenditure on social objectives in the same period reducing from £83 million to £57 million while expenditure on economic objectives for the inner city rose from £101 million to £121 million. In addition the Minister for Sport in an open letter to the Chairman of the Sports Council, in 1987 indicated quite strongly that the government was actively considering reducing the Sports Council's role to one of dealing predominantly with social provision for disadvantaged groups in the inner city, while placing responsibility for funding elite sports and competitors more clearly in the hands of commercial sponsors (Moynihan, 1987). The Minister also required that the management of the National Sports Centres be opened up to commercial competition. Although competitive tendering was introduced in the National Centres, the review of the Sports Council's future was completed ensued did not straightforwardly follow the New Right agenda hinted at in the Minister's original letter.

A corollary of the move to render public sector management and policy more responsive and flexible has been the sacrificing of some accountability to the electorate of such bodies. Commercial companies which win contracts to manage public facilities, for example, will not be required to account to local government except in respect of fulfilling the specific conditions of their contracts. Urban Development Corporations set up in urban areas to facilitate economic regeneration, have taken over the power of locally elected government. Such Corporations, made up of individuals directly appointed by the Minister for the Environment, usually from the world of business, are able to plan in secret, without reference to the local community, and though leisure has played an important part in many of the redevelopment plans of Urban Development Corporations with the use of urban waterways and the development of commercial facilities such as multi-screen cinemas and marinas, these have predominantly been designed to foster incoming investment rather than to meet the needs of existing communities. The key elements of UDCs in promoting investment n leisure are, firstly, to provide opportunities for profitable leisure investment, and, secondly, to generate a cultural infrastructure which will provide an attractive social environment for the new service class (Lash and Urry, 1987), from which will be drawn the core workforce of the new industries in urban regeneration. Neither of these roles is likely to generate significant investment for existing and disadvantaged local urban communities. Thus, reduced accountability is likely to be accompanied by a decline in responsiveness to local social needs.

The traditional independence or quasi autonomy of the leisure quangos from government, was perhaps always a myth which it has been increasingly difficult to sustain in the 1980s. The use of the term 'quango' (signifying quasi-autonomous non-governmental organisation) has given way in the rhetoric of the 1980s and 1990s to that of government 'agencies', reflecting the direct use of such organisations as policy tools by government. In the 1980s, government expenditure white papers regularly indicated, not only the level of funding to be given to the leisure quangos (The Countryside Commission became a quango in 1982, joining the Arts and Sports Councils). but also stipulating the use to which such funding should be put (Henry, 1993, Chapter 3). Furthermore, government appointments to the leisure quangos in the 1980s increasingly reflected political leanings sympathetic to the new Right, as well as policy interests in the sub-fields of leisure, of sport, the arts or the countryside. Thus ironically a government declaring itself to be against state intervention in all areas of social and economic policy, was exhibiting a growing willingness to intervene in the activities of 'quai-autonomous' leisure bodies.

Post-1991: the Post-Thatcher Era

In 1992 the Conservative Government succeeded in winning its first election under the leadership of John Major, who had replaced Margaret Thatcher as Prime Minister in the previous year. The new leader made some clear changes in leadership style, eschewing the more confrontational style of his predecessor, agreeing for example to rescind the unpopular community charge or poll tax. He also gave notice of some differences in policy emphasis, declaring a more positive position in respect of European integration. Whether these changes were likely to lead to a difference in terms of leisure policy is, at the time of writing, perhaps a little early to say, though there are some significant pointers.

However, perhaps the most significant feature of the leisure policy system was the continuity between the Thatcher and Major administrations, a function of over a decade of Thatcherism. Local government has been the principal provider of public sector leisure services in the British system and the control of local government expenditures put in place by the Thatcher administration, and finally becoming effective in the later 1980s, was continued by the Major Government. The reduction of inner city social spending, and the primary emphasis on economic rather than social regeneration, also continued. Furthermore the government maintained its programme of promoting the local management of schools by school boards (rather than by local government) and the process of competitive tendering to manage local government owned leisure facilities. Thus the loss of local accountability evident in the more centralised control of the Thatcher governments was to continue to provide a backdrop to the leisure policy of the 1990s.

Nevertheless, some policy shifts have been evident. The ministerial review of the future of the Sports Council, initiated by the Minister for Sport under Mrs Thatcher, was completed in 1991. However, far from reducing the size and influence of the sports quango, the government accepted the proposal that a new sports organisation be set up, the UK Sports Commission, which would take over the Sports Council's concern for international affairs, and for elite sport, with the Sports Council itself to be transformed into a Sports Council for England to parallel those Councils already in existence in Scotland, Wales and Northern Ireland. Although this new agency may well be charged with stimulating commercial involvement in elite sport through sponsorship, its existence would seem to signal that the government had not been prepared to countenance a wholesale reduction in intervention in sport on the part of the public sector at national level.

A further initiative in the leisure field might provide some clues as to government thinking in this area of policy. When John Major announced his post-election cabinet in 1992, he appointed David Mellor, a charismatic and energetic member of the Conservative administration to a new Ministry of national Heritage which was to combine responsibility for the arts, sport, and tourism. In the early 1980s the Thatcher administration had declared itself to be firmly against a proposal for the formation of a Ministry of Leisure, with its spokesperson arguing in the parliamentary debate that such an arrangement would imply too great a level of state intervention in the leisure field, and thus the encouragement of inefficiency and the suppression of individual initiative (Henry, 1993, Chapter 2). The new grouping of responsibilities in the National Heritage Ministry, however, seems to indicate two strands of thinking. The first is the notion that there is a single, unitary, national heritage, a view consistent with the traditional 'one nation Conservatism' of the pre-Thatcher Conservative Party. Mrs Thatcher once declared that there was no such thing as society, only individuals, and hence it might have been difficult, philosophically, to argue for a notion of a 'collective heritage'. However, the second strand of thinking evident in this move reflects the identification of sport and the arts, on the one hand, with tourism, on the other. Tourism had been supported by the state since the late 1960s because of the economic benefits it might generate. (Social tourism had never really been a feature of government policy in Britain). Sport and the arts were to be linked with tourism because of their use as tools of both national and city specific marketing. The promotion of a unitary heritage was thus to accompanied by the promotion of the process of the commodification of culture established in the later 1980s in the promotion of sport and the arts for their economic value (Myerscough, 1988; Henley Centre, 1986).

Conclusion

The changes which have affected leisure policy in Britain over the last two decades have been considerable. The period has covered the move from the end of the post-war boom through a series of major recessions, and has witnessed pressures both external (e.g. the International Monetary Fund's pressure on government spending) and internal (the Thatcherite squeeze on public spending and its hegemonic programme of market individualism) which have had profound effects on the role of the state in leisure. In the concluding chapter we employ the framework of regulation theory to characterise the nature of these changes, and to draw some parallels and contrasts with other systems. Certainly, British society with the loss of full employment has become a two tier society with the gap between rich and poor growing in the 1980s for the first time since such information was recorded in the 1930s (Pond, 1989). In this two tier society, leisure is no longer viewed as a welfare right for all, since welfare rights are replaced by a dual system of consumer rights and 'safety net' residual forms of welfare. The state's continuing interest in leisure has been predominantly economic in motivation rather than social, as the culture of welfarism was superseded in the later 1980s by the entrepreeurialism of the New Right, and the public sector leisure profession, which had its origins in the liberal welfare professionalism of the welfare state, has developed in ways much close to the industrial semi-professions of marketing and accountancy, or even in the anti-professional mode of Thatcherite 'meritocratic' individualism.

One way of conceptualising the shift in leisure policy which has taken place is by reference to O'Connor's (1973) typology of state expenditures. O'Connor argues that state expenditures can be categorised under three headings; social consumption (the provision of social services - e.g. education, public housing); social expenses (to maintain social order - e.g. policing and defence); and social investment - e.g. roads, cultural infrastructure). The history of leisure provision by the state in Britain in the last two decades can be characterised as a move from social consumption (leisure services as a welfare right), through social expenses (leisure as a means of promoting social order in the inner city), to social investment (leisure provision and cultural infrastructure as a means of attracting investment by the new service industries). Whether more recent moves by the state, such as that to establish a unitary Ministry of National Heritage, mark a departure from, or merely a consolidation of, such trends remains to be seen.

REFERENCES

Alexander, S. (1990) 'Women, Class and Sexual Differences in the 1830s and 1840s: Some Reflections on the Writing of a Feminist History', in Lovell, T. (ed.) *British Feminist Thought*, Oxford: Blackwell.

Arts Council (1974) *Research and Information Statistical Reports*, nos. 2-4, Arts Council, London.

Arts Council (1984) *The Glory of the garden: Strategy for a Decade*, London: Williams Lea.

Atkins, R. (1990) Open Letter to the Chairman of the Sports Council, December 1990.

Bailey, P. (1987) *Leisure and Class in Victorian England*, London: Methuen, 2nd edn.

Baldry, H. (1981) *The Case for the Arts*, London: Secker and Warburg.

Blunden, J. and Curry, N. (1985) *The Changing Countryside*, London: Croom Helm.

Braden, S. (1978) *Artists and People*, London: Routledge and Kegan Paul

Brailsford (1969) *Sport and Society: Elizabeth to Anne*, London: Routledge and Kegan Paul.

Bramham, P., Henry, I. and Spink, J. (1990) 'Leisure, Culture and the Political Economy of the City: the Case of Leeds', paper presented to the International Sociological Association, World Congress, Madrid, July 1990 (Working Group 13).

CIPFA (1990) *Leisure and Recreation Estimates 1990/91*, London: Chartered Institute of Public Finance Accountants.

Clark, R. (1980) *The Arts Council*, Centre for Leisure Studies, University of Salford (monograph).

Coghlan, J. (with Webb, I.) (1990) *Sport and British Politics Since 1960*, Brighton: Falmer Press.

Cunningham, H. (1980) *Leisure in the Industrial Revolution, c.1780-1880*, London: Croom Helm.

Department of Environment (1975) *Sport and Recreation*, London: HMSO.

Doyle, W. (1978) *The Old European Order 1660 - 1800*, Oxford: Oxford University Press.

Dunning, E. and Sheard, K. (1976) *Barbarians, Gentlemen and Players*, London: Martin Robertson.

Evans, H.J. (1974) *Service to Sport: the Story of the CCPR 1935-1972*, London: Pelham.

Golby, J. and Purdue, A. (1984) *The Civilisation of the Crowd*, London: Batsford Press.

Gough, I. (1979) *The Political Economy of the Welfare State*, London: Macmillan.

Grazia, V. de. (1981) *The Culture of Consent: Mass Organisation of Leisure in Fascist Italy*, Cambridge: Cambridge University Press.

Gregory, S. (1977) *Badminton at Three Sports Centres*, Sports Council Working Papers No. 11, London: Sports Council.

Grimshaw, P. and Prescott-Clarke, S. (1978) *Sport, School and the Community*, Sports Council Working Papers No. 9, London: Sports Council.

Hall, C. (1990) 'Private Persons versus Public Someones: Class, Gender and Politics in England 1780-1850' in Lovell, T. (ed.) *British Feminist Thought*, Oxford: Blackwell.

Hargreaves, John (1986) *Sport, Power and Culture*, Oxford: Polity Press.

Harrison, B. (1967) 'Religion and Recreation in Nineteenth Century England', *Past and Present*, no. 38, December.

Harrison, B. (1971) *Drink and the Victorians: the Temperance Question in England 1815-1872*, London: Faber.

Hasard, P. (1973) *The European Mind 1680-1715*, Harmondsworth: Penguin.

Henley Centre for Forecasting (1986) *The Economic Impact and Importance of Sport in the UK*, London: Sports Council.

Henry, I. (1993) *The Politics of Leisure Policy*, London: Macmillan.

Hill, C. (1964) *Society and Puritanism in Pre-revolutionary England*, London: Secker and Warburg.

Hillman, M. and Whalley, A. (1977) *Fair Play for All*, Political and Economic Planning Report, London: P.E.P.

Howkins, A. and Lowerson, J. (1979) *Trends in Leisure 1919-1939*, London: Sports Council / ESRC.

Hutchinson, R. (1977) *Three Arts Centres*, London: Arts Council.

Jones, S. (1986) *Workers at Play*, London: Routledge and Kegan Paul.

Kelly, O. (1984) *Community, Art and the State*, London: Comedia

Lash, S. and Urry, J. (1987) *The End of Organised Capitalism*, Oxford: Polity Press.

Malcolmson, R. (1973) *Popular Recreations in English Society 1700-1850*, Cambridge: Cambridge University Press.

McIntosh, P. (1963) *Sport and Society*, London: Brailsford.

Mooers, C. (1991) *The Making of Bourgeois Europe: Absolutism, Relativism, and the Rise of Capitalism in England, France and Germany*, London: Verso.

Moynihan, C. (1987) Open Letter to the Chairman of the Sports Council, November 1987.

Myerscough, J. (1988) *The Economic Importance of the Arts in Britain*, London: Policy Studies Institute.

O'Connor, J. (1973) *The Fiscal Crisis of the State*, London: St. James's Press.

Perkin, J. (1969) *The Origins of the Modern English Society 1980-1880*, London: Secker and Warburg.

Pond, C. (1989) 'The Changing Distribution of Income, Wealth and Poverty' in Hamnett, C. McDowell, L. and Sarre, P. (eds.) *The Changing Social Structure*, London: Sage.

Shoard, M. (1980) *The Theft of the Countryside*, Aldershot: Temple Smith.

Travis, A. and Veal, A. (1979) *The State and Leisure Provision*, London: Sports Council / Social Sciences Research Council.

Treasury (1981) *The Government's Expenditure Plans 1982/3 - 1984/5*, London: H.M.S.O.

Treasury (1986) *The Government's Expenditure Plans 1987/8 - 1989/90*, London: H.M.S.O.

Treasury (1987) *The Government's Expenditure Plans 1988/9 - 1990/1* London: H.M.S.O.

Treasury (1988) *The Government's Expenditure Plans 1989/90 - 1991/2* London: H.M.S.O.

Walvin, J. (1978) *Leisure and Society 1830-1950*, London: Longman.

Waters, C. (1990) *British Socialism and the Politics of Popular Culture, 1884-1914*, Manchester: Manchester University Press.

Whannel, G. (1983) *Blowing the Whistle: the Politics of Sport*, London: Pluto Press.

Wolfenden Committee (1960) *Sport and the Community*, London: CCPR.

Chapter 6

Leisure Policy in Germany

Wolfgang Nahrstedt

German Understanding of Leisure Policy

Leisure policy can be understood as referring to all policy which seeks to improve the leisure lives of the population. The most common translation in German for leisure, however, really means 'free time' (Freizeit). In a broad sense 'Freizeit' corresponds to the wider meanings of leisure (see Mommaas, 1992, p. 2), but in more specialised instances, however, leisure should be translated in subtly different ways. Closest to 'leisure as a state of mind' would be the German word 'Muße', meaning 'having time', 'contemplation', or 'spiritual development'. Other translations include recreation (Erholung), entertainment (Unterhaltung), creativity (Kreativität). 'Freizeit', by contrast, is more suggestive of time rather than the quality of the experience. Leisure policy will thus be treated as referring to policy which seeks to improve the conditions for free choice of activity during free time. Such activity may be readily recognisable as leisure-like, but it may also take unconventional forms, such as voluntary work.

Although policy predominantly refers to the activities of government at all levels (local, state, federal, European), nevertheless, civic groups, clubs, and associations also formulate their own leisure policies, while trade unions have done so for more than a century. Business policies, such as the marketing strategies of organisations in the leisure industry may also have a considerable impact on leisure opportunities. Thus, the concerns of leisure policy can be said to relate to policy-oriented activities and initiatives in the public, private and voluntary sectors which seek to improve leisure conditions. This chapter will however, focus almost exclusively on leisure policy in the public, governmental sector.

Before going on to consider in detail the state's involvement in leisure policy, some general observations concerning the role of leisure in German society should be made. Most of the data to which reference will be made relate to the old Federal Republic, the former West Germany. However, since the dominant political, economic, and cultural characteristics of the unified German state are likely to be derived from the West rather than the former communist state of the German Democratic Republic, these data are perhaps more germane to a discussion of Germany's future.

German Leisure: Rapid Growth with Little Co-ordinated State Intervention

The Germans may be considered world leaders in terms of consumption of leisure and tourism. From 1950 to 1988 the working week reduced from 50 hours to less than 40 hours in the (old) Federal Republic of Germany (Table 6. 1), and since 1978 the trade unions have been fighting for a reduction of the 40 hour week to 35 hours. Indeed, in 1991, for the first time, the demand for a 30 hour week was voiced by a German trade union. Since the early 1980s, six weeks of vacation have been enjoyed by 80 per cent of those in full-time employment. Between 1972 and 1990 the proportion of adults taking vacations grew in the Länder of the former West Germany from 65.4 per cent to 74.8 per cent, with those taking trips of five days or more increasing from 49.0 per cent to 68.2 per cent, and those taking shorter breaks (of from two to four days) growing from 25 per cent to 37 per cent (Figure 6.1). From 1979 to 1989 the amount spent on travel abroad rose sharply from 29 to more than 46 billion DM (Figure 6.2).

The span of working life has also been reduced. The 'post-adolescence' phase, for students and other groups in education and further training (which accounts for nearly 30 per cent of the younger generation) lasts well into the third decade of their lives, while with people retiring earlier, Germans join the 'new elderly' earlier, that is between the ages of 50 and 60. This group already accounts for, about 15 per cent of the population, with forecasts for the year 2010 estimating a growth of up to 30 per cent. An overview of the shift from work time to leisure for the general population between 1964 and 1980 (Tokarski and Schmitz-Scherzer, 1985), reveals that in 1964 the average working time (7 hours 53 minutes), exceeded the average time for leisure (5 hours 41 minutes). By 1980, these proportions were reversed with leisure (7 hours 29 minutes) exceeding working time (6 hours 26 minutes). Such generalised data obviously mask real differences within the population, particularly between the sexes, and between those in and out of employment, but the figures illustrate an interesting trend.

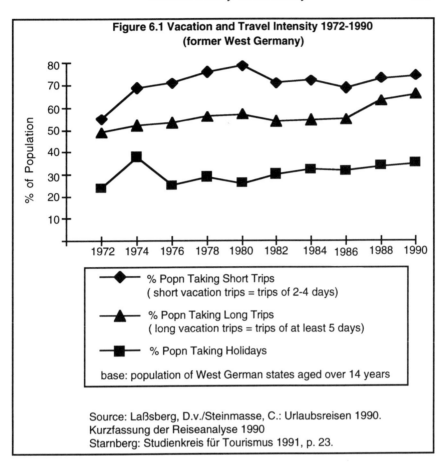

Figure 6.1 Vacation and Travel Intensity 1972-1990
(former West Germany)

- ◆— % Popn Taking Short Trips
  (short vacation trips = trips of 2-4 days)

- ▲— % Popn Taking Long Trips
  (long vacation trips = trips of at least 5 days)

- ■— % Popn Taking Holidays

base: population of West German states aged over 14 years

Source: Laßsberg, D.v./Steinmasse, C.: Urlaubsreisen 1990.
Kurzfassung der Reiseanalyse 1990
Starnberg: Studienkreis für Tourismus 1991, p. 23.

The figures cited by Tokarski and Schmitz-Scherzer demonstrate some of the differences in the length of leisure for various groups. Full-time workers have nearly three hours less free time (6 hours 22 minutes) than pensioners and the unemployed (9 hours 40 minutes), though whether this can be described as increased leisure is highly debatable. There are also great differences between the leisure spent in and out of the home. The increase in free time between 1964 and 1980 seems evident only in the increase in the average time spent on indoor activities, a consequence of the spread of television, but also, perhaps, a reflection of the lack of an effective leisure policy. Although considerable free time is available as leisure in Germany, significant differences exist between different sectors of the population in terms of both the length, and the structure of leisure. Leisure innovations (in particular television) have affected the weekly time structure of the whole population (e.g. the relation between time spent indoors and outdoors). To counteract this, a clearly defined, effectively structured, and very active leisure policy might thus be expected.

Table 6.1 Weekly Working time in Federal Republic of Germany 1950-2010	
1950	50 hours
1955	48 hours
1958	45.2 hours
1973	40 hours[1]
1983	40 hours[2]
1988	39.2 hours

[1] 40% of workforce
[2] 99% of workforce

Source: Federal Agency for Work. In: Neue Westfälische 9.12.1988

Germany is, however, also a highly industrialised and export-oriented country. More than half of its industrial products are sold abroad. Work and productivity are the basis of wealth and leisure, and German unification and the new orientation towards the East, seem to have reactivated old work-ethic values. In the old states of West Germany, unemployment had almost disappeared. The autobahns are overcrowded 24 hours a day and the gross national product has been growing rapidly. Leisure and leisure policy have been thus overshadowed by work and industrial policy, which provide the basis of economic policy. Thus,while in Germany a clearly developed economic policy does exist, there is no identifiable, developed leisure policy as such. There is no ministry in federal or state government with specific responsibility for leisure. Many elements exist which might be regarded as belonging to leisure policy, but there is no clearly defined government focus on leisure nor is leisure a signifcant focus of academic enquiry.

A chapter on leisure policy in Germany must, therefore, relate to leisure-relevant policy rather than leisure policy per se, and one goal of this chapter will be to demonstrate the contradiction between the social importance of leisure and the lack of a clear definition of leisure policy. However, we will begin this analysis with an historical overview of the development of elements of policies of relevance to leisure.

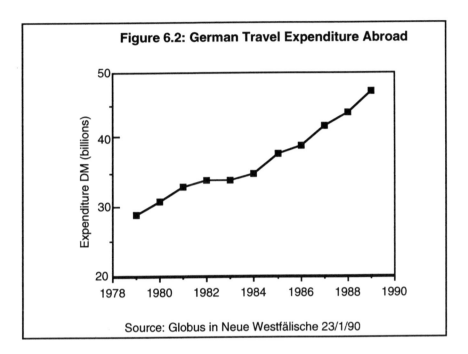

Figure 6.2: German Travel Expenditure Abroad

Source: Globus in Neue Westfälische 23/1/90

From Work Policy to Leisure Policy: Some First Steps Towards Leisure-related Policy

The Leisure of the Gentry and the Citizens' Movement (1789-1848)

If the leisure of the gentry is regarded the precursor to the leisure of ordinary citizens and workers, a leisure policy has been in existence in Germany for centuries. The parks, castles, festivals and chases of the gentry were early forms of leisure facilities, and such provis,ion might be regarded as examples of early leisure policy (Nahrstedt, 1990). The modern epoch in leisure began with the Enlightenment and the political revolutions in the United States in 1776, and in France in 1789. In the development of citizen power between 1789 and 1848, ideas of individual freedom were propagated which are essential to the notion of leisure policy. Indeed, German intellectuals, such as Immanuel Kant, Friedrich Schiller and Friedrich Schleiermacher discussed the new 'problem' of leisure for working people. The growing power of citizens fostered the development of demands for leisure, and the first intellectual discussions relating to leisure date back to the beginning of the nineteenth century. The word 'freizeit' first appeared in 1823 in the writings of the educationalist, Friedrich Frobel (Nahrstedt, 1988, p. 31).

The Workers' Movement and Social Policy (1848-1918)

Trade unions and political parties for workers developed after the unsuccessful revolution of 1848, and one of their demands was for a reduction in work time. With the onset of industrialisation daily working time had grown and the pace of work had intensified. Sixteen hour days, 80 to 90 hour weeks, with no free Sundays or holidays were not untypical. Between 1850 and 1890, the first attempts were made to formulate a policy with the goal of reducing working hours. This initiative can be regarded as the second significant step towards a leisure policy. Gradual reductions, first to a twelve-hour day, and subsequently to a ten hour day, and finally to an eight-hour day and a 48 hour week, were achieved through trade union struggle. This reduction of working time opened the way for the expansion of leisure related activities.

Bismarck's Conservative Government, after the founding of the Second German Reich in 1871, created the basis of modern social policy. In 1892 legislation was introduced to declare Sunday a day free from work once more. The bourgeoisie, however, feared political misuse of the new leisure by workers, and some forms of leisure provision and leisure education were stimulated by this fear (Giesecke, 1983). Both the workers' movement, and the social policy promoted by the middle class and the gentry, sought to influence the leisure behaviour of workers, with education and culture as major goals. Provision of adult education and libraries were part of a strategy aimed at both improving, and controlling leisure behaviour. Thus the beginnings of a leisure policy were evident in Germany from 1890.

The Weimar Republic and the New Leisure Market (1918-1932)

The Weimar Republic was founded after the First World War, and lasted from 1918 to 1932. The first governments were run by Social Democrats and an attempt was made to guarantee the 8 hour day and the 48 hour week. The first real political and academic discussions on leisure began during this period (Klatt, 1929; Geck, 1966). At a local level, the first programmes for leisure centres for young girls and boys were set up (e.g. in Berlin and in Hamburg, Gebhard and Nahrstedt, 1963). In the 'golden twenties' the development of leisure opportunities was promoted mainly by the market, particularly the emergent leisure and entertainment industry. Film and broadcast systems spread rapidly. Sport and the Schreber 'garden movement' became increasingly important in the leisure of workers. However, no clearly formulated leisure policy was developed by government agencies to give a political framework to these different movements and the economic and political crisis between 1929 and 1933 focused attention on other matters.

National Socialists, Leisure Policy and the 'Führer' Cult (1933-1945)

The significance of leisure was clearly recognised by the National Socialists (Nazis). They made leisure an important policy issue, and organised it around the cult of the strong leader. Young people and adults were organised in political associations during their leisure. For leisure and recreation a special organisation called 'Power through Joy' ('Kraft durch Freude') was formed. A very rigid control of popular leisure was sought by the National Socialist Government and the National Socialist Party in pursuit of ideological goals (Nahrstedt, 1990, p. 105; Wilson, 1988).

Debate about the democratic approach to leisure policy, fostered during the Weimar Republic, continued, though in a covert manner. The educationalist Wilhelm Flitner (1890-1940) first used the term 'Freizeitpolitik' writing in 1937, in the context of the Second World Conference on Leisure and Recreation in Hamburg. He argued that the industrial revolution, had led to a 'decollectivisation' of the 'old social order' and there was a need for a reconstruction of society. The goal of policy, Flitner suggested, should be to re-establish the traditional notion of 'a social, common leisure after work, but adapted to the new conditions'. The core tasks for a leisure policy should thus be, the regulation of work time, and of the kind of work undertaken; the construction of city leisure facilities, and the development of leisure programmes.'Leisure education and leisure research ... [were to be] ... necessary components of a leisure policy ... [since] ... science may clarify problems, but only, if there exists a political will and educational purpose, will progress be made' (Flitner, 1937, p. 34).

Later in the 1970s the first attempts to develop a structure for leisure policy along these lines were made, but in National Socialist Germany no real progress was possible for a leisure policy independent of Nazi ideology.

Federal Republic of Germany: the Reconstruction of Leisure Markets (1949-1969)

After World War II West Germany was reconstructed on the basis of a 'social market economy'. The German economic miracle of the 1950s also brought about shorter working hours. Step by step it was possible for the trade unions to re-establish the 48 hour week, and then to reduce it to 40 hours in 1958, and to begin the struggle for a 35 hour week. Vacation time was gradually lengthened from two weeks to six weeks. The age of retirement was reduced from 65 to 62, and then from 60 to 58, with many people entering retirement at an even earlier age.

Although Germany purportedly led the world in the consumption of leisure and holiday time, during the term of office of the Conservative Governments, from 1949 to 1969, no attempt to construct a leisure policy was made. The government regarded leisure as a non-political issue. The example of Nazi Germany was used as an argument against political involvement in leisure affairs. The quality of leisure was seen as an issue for the market and voluntary sector, rather than for governments, and this has continued to be the position of the Conservatives and Liberals.

Nevertheless, the awareness of the importance of a policy for leisure grew during this period among various social groups and organisations such as the churches, trade unions, universities, academies, sports organisations and so on. In 1963 at a meeting on 'Political Responsibility for Leisure' within the Evangelical Academy at Tutzing, attended by 33 representatives of these different types of groups, it was argued that leisure policy was an indispensable part of cultural and social policy (Rieger, 1964, p.13). Thus a growing awareness (at least in some quarters) of the necessity for a leisure policy had begun to develop in the 1960s.

Developments of the First Policy Frameworks for Leisure

Leisure Policy 1969-1982

During the Social Democrat-Liberal coalition Federal Government, from 1969-1982, the first attempt to plan a leisure policy was made, though with little effect. Between 1969 and 1972 (the first Federal Government led by Willy Brandt of the Social Democrats and Walter Scheel of the Liberal Party) a positive climate for leisure policy in Germany was developed. The very densely populated Ruhr-district (the 'Siedlungsverband Ruhr-Distrikt'; SVR) organised regular conferences on leisure from 1970. Large scale community leisure parks ('Revierparks') were also constructed in the 1970s, and, in 1973, the German Association of Cities and Communities ('Deutscher Städte und Gemeindebund') formulated explicit demands for 'cities conducive to leisure' (freizeitfreundliche Stadt). Even conservative state governments such as the Bavarian State Government presented a 'Programme for Leisure and Recreation' in 1970, while the Liberals also articulated their own *Reflections on a Policy for Leisure* (Giesecke, 1973).

Attempts to establish a framework for leisure policy were made in the 1970s. In 1973 the second Social Democrat-Liberal Coalition promoted leisure as a political issue. Willy Brandt in his first declaration as Prime Minister of the second Brandt/Scheel Cabinet on 18 January, 1973 argued that:

The quality of life is more than merely the standard of living. It means enrichment of life and more than income and consumption ... the improvement of standards of living, the improvement of work, of leisure and of recreation have to be focused upon.

To foster this initiative a new approach to leisure policy was to be developed. In 1973 a governmental unit for 'leisure and recreation' ('Freizeit und Erholung') was formed within the Federal Ministry for Youth, Family and Health. Ten research projects on special leisure problems in different areas were commissioned. Two major leisure conferences were held on 'Leisure Policy in the Federal Republic, States and Communities' (under the auspices of the Deutsche Gesellschaft für Freizeit, 1975) and on 'Leisure Policy in Europe' (organised by the Deutsche Gesellschaft für Freizeit / European Leisure and Recreation Association in 1976), and the first books on leisure policy were published (Lenz/Romeiß, 1975; Kohl, 1976).

A broad discussion of the meaning and importance of leisure policy was stimulated by these debates in the Bundestag, and by conferences and research projects. On 2 February, 1974, the Federal Government defined its understanding of leisure policy in a response to a Member of Parliament's question. Leisure policy was seen as 'policy, which would improve the leisure opportunities for wide sections of the population'. The position of leisure policy in German politics was however still weak, and the government's statement went on to identify leisure policy as subordinate, but complimentary to other areas of policy concern.

> Leisure policy is part of a social policy, which is directed to the achievement of an adequate standard of human, social and democratic life, and of working conditions for all citizens. Leisure policy does not replace, but supports other policies.

The statement went on to define what the government considered to be the main areas with which leisure policy should be concerned. These were

(1) the development of leisure spaces;
(2) further education as an essential element of leisure development;
(3) the promotion of sport for all and of recreational sport;
(4) the promotion of leisure opportunities for special needs groups;
(5) the development of leisure research;
(6) support for central 'umbrella' organisations in leisure.

Leisure policy impinges on virtually all areas and problems of society, but for all such problems and policy areas, institutions and policy communities already exist. Establishing a comprehensive leisure policy would, therefore, invariably involve a political struggle with existing professional groups. However, this first governmental definition of leisure policy demonstrated the government's conservative approach, which sought not to provoke any resistance from already established policy communities. A carefully limited attempt to define the appropriate range for leisure policy had been made.

The Era of Leisure Conferences and Congresses (1970-1978)

From 1970 to 1978, the SVR organised conferences on leisure virtually every two years in its new leisure parks within the Ruhr-region, fostering debate and publishing the proceedings (Sieglundsverband, Ruhrkohlenbezirk : SVR *et al.* 1970, 1973, 1975, 1978). In 1970 the first 'European Leisure Congress' was also organised in Geneva, Switzerland. This congress was promoted by the World Leisure and Recreation Association (WLRA), and was organised by the Swiss Organisation, Pro Juventute The foundation of the European Leisure and Recreation Association (ELRA), two years later in 1972, was one outcome of this congress. Typical of the flavour of the debate in this period were the proposals put forward by Lederman (1971, pp. 18-22) for a 'leisure charter'. These incorporated the following demands;

(1) adequate leisure space and resources in the home;
(2) play spaces for children and leisure facilities for all ages and social groups close to home;
(3) neighbourhood public leisure facilities should combine sports facilities, pools, school facilities, and shopping centres;
(4) in each city and community a co-ordination group, from different local government departments and other institutions, should be established, to engage in leisure planning and provision. Educators, sociologists, planners, and landscape architects should work together to co-ordinate and plan leisure provision for the city;
(5) regional leisure parks and recreational landscapes should be established, following the model of the Ruhr, to improve opportunities for week-end leisure;
(6) a cultural infrastructure to support active holidays was urgently required;
(7) education for leisure should be developed in school and family;
(8) architectural competitions should be established to promote adequate leisure environments in homes, neighbourhoods, villages and towns;
(9) a European agency for documentation of good practice and advice should be set up;
(10) a European 'discussion group' on 'daily', 'weekly' and 'vacation leisure' should be established.

In autumn 1974 another German Leisure Congress was organised in Garmisch-Partenkirchen by the German Association for Leisure (Deutsche Gesellschaft für Freizeit: DGF). During this congress leisure policy issues and demands were formulated by members of the Association. These emphasised the importance of leisure given the changing time structures experienced by German society, and therefore the need to provide opportunities and education for leisure. The DGF recognised that leisure would be provided by all sectors, public, private, and voluntary, but stressed the government's role at federal, state and city level in co-ordinating leisure provision, in making direct provision, in spatial planning, and in researching leisure needs.

Areas of Leisure Policy

Figure 6.3 illustrates the structure of the developing emphasis on leisure and leisure-related policy topics. Since the nineteenth century, recreation, health and sport had been related to leisure and leisure policy. In the 1920s, leisure policy for youth and families was recognised as significant. Since the beginning of the 1970s, culture, education, and media had gained recognition as important components of leisure and objects of leisure policy. The importance of space and the environment, the problem of traffic and the relation of leisure to other time structures, especially to work time, had also increasingly been seen as new and essential issues for leisure and leisure policy.

The role of scientific enquiry in relation to leisure has not, to date, been central to policy development. Only specific enquiries on very limited questions of leisure and leisure policy have been undertaken to date. Nevertheless it seems that there is a growing awareness that an understanding of leisure implies an understanding of a complex set of relationships between economic, cultural, social and political phenomena, and that leisure science has an important part to play in furthering the understanding of such relationships necessary for informed leisure policy development.

Leisure Policy in the 1980s

The development of leisure policy has continued in the 1980s, though largely in states with Social Democratic Governments, and particularly in North-Rhine-Westfalia. In 1982 a new Federal Government was elected, the conservative Christian Democrats governing in coalition with the Liberals (Helmut Kohl CDU, Hans-Dietrich Genscher FDP). The Christian Democrats and Liberals saw the development of leisure opportunities as a responsibility of the market, and thus government intervention and associated leisure policy were neglected. Government investment was not to be in the social sphere but in industrial and economic policy, with huge sums spent in the areas of new technology, particularly the computer and aerospace industries, and atomic power.

A new, single-party government in North-Rhine-Westfalia in 1980 was formed by the Social Democrats, under the leadership of

Johannes Rau. It entrusted the responsibility for leisure policy to the Ministry for Landscape Development, City Construction and Traffic (MSWV). In his first declaration as Prime Minister, Rau demonstrated a firm commitment in principle to the development of the state's role in leisure:

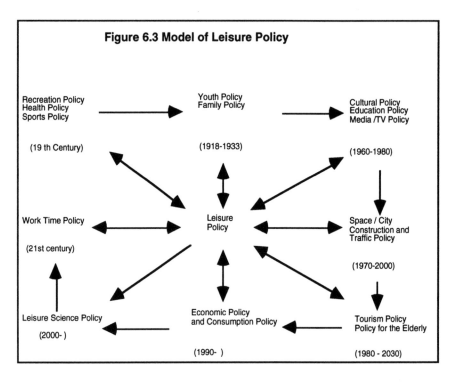

Figure 6.3 Model of Leisure Policy

> In so far as it is the state's task to administer the leisure of its citizens, the state will not accept the total commercialisation of leisure. The state government can and will secure free rooms, and together with other agencies - present proposals to its citizens. Space for play and leisure, for talks and meetings are necessary primarily in densely inhabited living areas. Our cities and communities must offer also space for leisure, sport and culture.

This statement clarifies the line which Social Democrats wished to follow for leisure policy, establishing a balance between market and state, and promoting the self-organisation of citizens in the area of play and leisure, sport and culture.

The SPD in North Rhine Westfalia also organised a 'Commission for Leisure Policy and Sports, which was to advise the ruling government. They formulated 7 'theses' on state policy including one on leisure policy, and organised a conference on 'Leisure Policy in the Community' in September 1983 within the new 'Leisure House' ('Freizeithaus') of the 'Revierpark Wischlingen' in Dortmund.

In 1983 the *First Leisure Report of the Government of North-Rhine-Westfalia* was also published. The Minister responsible, Christoph Zöpel legitimated this by pointing out that 'the relation of working time to free time will be a dominant social problem in the next ten to twenty years'. In 1984, the Social Democratic Party in North-Rhine-Westfalia published a small brochure (52 pages) entitled *Sensible Leisure for All: Tasks for the Local SPD-Clubs* The State Government also supported a number of leisure research projects including *Self-organised Leisure and Culture in the Neighbourhood* (Forschungsteam Self, 1987) and *Leisure Initiatives Bridging Work and Retirement*. In 1985, after the re-election of the Social Democrats a new commission for the State Party on 'Culture and Leisure' was founded. This was a signal that culture, rather than leisure, had become the government's principal concern. Though a second leisure report of the state Government was prepared, it was never published. The Minister responsible for leisure policy, Christoph Zöpel organised a forum under the heading *The New Organisation of Time* (Hesse and Zöpel, 1987), but, significantly, time not leisure was the key subject.

Of the leading figures in the SDP only Bjorn Engholm who was to become Prime Minister of Schleswig-Holstein in 1988, and Chairman of the Social Democrats of the Federal Republic in 1991, showed any real interest in the topic of leisure policy, and in 1987 he published a book entitled *The Future of Leisure*.

While interest in the field of leisure policy diminished in the 1980s, a new concern with tourism policy emerged. In 1987 the *First Tourism Report of North-Rhine-Westfalia* was published, and the State Government began to invest more heavily in tourism development. However the demise of leisure policy per se was underlined when, after the re-election of the Social Democrats in 1990, no commission on leisure policy was established, and no research projects were commissioned involving leisure policy. Although investment in tourism in the new Länder, especially in Brandenburg, was promoted, in the period after 1989, leisure policy was no longer a significant topic for policy discussion either within the Social Democratic Party in general, nor in the North-Rhine-Westfalia Government.

In the 1990s, work policy and work-place policy were once again the main preocupations of government. Even the Social Democrats seemed to have neglected the argument that future work would depend upon development of the service sector, and that leisure (as well as culture and tourism) is of considerable significance within this sector. Leisure policy in the 1970s and 1980s was discussed within the programmes of the political parties predominantly by the Social Democrats (Forschungsteam Self, 1987, pp. 80-89). The Social Democrats saw leisure policy as part of a comprehensive social policy. In 1979 they voted for the establishment of local government

Departments of Leisure, whose main focus was to be on furthering self-organised leisure and culture in local communities. By contrast the Christian Democrats and the Free Democrats saw no great necessity for leisure policy, indeed, they viewed it as a danger. The conservative political groups wanted no planning of leisure by the state. The leisure problem for them would to a great extent be solved by the market and the voluntary sector. Thus, while the emphasis in Social Democratic thinking shifted to work, or tourism development, its new emphasis was similar to that of the political right which had traditionally been antipathetic to government involvement in leisure.

1989 Leisure in the Former German Democratic Republic and the Impact of Unification

In the 'other' Germany, the German Democratic Republic, from 1949-1989 an alternative model of a totally government controlled leisure policy held sway. On the basis of socialist ideology a very detailed leisure regulation system for children, youth, and adults was constructed. Pioneer houses, youth clubs, cultural centres were set up in great numbers by the organisations of the ruling political party the United Socialist Party (SED), but they were neither democratically organised, nor particularly leisure-oriented. By virtue of the heritage of the workers movement and for economic reasons, socialist countries followed a work-based ideology in contrast to western societies which were exploring a new form of leisure ethic.

The contrast between the value orientation of Eastern and Western Europe was experienced particularly sharply by the inhabitants of the German Democratic Republic. Daily television and radio broadcasts brought news of a 'better' (West) Germany. Through visits of relatives and friends, and through contacts with West German tourists in holiday camps, especially in Hungary, they were able to perceive the great difference between the lifestyles of East and West. The 1989 revolution was, in some senses, a leisure revolution, inspired by lifestyle contrasts, and 'freedom to travel' was one of its first demands. Western cars were the first consumption goods purchased, and travelling west was one of the first steps of freedom.

Leisure Policy as Transformation Policy

A deep depression followed after the political and economic changes associated with unification. The ensuing months brought about, not a leisure society but unemployment in many regions. The entire infrastructure had to be changed, and the centralised leisure system of the German Democratic Republic had to be transformed into an open democratic structure operating on a new financial basis. This task of transformation meant a challenge for the whole leisure system of the enlarged Federal Republic of Germany. Leisure, like many other areas of policy, was to be employed to facilitate the transformation of

German society. In fact many co-operative initiatives between leisure facilities and agencies in East and West Germany were established in the post-unification period, and leisure organisations from West Germany provided further training for leisure experts in East Germany. Academics from universities in the Eastern and Western Länder organised research into the social transformation of, for example, 'pioneer houses' into 'leisure centres for the young'. Curricula in leisure studies and leisure education were developed at universities within the new States. However, all these initiatives were independent, rather than the result of co-ordinated policy at the federal level.

Leisure policy in Germany by the beginning of the 1990s was not a topic of great importance. The public sphere in federal, state and community governments remained very much an observer of the innovations in leisure developed within the commercial and voluntary sectors. Despite the pressing social problems which resulted from the unification of Germany in 1989, and perhaps because of them, leisure policy had not grown in significance.

Units and Levels of Leisure Policy

Germany is a Federal Republic which now has nearly 80 million inhabitants within 15 Länder (states) and the independent city of Berlin. The nature of federal government means that political power resides with the Länder, and federal government only has competence in areas which are stipulated in the constitution, and declared specifically as tasks of federal government. All other areas remain the responsibility of the Länder, and leisure policy is thus mainly a duty of the states.

The ten 'old' states are, from North to South: Schleswig-Holstein, Hamburg, Lower Saxony, Bremen, Nordrhein-Westfalia, Hessa, Rheinland-Pfalz, Saarland, Baden-Wurttemberg, and Bavaria. The five 'new' states in the area of the Ex-German Democratic Republic, which joined in 1990, are: Mecklenburg-Vorpommern, Brandenburg (including Berlin), Sachsen-Anhalt, Thuringia, and Saxonia. The states differ very much in size, number of inhabitants and density of population. In Nordrhein-Westfalia there are 17 million inhabitants; in Hamburg only 1.7 million. Brandenburg (30,000 sq. km) is nearly as large as Nordrhein-Westfalia in area, but has only 2.5 million inhabitants. The bigger states include a large number of 'communities', or local government units.

In the Federal Republic of Germany policy in general is organised at different levels. The three main levels are federal, state and community government. In large states there are also districts ('Regierungsbezirke') and boroughs ('Landkreise') which exist between the state and the community level. Responsibility for leisure policy lies with all levels, but the community and the state are the most significant. Although not specifically termed leisure policy, a lot of political decisions are made which can be regarded as elements of a leisure policy. Community departments for youth, for culture, for sport, for tourism etc. manage or subsidise leisure facilities such as adventure playgrounds, youth centres, community centres, cultural centres, and tourist information systems. The state supports the communities by funding special programmes to erect leisure facilities (e.g. by donating 80 per cent of the costs of construction), while the community is responsible for revenue costs associated with running such facilities.

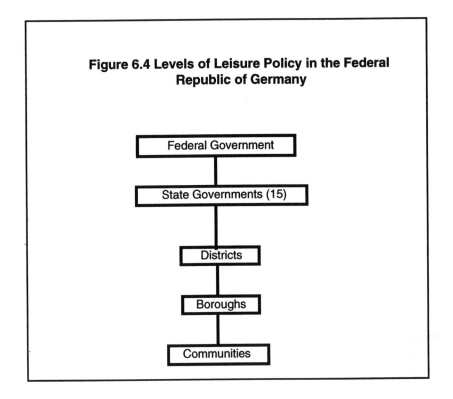

Figure 6.4 Levels of Leisure Policy in the Federal Republic of Germany

An integrated leisure policy demands communication and co-operation between the different policy levels. This co-operation system between relatively independent political bodies on different levels might also be seen as a model for an United Europe of independent countries in the area of leisure policy.

Perspectives

In considering the history of leisure policy in Germany it seems that democratic leisure policy can only exist at a point somewhere between the extremes of a free market non-intervention and government control. To date only Social Democratic Governments have promoted mixed market approaches to leisure. The reality of the weak position of Socialist and Social Democratic policy in Germany and elsewhere in Europe may thus go some way towards explaining the weak position of leisure policy.

There were two stages in modern German history, in which leisure policy was defined in any detail (excluding the Nazi totalitarian state). The first was the development of leisure as a new social and political problem within the Weimar Republic (1918-1933), and this was brought to an end with the development of the National Socialist regime. The second period was after the reconstruction of Germany and the development of the German 'economic miracle' in the 1960s, when (West) Germany re-entered the modern era, with increasing wealth and reduced work time. The end of rapid economic growth and the triumph of economic liberalism (at least at Federal level) marked the end of this era of concerted state intervention in leisure.

Although, in the political landscape of the Federal Republic of Germany the necessity for leisure policy has been voiced, no comprehensive approach to leisure policy has ever been developed. One reason for this is, that the values of traditional, work-oriented society have never been wholly displaced. The second major post-war economic depression experienced in Germany in 1977, with growing unemployment rates, which jumped to more than 10 per cent, that is more than two million unemployed, in the early 1980s, suppressed discussion of leisure policy. With new technology and new media, with longer vacation time and growing numbers of 'new elderly', a new debate on the 'Crisis of Working Society' was raised and, for example, debated at the Congress of the German Association of Sociology in 1982 (Matthes, 1983). This provided a new stimulation for discussion of leisure policy, but with the economic impact of German Unification in 1990, the value system again seemed to revert to that of the 1950s, with its emphasis on work priorities

The institutionalisation of leisure policy in the task forces of Parliament, and the administration units, of local, state and federal governments have not yet developed, nor has a clear understanding of leisure policy. It seems that given the hegemony of economic liberalism and the pressures of economic restructuring the development of comprehensive leisure policy is unlikely to take place.

REFERENCES

Deutsche Gesellschaft für Freizeit / European Leisure and Recreation Association / Europäisches Zentrum für Freizeit und Bildung (ed.) (1976) *Freizeitpolitik in Europa*, Dusseldorf: Editon Freizeit 19.
Flitner, W. (1937) 'Freizeit' in *Die Erziehung*, 12. Jg. 1/1937, 26-38.

Forschungsteam Self (Nahrstedt / Hey / Stehr) (1987) *Selbstorganisierte Freizeitkultur in Wohnumfeld: Analysen - Modelle - Ergebnisse*, Dortmund: (ILS-Schriftenreihe).

Geck, H.A. (1966) 'Geschichtliche Entwicklung der Arbeitbildungsbestrebungn in den Vereinigten Staten von Amerika' in *Archiv für Geschichte des Sozialismus und der Arbeiterbewegung*, 14, Jg. Leipzig 1929, Nachdruck, Graz, 1966.

Giesecke, H. (1983) *Leben nach der Arbeit: Ursprünge und Perspektiven der Freizeitpädagogik*, Munchen.

Giesecke, W. (1973) 'Gedanken zu einer Politik für die Freizeit' in *Liberal* 5/73, 369-376.

Grazia, V. de, (1981) *The Culture of Consent: Mass Organisation of Leisure in Fascist Italy*, Cambridge: Cambridge University Press.

Hesse, J.j. and Zöpel. C. (ed.) (1987) *Neuorganisation der Zeit*, Baden-Baden, (Forum Zukunft 2).

Klatt, F. (1929) *Freizeitgestaltung: Grundsätze und Erfahrungen zur Erziehung des berufsgebundenen Menschen*, Stuttgart.

Kohl, H. (1976) *Freizeitpolitik: Ziele und Zielgruppen verbessertrer Freizeitbedingungen*, Köln.

Lederman, A. (1971) 'Freizeiteinrichtungen gestern und heute' in Sieglundsverband, Ruhrkohlenbezirk (SVR) (ed.) (1971) *Freizeit '70: erster Deutscher Freizeitkongreß*, Essen: SVR: pp. 17-22.

Lenz-Romeiß, F. (1975) *Freizeitpolitik in der Bundesrepublik*, Göttingen: Kommission für wirtschaftlichen und sozialen Wandel 67.

Mandell, R. (1971) *The Nazi Olympics*, New York: Macmillan.

Matthes, J. (ed.) (1983) 'Krise der Arbeitsgeselleschaft?', *Verhandlungen des 21 Deutschen Soziologentages in Bamberg 1982*, Frankfurt.

Mommaas, H. (1992) 'Het Vraagstuk van den Vrijetijd: The Study of Free Time in the Netherlands' unpublished paper, European Consortium for Leisure Studies and Research.

Nahrstedt, W. (1988) 'Die Enstehung der Auflage' Bielefeld: 2, Auflage, IFKA-Faksimile.

Nahrstedt, W. (1990) *Leben in freier Zeit: Grundlagen und Aufgaben der freizeitpädagogik*, Darmstadt.

Rieger, P. (1964) *Politische Verantwortung für die Freizeit: Aktuelle Beiotruage*, Munchen.

Sieglundsverband, Ruhrkohlenbezirk (SVR) (ed.) (1971) *Freizeit '70: erster Deutscher Freizeitkongreß*, Essen.

Sieglundsverband, Ruhrkohlenbezirk (SVR) / Deutsche Gesellschaft für Freizeit (eds) (1973) *Freizeit '72: zweiter Deutscher Freizeitkongreß*, Essen.

Sieglundsverband, Ruhrkohlenbezirk (SVR) / Deutsche Gesellschaft für Freizeit (eds) (1988) *Freizeitpolitik als Gesellschaftpolitik*, Erkrath: Deutscher kongreß 1987.

Sieglundsverband, Ruhrkohlenbezirk (SVR) / Deutsche Gesellschaft für Freizeit (eds) (1974) *Freizeit '74: dritter Deutscher Freizeitkongreß*, Essen.

Sieglundsverband, Ruhrkohlenbezirk (SVR) / Deutsche Gesellschaft für Freizeit (eds) (1978) *Freizeit '78: Freizeitkongreß 7*, Essen.

Tokarski, W. and Schmitz-Scherzer, R. (1985) *Freizeit*, Stuttgart.

Wilson, J. (1988) *Politics and Leisure*, Boston: Unwin Hyman.

BIBLIOGRAPHY

Agricola, S. (ed.) (1972) *Freizeitpädagogik als kommunal Aufgabe. Das Amt für Freizeit in Erlangen*: Erlangen: Deutshe Geselleschaft für Freizeit.

Bayerische Staatsregieerung (1972) *Programm Freizeit und Erholung*:Munchen: Bayerische Staatsregieerung .

Brandt, W. (1973) 'Regierungerklärung des 2': Kabinetts Brandt / Scheek vom 18 Januar 1973: Bonn: SPD.

Browne, D.R. (1989) *Comparing Broadcast Systems: the Experience of Six Industrialised Nations*, Ames: Iowa State University Press.

Bundesminister für Jugend, Familie, Gesundheit: Antwort der Bundesregierung auf die kleine Anfrage der Abgeordnetan Schirmer u.a. betr. 'Frizeitpolitik', Bonn, 1974; Deutcher Bundestag, 7 Wahlperods: Drucksache 7/1948 vom 2.4.1974.

Deutscher Städte- und Gemeindebund (ed.) (1973) 'Hinweisse zur freizeitgerechten Stadt' in *Deutscher Städte- und Gemeindebund* : Göttingen.

Deutsche Geselleschaft für Freizeit (ed.) (1975) *Friezeitpolitik in Bund, Ländern und Gemeinden*, Dokumentation des Deutschen Freizeitkongress 1974 in Garmsich-Partenkirchen, Dusseldorf.

Engholm, B. (ed.) (1987) *Die Zukunft der Freizeit*, Weinhiem: Psychologie heute.

Filipec, J. and Nahrstedt, W. (1992) 'World Culture in Everyday Life: the role of post-socialist societies in postmodernity' in Muskens, G. (ed.) *Creativity, Cultural Insititutions and the Market, with special reference to post-communist conditions*, Vienna: European Coordination Centre for Research and Documentation in the Social Sciences.

Gieße, M. and Schneider, W. (ed.) (1982) *Freizeitamt Erlangen: Sozialkulturelle Stadtteilarbeit*, Erlangen.

Hoberman, J. (1984) *Sport and Political Ideology*, Austin: University of Texas Press.

Maase, K. (1976) *Arbeitszeit - Freizeit - Freizeitpolitik*, Frankfurt: Institut für marxistische Studien und Forschungen - Informationsbericht, 27.

Minister für Landes- und Stadtenwicklung des Landes Nordrhein-Westfalen (ed.) (1987) *Arbietsfreie Zeit und Folgerungen für Freizeitpolitik: Erster Freizeitbericht der Landesregierungen Nordrhein-Westfalen* : Dusseldorf (Schriftenreihe des Ministers für Landes- und Stadtenwicklung des Landes Nordrhein-Westfalen 5).

Minister für Stadtenwicklung, Wohnen und Verkher des Landes Nordrhein-Westfalen (ed.) (1987) *Bericht über die Förderung von Freizeitinitiativen 'Zwischen Arbeit und Ruhestand (ZWAR)'*: Dusseldorf (Schriftenreihe des Ministers 7/87).

Nahrstedt, W. (1989a) *Die Wiederentdeckung der Muße*, Baltmannsweiler.

Nahrstedt, W. (1989b) 'Leisure Education 2000: in Search of a Concept for Leadership Training in Europe' in *World Leisure and Recreation* 31, 2, 32-41.

Nahrstedt, W. (1990) 'The Leisure Revolution: Towards a European Culture through Freetime and Tourim Education?' presentation at the European Leisure Studies Winter University at Katholieke Universiteit Brabant,Tilburg.

Nahrstedt, W. (1992) 'Freizeitforschung und Freizeitpolitik in Europa' in Gräßler, E. (ed.) *Freizeitwissenschaften in Europa*, Zwickau: 2 Zwickauer Freizeittage .

Opaschowski, H.W. (1977) 'Freizeitpolitik als Gesellschaftspolitik: die politische Aufgabe der Humanisierung des Alltags', in Ders (ed.) *Freizeitpädagogik in der Leistungsgesellschaft*, 3, Auflage, Bad Heilbrunn/Obb., 33-49.

Poggeler, F. (1981) 'Freizeitpolitik ' in *Die Heimstadt,* 1-2, 88-99.

SPO-Landesvorstand Nordrhein-Westfalen Kommission Freitzeitpolitik und Sport (ed.) (1984) *Sinnvolle Freizeit für alle*, Dusseldorf, Aufgaben der SPD-Ortsvereine.

Sternheim, A. (1932) 'Zum Problem der Freaizeitgestaltung', *Zeitschrift für Sozialforschung*, 336-355.

Turner, B.S. (1991) *Theories of Modernity and Postmodernity*, London: Sage.

Williams, A.M. and Shaw, G. (eds) (1991) *Tourism and Economic Development: Western European Experiences*, London: Belhaven Press, 2nd edn.

Chapter 7

Leisure Policy in Spain

Julia Gonzalez and Aitor Urkiola

Introduction

It is impossible to understand the development of leisure policy in Spain without first understanding the cultural roots and history which have provided the background to the development of the Spanish state. Located in the subtropical belt of the Northern Hemisphere, Spain represents a cross-roads. Its history has been continuously influenced by the land masses (Europe and Africa) and the oceans (the Mediterranean and the Atlantic), at whose point of convergence Spain is located.

Various waves of invaders have left their mark on the Iberian Peninsula. The first invasions, the Phoenicians, the Carthaginians, the Greeks and in the second century the Romans, came from the South-East, and were followed by the arrival of Celts the first northern people to settle in the Peninsula. In the fifth century Spain was overrun by Germanic invaders and a Visigothic kingdom was established. However, the strongest influence was to come from the South. After 711, the country was invaded by Muslim Berbers. The Moors, as the Muslim invaders were known, conquered the entire Peninsula except for Asturias and the Basque region. During the following 800 years, periods of violent turmoil alternated with times of tolerance, when intensive cultural exchange took place in the country. The two dominant groups - Christians and Moors - were joined by a third ethnic group, the Jews, and during periods of peaceful exchange, industry and agriculture prospered greatly as did Spanish cities such as Cordoba and Grenada. This combination of influences, together with the diversity of its lands and peoples, is present in the variety of music, folklore, traditional patterns and the architecture of Spain.

In 1992 Spain celebrated its fifth centenary as a single State united initially under Ferdinand of Aragon and Isabela of Castille. The fifteenth and sixteenth centuries saw growing affluence and the development of a great empire. The country had traditionally been an absolute monarchy, until it was invaded by Napoleon. When the French left, brief attempts were made to establish a constitutional monarchy, before absolutism returned.

During the nineteenth century, liberals and conservatives fought for power, and the country threatened to fall into the hands of the military on several occasions. In this period, three civil wars shook the north. This was accompanied by the dismemberment of the last vestiges of the Spanish Empire, the loss of Central and South America at the beginning of the century, and of the Philippines and Cuba at the end of it.

In the twentieth century, Spain remained neutral during the First World War, and sought to increase its maritime commerce and to develop industrially. This was especially evident in the Basque region where heavy industry grew rapidly. In 1931, the victory of the Left wing in national elections forced the King to leave the country, and the Second Republic was proclaimed. However, the victory of the left was short lived; 'Born with obvious congenital defects, Spain's incipient democracy was from the very outset an impossible Republic' (Ben-Ami, 1983). It was also the prelude to the Spanish Civil War of 1936-39, which left the country divided, in ruins, and under the rule of Franco.

Franco's dictatorship lasted for 36 years and was characterised by the absence of democratic freedom and the suppression of political parties and trade unions. This resulted in international isolation, which only began to be breached at the end of the 1950s, but remained as a dominant feature of Spanish life. The 1960s, however, was a period of economic development, with a boom in European tourism. This was accompanied by intense migration of unskilled labour to other countries in Western Europe and large flows of people from rural to urban areas. The gap between the rich periphery and Madrid on the one hand, and the poor interior of Spain on the other grew wider. Following Franco's death in 1975, a constitutional monarchy was established under King Juan Carlos, and Spain was steered towards parliamentary democracy. With all the political parties legalised by 1977, and the first parliamentary elections held, the Spanish Constitution was promulgated in 1978.

Spain is a country with a pluralist culture. Basque, Catalan and Galician languages are used in their respective 'Autonomous Communities' (*Comunidades Autónomas*), as well as Spanish, which is the major language spoken throughout the country. Spain is a member of the United Nations, the Western Alliance for Defense, NATO, and is a firm supporter of the concept of a united Europe, with active membership of the European Community and the Council of Europe.

The Political Organisation of the Spanish State

Spain, according to the 1978 Constitution, is a social and democratic state in its own right. In this Constitution, freedom, justice, equality and political pluralism are enshrined as the key values. The Parliament consists of a Lower House of 350 elected members and an Upper House of 207 elected members and 41 members appointed by the Autonomous Communities. The Crown of Spain is hereditary, and it is the King's task, after he has consulted all the political parties, to nominate the Prime Minister once the country has expressed its choice in the general election. When the Prime Minister obtains an absolute majority in Congress, he remains in office for four years, assisted by the Council of Ministers. 'Las Cortes Generales' (The Parliament), elected for the first time in June 1977, is renewed every four years by universal suffrage. When they met for the first time in July 1977 they formed the *Asamblea Constituyente* and drafted the Constitution, which was then carried in a referendum in December 1978.

The political infrastructure of Spain is often thought of as having a dominant or hegemonic party, but it is also considered bipartisan - or even pluralist - in an imperfect sense. It is a system with three clear characteristics. Firstly, its political parties have only been active for a relatively short time. Secondly, the parties represent a varied set of ideological and geographical constituencies. Thirdly, and as a consequence of the other two features, the political system has been in a state of perpetual flux. In fact, since its formation, parties have appeared and disappeared and others have fragmented, while at the same time the number of regional parties has steadily increased. Thus, one way of classifying the political parties in Spain is in chronological order (see Table 7.1).

A further characteristic of the system was that all the major left-wing parties had already been in existence before 1975, whereas the right-wing had been in disarray, and was unable to develop in the period between Franco's death and the elections, resulting in a lack of political stability in the period that followed.

The speed with which the political system was organised and the enthusiasm evident in its deployment accounts for the fact that the political parties are looked upon as something of a panacea. In the process however, the significance of popular movements has declined.

The dominant ideology at state level over the last ten years has been socialism. The Socialist Party (PSOE) has been in power without interruption since 1982. The rest of Parliament currently consists of the Christian Democratic parties (PP, PNV, UDC) with more Conservative appendices (UPN, AP) in recession, the Liberals (CDS, PL), who are in the process of becoming obsolete and the Communists, who are evolving towards a social-populist party with the participation of civic organisations (PCE, IU).

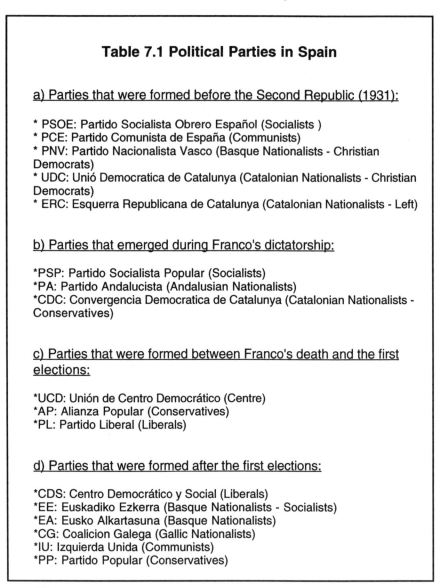

Table 7.1 Political Parties in Spain

a) Parties that were formed before the Second Republic (1931):

* PSOE: Partido Socialista Obrero Español (Socialists)
* PCE: Partido Comunista de España (Communists)
* PNV: Partido Nacionalista Vasco (Basque Nationalists - Christian Democrats)
* UDC: Unió Democratica de Catalunya (Catalonian Nationalists - Christian Democrats)
* ERC: Esquerra Republicana de Catalunya (Catalonian Nationalists - Left)

b) Parties that emerged during Franco's dictatorship:

*PSP: Partido Socialista Popular (Socialists)
*PA: Partido Andalucista (Andalusian Nationalists)
*CDC: Convergencia Democratica de Catalunya (Catalonian Nationalists - Conservatives)

c) Parties that were formed between Franco's death and the first elections:

*UCD: Unión de Centro Democrático (Centre)
*AP: Alianza Popular (Conservatives)
*PL: Partido Liberal (Liberals)

d) Parties that were formed after the first elections:

*CDS: Centro Democrático y Social (Liberals)
*EE: Euskadiko Ezkerra (Basque Nationalists - Socialists)
*EA: Eusko Alkartasuna (Basque Nationalists)
*CG: Coalicion Galega (Gallic Nationalists)
*IU: Izquierda Unida (Communists)
*PP: Partido Popular (Conservatives)

The regional parties and those formed with clear nationalist ideals are of considerable significance. These form subsystems in their respective Autonomous Communities as well as in the central State system:

-Basque Country: PNV, EA, EE, HB.
-Catalonia: CDC, UDC, ERC.
-Galicia: CG, BNPG.

On the whole, the Spanish political system can be characterised by its low level of militancy, its high degree of internal discipline and its low tolerance towards dissidence and anti-system parties such as Herri Batasuna (HB), the political wing of the ETA Basque separatist group (despite the fact that the HB prints an anti-system newspaper that has the highest circulation of its class in Europe).

The Spanish State had traditionally been organised along the lines of the Napoleonic model developed during the nineteenth century, with strong central power and an administrative division into provinces. With the advent of democracy, a new pattern came into being, namely 'El Estado de las Autonomias'. The State 'recreated' the autonomous communities which had been suppressed under the Franco regime. This reflected a recognition that power 'belonged' to communities and their citizens, which preceded the central State.

The 17 Autonomous Communities have legislative powers specific to their own territory. They have their own autonomous government, and jurisdictional powers in the application of laws approved by their parliaments. In a federal system power is normally delegated by the federal 'units' to the central State. The Spanish state is, however, not a federal state, since power is delegated downwards, from the centre to the Autonomous Communities. The relationship between the different components of the Spanish state is illustrated in Figure 7.1.

The municipalities are perhaps the weakest element in this system, since their budgets are dependent on subvention from various higher levels of government, and there is a lack of definition as to their specific competencies. Local government expenditure is only 4.7 per cent of the GDP out of a total public expenditure of 40.3 per cent. One reason for this situation is that the process of change has been slower than desired, and has tended to concentrate on partial reforms and the provision of new services.

Major Post-war Trends in Leisure Patterns

In Spain, any meaningful periodisation has to take the Spanish Civil War (which ended in 1939), rather than the Second World War, as its point of reference. In fact, the political system which was developed after the Civil War is reflected in the patterns of leisure and its development during the last few decades. Initially, in the post-Civil War period, all efforts centred on reconstruction. The State had been established within a dictatorship where political freedom was reduced to a minimum. The totalitarian state and its political wing, the National Movement, assumed complete power, and the move to regulate, control, and supervise social development on behalf of the political regime affected all spheres of life. Everything was subject to censorship unless officially excluded. The only institution that was given any power was the Church (which had allied with the Army during the war).

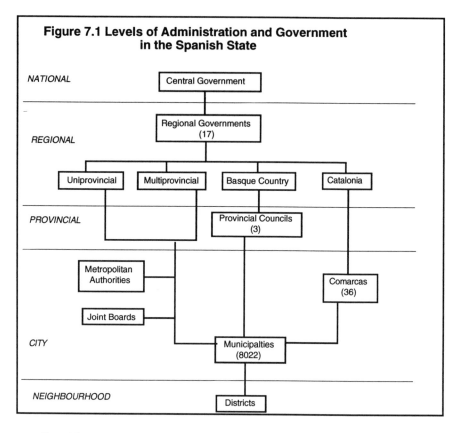

Figure 7.1 Levels of Administration and Government in the Spanish State

In this context, the radio was the most important means of communication for large numbers of people, but all broadcasts were subject to censorship, and the State used the radio to spread propaganda. The press, books, cinema and every other aspect of cultural life was also subject to censorship. In the 1950s, in an attempt to counter international isolation, the system looked towards the American way of life as a model to be emulated, because the United States was seen as anti-communist, and therefore represented a natural ally. This movement coincided with the arrival of Americans at newly established military bases in Spain. Others were drawn to Spain by the imaginative descriptions of writers such as Ernest Hemingway, and it was also at this time that Caribbean and Spanish music was making inroads into Hollywood.

These outward-looking policies merely diverted attention from the real problems of an impoverished society locked into a precarious pattern of subsistence existence. The major leisure pursuits of rural Spain were limited to Sunday dances, playing cards and 'gossiping', with the occasional diversion of village feasts and either social or seasonal celebrations. This almost medieval pattern of leisure was particularly marked in the case of women.

The 1960s, however, brought about economic development. There was a significant growth in national income and industrial production. Modernisation became apparent in the large cities, and consumer goods began to be more widely available. Thus, the expenditure patterns of the average person in Spain began to reflect the patterns of modern life. This was a time of prosperity for the regime, with continued economic development, the promotion of tourism, an increase in wages, growing consumption, housing subsidies, the introduction of social security, and of foreign languages in education. Home ownership or the purchase of a car were beginning to be within the financial means of the 'average' citizen. This period also witnessed a peak in the migration of people into the cities. Congestion in high rise buildings and the desire to go to the country or the beach for a break, together with an emphasis on family values gave birth to the development of second home ownership, a characteristic which is significant in terms of trends in domestic holiday-making.

Tourism was promoted in official spheres with improvements to transport and the hotel industry and advertising campaigns in other countries. A crucial change to the infrastructure was the renovation of palaces, castles and mansion houses into stylish hotels and 'Paradores' which were considered to be part of the national heritage. Parallel to this, a leisure oriented mentality evolved and this was clearly evident in changes in leisure patterns for holidays and sport. Women, who had been constrained by traditional gender roles, and young people, were particularly influenced, by exposure to these new patterns of behaviour and to the goods introduced through tourism.

In 1964 legislation liberalising the activities of voluntary associations was introduced. Groups with sporting, educational and cultural aims began to emerge, particularly in Church circles. They searched for new and more personal patterns of leisure. This new growth of voluntary organisations, many operating in areas of urban deprivation, sought to improve the quality of life in the (socially and geographically) marginal areas of towns. They sought to establish a quality of life in which education, culture and recreation played a major part. In the mass media, television became more widely available and grew in importance, as it became possible to broadcast to a wider set of social strata.

In the 1970s, leisure continued to symbolise the aspirations of freedom for citizens. These aspirations were particularly manifest with the arrival of democracy. However, the initial hope that the restoration of political freedom would bring about a flowering of artistic and cultural creation, resulting in works of art of higher quality, was soon quashed as the change in political regime produced few immediate cultural changes. In fact, there were no major works that were awaiting the end of censorship, as Spanish artists had long since escaped from the limits of cultural isolation. The return to Spain from exile of a group of leading figures had no significant impact, their return representing an act of faith in the new system, rather than a powerful push towards cultural creation. In general terms, democratic Spain followed the trends which had been set in the previous period, cosmopolitanism and eclecticism, reflecting the growing importance of the cultural industries (López Alvarez, 1991).

What was really relevant for leisure was the growth of consumer culture. Spanish society had experienced a considerable political and economic change, and this was accompanied by a change in mentality, in ways of thinking and behaving. Against the pattern of the traditional family, new family structures became more common. While male and female roles moved towards greater equality, the number of young consumers grew and there was an increase in material well-being. In fact, by the 1990s, almost all Spanish households had a television set, and most had colour television. Ninety five per cent had a refrigerator, 94 per cent a radio, 88 per cent a washing machine, 61 per cent a car, 37 per cent a record player and 29 per cent a video player.

Studies of leisure and leisure policy in Spain are conspicuous by their absence. Only in Bilbao has research been conducted in this field, with a study sponsored by local government, and conducted by researchers at Deusto University (EIIO, Deusto, 1992). The study, conducted in 1989/90 investigated the leisure habits of the population of Bilbao and concluded that, for the majority, leisure was predominantly passive and spent within the home; 80.3 per cent watched television daily, 84.7 per cent were regular radio listeners and 70 per cent listened to records several times per week. There were active options in home entertainment, such as playing table games (21 per cent), and pursuing hobbies, and there had been a clear increase in the amount of leisure time spent at home.

However, the study identified seven further types of leisure practice in the population of Bilbao. These included going to bars and cafeterias (a popular practice for over a third of the population) and engaging in sport and physical exercise (with numbers on the increase, particularly of women, and a growing variety of sports on offer). In addition, 15 to 20 per cent of the population were involved in sport as spectators. There were other minor activities identified, such as taking part in cultural events (between 5 and 10 per cent) and, in lower proportions, playing electronic games, athletics, fishing, hunting and mountaineering.

The rapid changes experienced by Spanish society have been particularly profound, and traditional ways of life have been left behind, supplanted by values and lifestyles from the West.

Leisure Policy

Despite the fact that leisure policy as such does not have a specific place in Spanish political organisation, it is significant that several political parties made references to leisure in their 1991 election manifestos. One should bear in mind that the historical context is, in the case of Spain, of crucial importance to an understanding of the development of policies related to leisure. Wilson's (1988) description of leisure in totalitarian regimes accurately characterises the state of affairs under Franco. Work and play, labour and leisure, were treated as a unity and administered by the State. There was no distinction between private and public spheres. All aspects of life, including how people chose to spend their free time, were assumed to have political significance. Sports festivals and the regular practice of gymnastics were common during the dictatorship. They were designed to entertain as well as to help with the development of a sporting temperament to provide a sense of competitive aggressiveness, physical self-consciousness, ascetic indifference to pain and political disinterestedness.

A strategy of creating celebrations, ceremonies, artificially created customs and staged folklore, was adopted in an attempt to fill free time and empty lives. As in the case of Italy under the fascists, sport was considered to be 'the best distraction for youth otherwise tempted by political activities' (De Grazia, 1981). Control over radio, cinema and television broadcasts was once a regular practice, but declined as the old regime deteriorated, while groups of differing shades of opinion began to organise, under the auspices of the Church, the only institution which still retained some power. These deregulating tendencies continued to become stronger in the period between 1978 and 1982, after which the socialists took up office, and a certain degree of stability was introduced. From a period of transition and confusion, leisure policies reflected a move to incorporate leisure within the general framework of a welfare state.

In relation to the leisure sectors, there were several issues which were the subject of state concern. These may be itemised as follows:

1. The lack of a clear scheme of leisure programmes, of sources of finance, or levels of administration for leisure in the public sector.

2. A significant concern, relating to two social groups, the young and the elderly, in respect of leisure.

3. The need to establish an appropriate cultural policy.

4. The preservation of cultural heritage.

5. The discovery of leisure as a key component in the quality of life and in urban regeneration (both social and economic).

6. The importance of cultural industries and markets.

7. The need to renew and develop new tourism policies.

8. The move towards adequate levels of leisure infrastructure and, in particular, concern with the provision of sport for all.

It is perhaps worth commenting on each of these aspects individually.

The Absence of a Policy Framework

One of the characteristics of the policies connected with all the leisure sectors was that the whole area was largely ill defined. In fact, the transference of power to the different Autonomous Communities had not yet been completed, and this was aggravated by the fact that responsibility for the leisure sectors was given to various levels of administration - central government, autonomous government, provincial government, and municipality. The division of responsibility between each of these levels is not easy to identify. Furthermore, the roles of different types of finance had not yet been identified. This was a period of predominantly public funding, where private initiative was accepted, and considered important in principle, but had very little effect, since incentives for private funding had not yet been provided. There was a similar lack of clarity over the requirements of, and the need for professional training in the leisure field.

Concern for the Young and the Elderly

The concern for the elderly was a very recent development, but has caused a considerable amount of public debate. The achievements, however, have not been very significant. The traditional arrangement, with the elderly living with their families wherever possible, or taken care of by charitable institutions, is still the commonest practice. The initial stages of development of a welfare state promise the beginnings of basic provision for health care and pensions. However, much remains to be accomplished, even in terms of basic services for this group.

Leisure policy for the elderly is limited to social tourism (a small but increasing supply of cheap holidays and trips) and to the development of pensioners' clubs. These are provided by both public and private institutions. Two recent trends should be highlighted here: the tendency for public institutions to take responsibility for what started as private ventures, and the emergence of voluntary sector centres for the elderly.

Youth represents an important focus of policy for all administrative levels of government, from central State to municipality. With a traditional base in the voluntary sector during the period of transition to democracy, the development of youth policies per se, began in the democratic system and can be divided into three stages: the initial years of democracy, the period around the International Year of Youth, and the early 1990s.

The policy void inherited from the Franco era was countered by the development of social and cultural services. The administrative structure of youth work was then created, from the municipal level up to the autonomies and central government. Young people who had taken a significant role in the political transition were regarded as a modernising element capable of transforming society, with revolutionary zeal and social commitment. However, although the majority of the municipalities had youth plans, they had only very small budgets and rather utopian ideas.

Leisure was central to youth policies in this period. The only organised groups with any real experience in this field were the 'free-time schools' provided by community associations. Youth policy during this period was mainly created by people who came from such associations. The importance of youth policy had been recognised but there was a lack of financial resources, and of policy goals.

The second phase in the development of policy in this field, began in 1982 (1983 at municipal level). With restructuring of government, policy direction in a variety of areas came under review. Two factors influenced youth policy significantly. The first was a general openness to influence from other European policy systems as Spain moved towards full participation in Europe. The second was the European Year of Youth, which brought with it a wide range of studies and policy debates. The principal points for action were thus clarified and included the following: professional qualifications for youth work, the question of compulsory military service, the problem of access to economic activity, and the need to effect incorporation of youth into wider society.

The image of youth changed from the utopian notion of a revolutionary group to a more realistic one, which recognised the difficulties of finding jobs and of social integration for young people who, because of economic difficulties, were often choosing to remain with their families for longer. The result was a shift from a policy in which leisure and free time were the principal concerns, to a policy with a more integrated approach, taking on board economic and political dimensions of youth needs.

The late 1980s and early 1990s may be characterised as a period of stabilisation, as concern with the elderly has become more evident and policy programmes have matured. Several of the Autonomies have already published their plans for youth, with some more developed than others (Catalonia is perhaps the leading community in developing youth policy). However, despite the attempt to give priority to areas other than leisure, programmes of *difusión cultural* and the creation of culture take up a large part of the efforts of government. The lead in policy development is taken by government with young people being regarded simply as cultural consumers rather than active participants in the policy development process.

With the exception of the programmes of assistance for young artists and those concerned with youth training in the areas of culture and sport, most youth policy lacks cohesion, representing systems of partial and disjointed action connected by a place, the *casa de juventud* (the youth centre) or a time, vacation periods when there is a burgeoning of youth camps, cultural exchanges, tourist activities and festivals proliferate.

Cultural Policy

In the field of culture, the central State developed a policy which has been progressively changed by the devolution of power to the Autonomous Communities. This process has witnessed the flourishing of other public institutions - municipalities, 'diputaciones' (provincial administrative centres) - and the reform of administration from local bureaucracy to a more proactive cultural service.

Despite decentralisation, it was decided that the central State should be active in cultural policy rather than simply delegating this power wholly to the autonomies, because it was felt that there was a need for combined action at all governmental levels to secure preservation of cultural heritage and to foster the promotion and distribution of culture. However, the role of the central State in relation to culture has been clearly delimited: 'Public intervention must be directed towards helping and stimulating cultural creation, freely developed rather than becoming a cultural enterprise in cultural matters substituting for private initiative'. But, 'the State has responsibility for providing the minimum conditions needed for the continuity of cultural creation and the preservation of cultural heritage' (Ministerio de Cultura, 1986).

In the cultural field, as in other fields, years of dictatorship had left their mark. Important elements of historical and cultural heritage had deteriorated with years of relatively uncontrolled development. There was a void in legislation relating to the protection of heritage, public cultural infrastructure was inadequate, and the cultural industries were in crisis. The reaction against patterns of behaviour imposed during the dictatorship dominated all the arts. In fact, the trends towards eclecticism and cosmopolitanism in Spain reflect a wish to break links with the past and to liberate the country from tradition. These trends are the cultural equivalent of political pluralism and are regarded as a concomitant of democracy. They are evident in a variety of cultural fields. Literature (Rico, 1989), music (Otero, 1989) and plastic art (Calvo Serraller, 1988) in particular have flourished, because of their tendency to look outwards, towards Europe and North America reflecting the international influence of post-modernism and the dominance of the cultural industries. As a consequence of the connection between Spanish artists and multinational cultural industries, artistic work has been produced which is highly influenced by transnational aspirations and appears to be almost wholly independent of the cultural roots of the country.

This movement is in clear opposition to the policy priorities of the State, which wishes to foster a revival of popular culture and the development of national talent. This is partly in response to the external demand created by cultural markets searching for a 'Spanish' product, and partly an attempt to establish the cultural identity of Spain. The State's strategy of fostering groups of writers who promote national tradition is a reflection of these goals, as are , policies backing young artists whose work presents an alternative to the mass production launched by multinationals. However, this approach to fostering 'Spanish' culture is regarded as having met with very limited success.

Two major pieces of legislation introduced during the 1980s, and with potentially important implications for cultural policy, were laws on 'intellectual ownership' and on 'protection of cultural heritage'. The former, promulgated in November 1987, sought to create an adequate framework for the protection of cultural production. This law went further than the mere recognition of the traditional rights of authors in artistic and literary creation, and introduced the notion of the moral rights of the authors in the reproduction and distribution of their work. Coverage under the law in this respect is quite significant since it addresses issues raised by the introduction of modern technology in the cultural industries. A further decree followed, to establish control over the number of copies of an artistic work to be published, favouring the rights of the artist over those of the publisher. However, according to the Association of Spanish Authors, this law has had little impact on what they consider to be established publishing practices.

The Law of Cultural Heritage (25 June 1985) had precedents in Spanish legislation (López Alvarez, 1991) both before Franco's regime (laws and decrees were enacted covering different aspects of exploitation of archaeological remains and historical documents in 1911, 1915, 1922, 1931 and 1933) and during the dictatorship itself (with legislation relating to 'Zones of Importance for Tourism' in 1964, 'Development of Coastal Areas' in 1969, and the 'Natural Parks' in 1975). With this new law Spain adopted a broader definition of culture and heritage covering not only historical and artistic productions but also those of archaeological, ethnographic, scientific and technological interest. In addition, the law regulated the market for artistic goods and established the principle of freedom of public access to them.

The legislation also introduced tax exemptions for restoration, improvement and provision of access to items of cultural significance. Despite this innovative approach, however, the administration proposed that only one per cent of the budget for public art works should be assigned to the fostering of artistic creation and to the protection or enrichment of cultural heritage. This factor, together with the lack of any clear guidelines on how the goals of this legislation are to be progressed, means that the legislation is relatively ineffective.

Long awaited legislation on 'Cultural Patronage' has not yet been drafted, and an analysis of the existing patterns of patronage reveals that it is private initiatives which are generally favoured by public protection and subsidy. Since different tiers of administration share responsibility for the same cultural areas, the tendency is to develop a pattern of subsidy where diverse public - and sometimes private - bodies, cooperate in the subsidy of a particular cultural work or event. This dilutes responsibility and tends to weaken the interest of public bodies. The consequence is the lack of a consistent policy and the effective use of resources (which represent only 0.6 per cent of the State budget).

The legislation on cultural heritage promulgated at central State level had a 'knock-on' effect at the level of the autonomies, with further legal development taking place and reinforcing the work of the councils and commissions which were already active at this level of administration. It was at the level of the Autonomies, their regions, and municipalities, that most work has been carried out in the renewal and restoration of old theatres and public monuments as well as in the creation of new cultural centres and improvement of the cultural infrastructure, which had deteriorated. In this respect, the State has had some significant achievements, such as the renewal of the Prado, the Royal Theatre, and the National Library and the creation of Centro Reina Sofia and the National Auditorium. Two other city regions shared the almost complete monopoly of central State intervention with Madrid in the later 1980s and early 1990s - these are the cities of Barcelona and Seville, which were focal points for major international events in 1992.

However, this is only one of the three major themes developed in cultural policy. The creation of cultural infrastructure is an attempt to develop a complete network of museums, libraries, archives, auditoriums, theatres, etc. The second priority is one of education and training to prepare people to utilise the infrastructure, and generate employment. The third priority relates to the fostering of the cultural industries.

The Cultural Industries

The processes of concentration and transnationalisation tend to dominate cultural industries in Spain (Bustamante and Zallo, 1988). These processes have taken place in an accelerated fashion but in a manner which is neither linear nor irreversible. In relation to ownership of the press, in 1975 seven major private groups accumulated 56 per cent of the total newspaper circulation (excluding papers in public ownership which were sold off in 1984). By 1986, with an increase in circulation of 0.9 million, 11 major groups owned 70 per cent of the total.

This tendency towards increased concentration also appears to be connected with diversification, a fact reflected in the rapid popularisation of the term 'multimedia' in Spain. During the economic crisis which faced the press in the 1980s the trend was to diversify, but this diversification was led by large groups, rather than small companies whose situation tended to deteriorate as their capacity to compete diminished.

The process of transnationalisation adds to this. During the period 1982-86, 19 per cent of periodicals were in the hands of four foreign groups. The growth of transnational investment began with magazines, but later shifted to the daily press. The control of 'Celta' and its connection with 'Edica' and 'Hachette' by the French group Hersant, the large share in 'Zeta' owned by the Kuwaiti group KIO, the alliance of Expansion-Dow Jones, and the activities of other groups, such as Bertelsmann, Bauer, VNU and Sarpe, provide some of the best examples of penetration of the Spanish market by transnational companies.

The State has played a decisive role in fostering these two processes by adopting various measures. The auctioning off of the State press in 1984 marked the beginning of a chain of amalgamations, and with the drafting of several laws in the period 1982-1988, subsidies were introduced which favoured concentration rather than backing small groups or new journalistic initiatives. In addition the general climate has been one of tolerance by the state of the activities of large transnational corporations, and their agglomeration strategies.

In relation to radio, from the end of the Civil War, the State established control over the media, and radio programming was used to further the ideology of the regime. The decade 1976-86 therefore saw considerable change. During this period, radio gained high levels of public confidence and large audiences, but the same period marked the beginnings of considerable market concentration. In 1981 the FM stations and several other groups formed 'Radio Cadena Española' (RCE). This development was to culminate in the 1990s when RCE and RNE (Radio Nacional de España) initiated a joint venture. This ran in parallel to the granting (as of 1981) of licences for commercial stations, which are now scattered around the country. In the same period, the independent public broadcasting networks were developed in Catalonia, the Basque country, Madrid and Galicia. These emerged by virtue of rights given to the Autonomous Communities which extended to the establishment by the Autonomies' governments of interests in the press and television broadcasting. However, despite the fact that it was anticipated that the autonomies' television channels would introduce a new dimension to the diet of programmes available, the reality has been that the programming patterns adopted by the central State have invariably been replicated, the only difference being that programmes are now broadcast in regional languages.

Basically, Spanish television is characterised by three main features: high levels of viewing, the dominance of advertising as a source of finance, and a strong relationship with American media interests. The audience level is not only high, but is on the increase, with 1990 figures showing an average of over 3 hours viewing per person and over 6 hours per household. This highlights the extent to which television can be used in the reproduction of social relations and of power, and its impact on economic, political, and cultural matters is clearly evident.

The statutes of TVE (introduced in January 1980) provide for three sources of finance: subsidy from the national budget, income through advertising and other resources, and a licence fee or tax on television sets. This last option is a practice which has never been employed and has consequently been abandoned. State subsidy, which in 1978 reached Pts 10,710 million against Pts 15,344 million from income by advertising, has decreased as a proportion of the rising total budget, and now accounts for a mere 1.6 per cent of the total, leaving what is supposedly a public entity to be financed almost entirely from advertising. Spain's three new private channels will have been able to learn from this experience and will have had the ground prepared for commercial exploitation.

The early incorporation of advertising revenue as a source of finance is also significant in the explanation of how Spanish television became an expansionary market for programmes from the United States. Without the protection of major State aid, it became dependent on the American market, not simply for programmes and films, but also for technical advice and even to some extent finance. In fact connections between Spanish television and CBS and UPI date from 1957. This pattern of dependence has proved difficult to break.

Since the onset of democracy, the State and the Autonomous Communities have enjoyed a monopoly over television and used it as a means to legitimate their cultural policies. However, television policy has been severely criticised for the failure to promote any sense of unity, of cultural identity, or of social responsibility, with programming decisions left largely to the market.

Publishing

In the field of book publishing in Spain, about 80 per cent of the titles printed are in Spanish, with Catalan, Basque and Galician making up the remaining 20 per cent. Book publishing has certainly provided a reasonable return on investment. According to the findings of the Centre of Socio-economic Research, the volume of business was high in 1987, reaching Pts 230,000 million and showing a rise in the following year of a further Pts 50,000 million. However, the significant boom experienced in this sector has attracted predatory foreign capital which has invested heavily in the Spanish market. At the beginning of the 1990s, the three largest transnational groups

(Bertelsmann, Mondadori and Hachette) had a volume of investment higher than all the national groups put together. Thus, the industry is faced with an expanding market but a low level of domestic capital investment, which is an obstacle to the regeneration of national firms. Although Latin America provides a large Spanish speaking market, the large external debt of Latin American countries means that a comparatively low number of copies are issued per edition in most cases, and it is in the area of translations that significantly higher numbers of books are sold.

In response to this situation, Spanish publishers banded together with a plan to foster the book industry, and sought subsidy from the Ministry of Culture totalling Pts 6,000 million, as well as a reduction of taxes on books, exemption from value added tax, creation of a foundation to help the publishing industry, a bureau for promotion of national products, subsidy for the translation of Spanish works into other languages, and a whole package of strategies and policies for the protection of the industry.

The Cinema

The film industry has also been witnessing a crisis due to a combination of factors, but in particular, the high level of competition from television and the video industry, escalating costs of production, and domination by multinational firms (seven out of ten films in Spain come from the USA).

Three stages can be identified in relation to the development of this industry in Spain. The first relates to the transition years when the cinema was nourished by a vein of criticism and self examination in Spanish society, which fostered critical artistic work. The second stage occurred during the six years of the so-called Miró Decree, which established a policy of subsidy for national productions. This measure made possible the production of a number of significant films. It was criticised for providing subsidies (which used up the resources of an already small national budget) which supported films that had no guarantee of a commercial future, but in reality it resulted in a large output of films (around 50 per year) and in efforts to consolidate some of the national producers.

The last stage was initiated by Jorge Semprún, who was critical of previous policies, suggesting that they represented only partial measures, which would not provide real solutions to the industry's problems. According to Semprún the whole structure of the film industry should have been questioned, not only in relation to production but also as regards taxation, reproduction and distribution. Whether the dependency on public subsidy has been stemmed remains to be seen, but by the beginning of the 1990s it was clear that the trend towards flooding of the market by foreign products had not abated.

Culture and Urban Regeneration

During the late 1980s, the consideration that leisure, culture, and tourism could become powerful tools in the process of urban regeneration began to have major repercussions among urban planners and the local authorities of the main cities in Spain. In fact, Spanish cities in particular had real reason to search for opportunities for, and means of, regeneration. This was conducted with two very specific sets of goals - improvement of the quality of life, and economic regeneration.

The 1960s were years of expansion, but had left urban areas in unplanned chaos. Meanwhile the sensitivity of the urban population to environmental issues and the aesthetics of the landscape had grown (Tinas, 1990). The unplanned growth and rapid urbanisation of the country produced a proliferation of new roads and industrial areas, severely reducing the amount of green space in and around cities. One of the common aspirations of the inhabitants of any large city is for the maintenance of some contact with nature, and this aspiration seems even stronger in Spanish cities since a significant proportion of the population are first or second-generation migrants from rural backgrounds (Castells, 1990). There is therefore a very high level of demand for parks and green spaces as places for rest and recreation. This became apparent in the study of Bilbao (EIIO, Deusto, 1992).

'Planes Generales de Ordenación Urbana' and urban environmental policies seek to increase the amount of open space available and to protect and renew existing areas. There is a conviction, particularly on the part of planners, that the availability of space contributes to well-being and to the quality of urban life (Wilheim, 1990).

There is another aspect of quality of urban life intimately linked with culture, since the city consists of more than just people and social services - it is more than a constellation of institutions. The city is a state of being, a combination of habits and traditions, of attitudes, and of the daily life of the people. It is in this context that culture is important not only as regards the quality of life but also as a defining feature of the city which imparts meaning to its inhabitants and to others.

Culture can thus become a significant element in the development of urban areas. The loss of sectors of industry and of agriculture, the capacity of the arts to generate income, the possibility of employment in new sectors connected with culture, and the attraction offered by cultural events has convinced authorities of the importance of a cultural sector. Thus urban cultural policy has become a priority for the Ministry of Culture and in the departments of culture at the lower level of the Autonomous Communities and their municipalities (Quintana, 1990).

Tourism

Spain is one of the world's major tourist countries, in relation to both the number of visitors received and the economic resources generated by this activity. The rapid growth of tourism in Spain has been one of its most outstanding features. This expansion was due to external factors such as the growth of paid holidays and improvements in communications, as well as to internal factors, such as cheap prices, availability of labour and the absence of social conflict.

The importance of tourism was strengthened by the fact that one of the most active ministries under Franco's regime was that of Information and Tourism. This combination was not a coincidence. Tourism was fostered as a powerful economic resource but also as a façade; a means of gaining a level of acceptance of the Franco government from the other countries of Europe.

The development of tourism is illustrated in Figure 7.2.

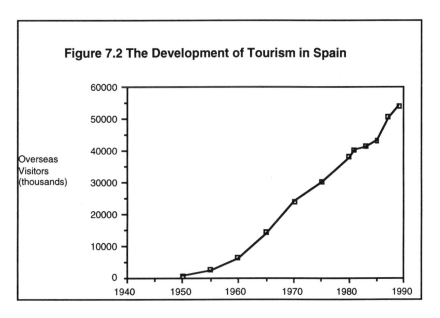

Figure 7.2 The Development of Tourism in Spain

This general trend, despite fluctuations, illustrates the rapid and consolidated nature of tourist growth. It should also be emphasised that these figures relate exclusively to foreign tourists, and the importance of domestic tourism should not be underestimated particularly in the period from the beginning of the 1970s. In fact, in the 1980s only 10 per cent of Spaniards took their holidays abroad (though this figure is clearly on the increase).

Significantly enough, tourism policy is one of the very few areas where the advent of democracy did not seem to have a major impact. After the initial years of discovery and growth, State attitudes to this sector remained basically the same from the 1960s to 1983. According to the *Libro Blanco del Turismo Español* (Secretaría General de Turismo, 1991) the most striking feature of the tourism marketing system in Spain, was that until the 1980s it had developed largely in an ad hoc, unplanned manner. This reflected the lack of any clear formulation of objectives for tourism development.

Tourism policy during this period concentrated on fostering existing markets. The attitude of government was that tourism was simply to be encouraged since it helped to stimulate economic development. There was a demand for enjoyable beach holidays in the sun at a low price, and this was mainly accommodated by foreign tour-operators (capitalising on the relatively down market 'sea, sun, sex, and sand' holiday image). State policies responded positively and unquestioningly to this buoyant demand. The substantial contribution which tourism made to the economy was self evident; it accumulated foreign exchange reserves, it stimulated the growth of several sectors such as transport, accommodation, travel agencies, commerce and recreation, and it contributed to job creation. Since the 1960s, Spanish economy had depended heavily on this sector for its development, and so the environmental and social costs of the tourist boom were never fully considered.

Tourism related demands were therefore almost invariably accommodated. However, the 'product dependence' which this created, as well as the impact of massive flows of people and the innate weakness of the tourism system, was underestimated. Since the demand was for 'sun and beach' the State concentrated on promoting an image of Spain predominantly based on these two commodities. The significant changes that ensued concentrated on providing good access to coastal areas, with detrimental effects for other regions in terms of transport planning. Furthermore, a number of measures were introduced to facilitate the development of tourism along the coast, including specific legislation in 1963 defining 'Centros y Zonas de Interés Turístico'. Leisure towns such as Benidorm, Torremolinos, Loret del Mar and Playa de San Juan emerged. Also, marinas and new sports harbours were developed, resulting in interesting urban patterns such as in La Manga and Sotogrande. In other instances, new tourist developments were added to existing settlements such as Mijas, Calvia and Calpe. The need for adequate accommodation was met by creating large hotels and by the policy of creating *Paradores Nacionales* (State owned hotels), which were usually located in renovated historical buildings.

The influx of retired foreigners taking up residence on the Costa del Sol or Costa Brava was welcomed as a way of limiting the heavy demands made on hotel accommodation and to combat seasonality. Spanish legislation placed little restriction on property acquisition, so large sections of seaside resorts had a considerable percentage of retired people from either West Germany or the United Kingdom, the two major sources of settlers in Spanish coastal regions. Issues such as environmental impact or the cost to local communities were never properly considered by policy-makers during this period, nor was consideration given to the fact that a large amount of investment came from outside the tourist areas and often produced little local benefit.

In 1983, La Secretaría General de Turismo issued a plan for marketing tourism, the main recommendations of which were to be adopted by several autonomous communities and municipalities. The main policies could be summed up as market strategies to counterbalance the weakness of the tourism system by focusing on the type of product offered, the concentration of tourists in very limited geographical areas, tourist origin, their socio-economic background, and the image of Spain. It aimed to promote an emphasis on diversity and quality. Strategies for a marketing-mix were proposed, and improvements were sought in service, the condition of the environment, the planning processes employed, commercialisation and communication channels. A further set of measures looked at the use of tourist resources. In fact, the main resources exploited represented only a small part of those available in a country with a great variety of landscapes, a diversity of water resources, abundant folklore, gastronomic variety and a rich archaeological and historical legacy. Finally, there were strategies to improve infrastructure and management systems, and this requirement was especially evident in aspects of hotel management and infrastructure, as well as in the development of professionals and the use of technology in the sector.

Perhaps the most significant action in the development of tourism policy began in 1988 with the official requisition of a thorough analysis of the sector, which culminated in the publication of a 'White Paper' on Spanish Tourism (*El Libro Blanco del Turismo Español*) in 1991. The Ministry of Transport, Tourism and Communication requested this analysis in view of changes in trends in tourism, commissioning a specialist consultancy, and consulting with the public and private sectors, trade unions and other interested parties. The document presents a thorough analysis of trends in tourism, with an evaluation of the major strengths and weakness of the field together with the main recommendations for future action. The thirty recommendations for action represented an advance in relation to the 1983 marketing plan. The measures are presented under five main themes, four of which relate to strategies in the earlier document. These four themes are: the tourist resources, tourist infrastructure and services, marketing, and tourism management. A fifth theme was added which related to the Institutional system.

In relation to resources *El Libro Blanco* demands a complete inventory of tourist resources to guarantee optimum usage; the elaboration of a national plan; a catalogue of natural areas; and information campaigns to encourage active citizen participation. Under the heading of tourism infrastructure and services a set of measures are presented for the improvement of roads and airports and the introduction of high speed rail links. Other measures include the modernisation of hotel catering, quality controls and alternative forms development for tourist areas. The marketing theme incorporates recommendations ranging from an increase in public investment for the promotion of new tourist products and new tourist areas, to the fostering of research on supply and demand, further utilisation of marketing techniques, and the development of new forms of commercial investment. Management recommendations promoted proposals for schools of catering management, and a higher quality and degree of technological development in tourist services. Finally, the institutional system presents the need for the development of tourism studies at University level, together with measures for co-ordinating the different levels of government to harmonise tourism legislation, to elaborate a plan for tourism development, and to develop and extend existing data banks.

Whether these measures succeed in reversing the recent decline of tourism remains to be seen. In 1991, the impact of the Gulf War clearly had an effect on the development of tourist areas. Furthermore, with the opening of alternative tourist destinations (the Aegean, North Africa, the Caribbean, Asia, and, more recently, Central Europe), it is possible that saturation point has been reached in respect of the European holiday market.

Sports Policy

While the approach of democratic government did not signify a break from that of the previous regime where tourism was concerned, the case of sports presents a completely different picture. From the tradition of sport and gymnastics as a means of training body and mind, the practice of sport has become a diverse and multi-form phenomenon. Initially a compulsory practice at school (with an almost total monopoly by soccer), sport has become characterised by choice and leisure, with a wide variety of options available to participants. In fact, this is one of the major characteristics of sports participation among the Spanish population - that is, a growth in the segmentation of tastes as a result of a growth in socio-economic standards and an increased individualism. The reduction of participation in 'community sports' had become apparent by the late the 1980s while sport practised at the individual level has tended to increase (Ruiz-Olabuenaga, 1991).

A growth in the level of individualism in society may well go some way to explaining this development, but other factors such as a greater variety of options, with better facilities, and a greater awareness should be taken into consideration. Also relevant in this respect is the increasing emphasis that people are placing on health, and on the role which sport can play in developing a healthy lifestyle.

The vast water resources available in Spain, and the experience of their exploitation by tourists, have made the practise of a wide variety of water sports possible (although not in all parts of the country and not for all social groups), and growth is also being seen in mountaineering and winter sports, while others like cycling, jogging, and adventure sports are all witnessing increased participation.

The diversity of this demand has presented problems of provision. Despite the fact that a significant effort has been made to develop new sports facilities, demand significantly outstrips supply. The municipalities have been particularly active in building 'polideportivos' - sports centres of considerable size that can accommodate various sports facilities, from swimming-pools to tennis courts, in the same area. Often located in peripheral areas of towns, usually serving two or three 'barrios', they have become centres brimming with social life, and are one of the major vehicles of the 'sport for all' policy adopted by democratic government. Another significant aspect of sport in Spain is the growth of spectating. The proportion of the population who are sports spectators is very significant. Related to this phenomenon is the issue of the coverage given to sport in the media, particularly in television, where decisions as to whether to televise a particular match or not can become a point of political debate.

The most significant influence on sports policy in the early 1990s, has undoubtedly been the staging of the 1992 Olympic Games in Barcelona. This provided a major stimulus to competitive sport in Spain, and has resulted in campaigns to raise competitiveness. Considerable finance has been put into the training of athletes and the development of centres of excellence (rendimiento). The Games were widely regarded as a success in the international arena, but it will take some time to evaluate the domestic legacy of the Games for Spain.

Towards the Future

For Spain, 1992 was an important year, not only the Olympic Games, but also the staging of the World Expo in Seville, and the celebration of Madrid's year as the European Capital of Culture brought Spain to centre stage in the world arena. These events together with other happenings in Europe, such as the Maastricht Treaty, are likely to further integrate Spain within what is an increasingly interdependent and rapidly changing world.

Looking further ahead, it is estimated that the population of Spain will rise to 40 million by 1995. This population will have a higher percentage of elderly than the European average. Indications point to continued growth in the Spanish economy (de la Dehesa 1990).The Spanish language, is currently spoken by 370 million people, and this figure will rise, according to estimates, to 500 million by the year 2000.

Looking at the country itself, the future as regards leisure policy may depend on five factors. Firstly, the pattern of development of the young democracy. Despite the rapid progress experienced, there are still vast areas which need to be articulated. The development of the Autonomous Communities implies a level of decentralisation which will require policy goals and responsibilities to be clearly specified for each of the administrative levels if the system is to be effective and capable of working without introducing duplication and confusion. The roles to be played by the different levels of municipality, province, region, autonomy and State require further clarification. Equally, social and economic policies in general, and those related to leisure in particular, need to be consolidated. In many instances they exist simply as concepts or statements of intent rather than as policy realities. Thirdly, there is a need to take a position in respect of the factors influencing the construction and development of cultural identity. At present, the United States has a dominant influence on the objectives and products of Spanish cultural markets, Europe has an influence as regards objectives and policies, and Japan exercises its influence in the means, tools and technology required. A search for cultural identity is a necessary task to be aided by government policy. Fourthly, Spain needs to build on its natural, historic, artistic and literary heritage. As it approaches the end of the century, it is expected to have human resources with high levels of professionalism, plural, defined, and affirmed cultures, and better use of its resources. Finally, just as the search for cultural identity is crucial, policies to protect and stimulate growth are necessary, particularly in respect of the cultural industries, which potentially provide the most powerful stimuli in cultural development.

REFERENCES

Ben-Ami, S. (1983) *Fascism from above. The Dictatorship of Primo de Rivera in Spain*, Oxford: Oxford Univesity Press.

Bustamante, E. and Zallo, R. (1988) *Las Industrias Culturales en España*, Madrid: Akal Comunicación.

Calvo Serraller, F. (1988) *Del Futuro al Pasado. Vanguardia y Tradición en el Arte Español Contemporáneo*, Madrid: Alianza.

Castells, M. (1990) 'Estrategias de Desarrollo Metropolitano en las Grandes Ciudades Españolas: la Articulación entre Crecimiento Económico y Calidad de Vida' in *Las Grandes Ciudades en la Década de los Noventa*, J. Borja *et al.* (eds) Madrid: Sistema.

Castillo, J. (1991) 'Consumo y Bienestar Social' in *España a Debate II. La Sociedad*, J. Vidal Beneyto (ed.), Madrid: Tecnos.

De Grazia, V. (1981) *The Culture of Consent: Mass Organization of Leisure in Fascist Italy*, New York: Cambridge University Press.

De la Dehesa, G. (1990) '¿Cómo será la Economía Española en 1999? in *España 1999*, Madrid: Ediciones Temas de Hoy.

EIIO, Deusto (1992) *El Ocio en el Area Metropolitano de Bilbao*, Equipo de Investigación Interdsciplinar en Ocio, Universidad de Deusto, Bilbao; Ayunamiento de Bilbao: Bilbao.

Fernández Prado, E.(1991) *La Política Cultural. Qué es y para qué sirve*, Gijón: Trea.

López Alvarez, L. (1991) 'La Política Cultural' in *España a Debate I. La Política*, J. Vidal Beneyto (ed.), Madrid: Tecnos.

Ministerio de Cultura (1986) *Cuatro Años de Política Cultural: 1982-1986*, Madrid: Officina Nacional de Cultura.

Otero, F. (1989) 'Brumas en la Estética de los Ochenta' in *Primer Encuentro sobre Composición Musical*, Valencia: Generalitat Valenciana.

Quintana, I. (1990) 'Políticas Culturales en las Grandes Ciudades' in *Las Grandes Ciudades en la Década de los Noventa*, J. Borja et al. (ed.) Madrid: Sistema.

Ramos, A. (1990) *Spain Today: in search of Modernity*, Madrid: Cátedra.

Rico, M. (1989) 'Nueva Narrativa: el acecho de la frivolidad' in *El Independiente*, Madrid 7/9/1989.

Ruiz-Olabuenaga, J.I. (1991) *El Ocio como factor de transformación*, unpublished.

Secretaría General de Turismo (1991) *El Libro Blanco Español del Turismo*, Madrid: Officina Nacional de Turismo.

Shubert, A. (1990) *Historia Social de España (1800-1990)*, Madrid: Nerea .

Tinas, J. (1990) 'Políticas de Medio Ambiente para las Grandes Ciudades Españolas' in *Las Grandes Ciudades en la Década de los Noventa*, J. Borja *et al.* (eds) Madrid: Sistema.

Urwin, D.W. and Paterson, W.E. (1990) *Politics in Western Europe Today*, London: Longman.

Wilheim, J. (1990) 'Medio Ambiente y Ciudad' in *Las Grandes Ciudades en la Década de los Noventa*, J. Borja et *et al.* (eds) Madrid: Sistema.

Wilson, J. (1988) *Politics and Leisure*, Leisure and Recreation Studies 5, London: Unwin Hyman.

Chapter 8

Leisure Policy in Greece

Fouli Papageorgiou

The Social, Political and Institutional Framework of Leisure Policy

Leisure policy is a nebulous area of responsibility in the political and administrative framework of government in Greece, without a defined position in the strategies of the political parties or the practices of the state bureaucracy. The reasons for this lack of institutional standing for leisure policy are varied, with perhaps three principal sets of factors explaining this situation. The first set of factors relates to the cultural outlook of modern Greek society, especially up to the end of the military dictatorship in 1974, which favoured a pattern of leisure activity that was mainly informal, family-based or friends-based, and as such did not require substantial facilities provided by the state. Whatever facilities were used for free time activities could be provided by the private sector and they tended to be of a minor scale (tavernas, cinemas). Sports were an exception. Here, state provision was necessary, but the demand was not manifest, because schools and open spaces, to a certain extent, met the needs of the young for play and physical education, while nature provided its own 'facilities' for popular sports, such as swimming, fishing or walking.

The second relevant set of factors relate to historical circumstances, in particular to the poverty experienced by Greek society after the Second World War and the Civil War which followed. This did not leave much margin for leisure spending for the average Greek family. The term 'free time' has not been in common use until recently, and was only meaningful for the higher social strata. Leisure itself, as a term, cannot be translated in modern Greek. Entertainment and recreation are the terms that substitute for leisure. Since the mid-1970s cultural activity has also been closely connected with the notion of free time and the search for meaningful leisure activity (rather than with 'self improvement'), particularly among the young.

The third set of factors relates to the prevailing political ideology during the 1950s and the 1960s, which was not particularly conducive to the development of leisure policy. Indeed, the political party which dominated the political scene during the 1950s and the 1960s, up to the coup staged by the military Junta in 1967, was closely identified with the new industrialist class which emerged after the Second World War, stimulating the Greek economy, which achieved a phenomenal annual rate of growth of 6 per cent during the 1950s. The main focus of government interest was economic development and growth, and very little was done in terms of welfare provision, health, education or culture. The prevailing political ideology was elitist and centralist, both in terms of government structure and operation, and in terms of political control. Both these aspects worked against the development of social welfare policies generally, and leisure policies more specifically.

The fall of the Junta marked the beginning of a completely new era in the political history of modern Greece. The political parties were reformed and regenerated. Elitism could no longer be sustained and decentralisation of government became a major political goal with popular support. Decentralisation of power to local government was finally implemented by government (though in limited form) in the early 1980s. Leisure, as entertainment, recreation, and cultural activity, took on a new meaning symbolic of a liberated and more meaningful life. The living standards of the population had been substantially improved in the late 1970s allowing the economic and social space for the development of leisure in Greek society, especially among the young. The change from the oppressive system of the dictatorship to the liberal democracy which succeeded it, created a climate of optimism and enthusiasm for the 'new life', a life of better quality in terms of both work and leisure.

However, institutional change in the 1980s was not as profound as expected. The attempt by parties in power, at both local and national level, to develop a populist appeal, militated against strategic planning, particularly in leisure, where decentralisation did not go as far as had been advocated. The provision of entertainment, such as the organisation of festivals and events, took precedence over the long term planning of a more permanent 'infrastructure' of facilities and services. In addition, although local government was allocated funds and was invited to take responsibility for local leisure provision, these funds were made available in a haphazard and unpredictable manner, and were not accompanied by assistance and advice as how they should be used. Thus, funds were used in a variety of ways, according to the capacity of the local authority to formulate a meaningful policy and to manage it. Inevitably, most local authorities, without any previous experience in formulating and managing autonomous local policies, did not make particularly good use of the funds. A few, like the outstanding case of Kalamata, provided lessons of good practice, both for other local authorities, and for central government, in the formulation and implementation of integrated policies for leisure and culture.

Nevertheless, overall the effect of decentralising responsibility for leisure policy to local government has been positive. Although the leisure policies developed by local government have been as haphazard and unpredictable as the central government funds that instigated them, they have increased the awareness of people regarding their leisure in two ways. Firstly, they offered alternatives to commercial entertainment, which could foster the development of more creative interests or the exploration of new opportunities (e.g. through informal education for leisure or culture). This was particularly important for a society whose values and leisure styles have been drastically re-defined by consumerism. Secondly, they created a new feeling of people's 'right to leisure' (similar to their right to work) and stimulated expectations for the provision of leisure facilities and services within the wider concept of welfare and quality of life standards (as recent research in three Greek cities has indicated: Papageorgiou, 1990).

The role of local government as leisure provider and policy maker therefore became much more significant in the 1980s in Greece. The remainder of this chapter will therefore be divided into three parts. The first section will review the key features of the governmental system; the ensuing section will focus on the role of central government in leisure and cultural policy; while the third section will identify the role of local government in this policy field, on the basis of recent research undertaken by the author which reviews the implementation of leisure policy in selected local authorities in Greece.

Centralisation and Political Control

One of the key features and a major structural dysfunction of public administration in Greece is its very high degree of centralisation. This is manifested in all tiers of government. Local government is minute compared to most other European countries both in terms of decision making powers, expenditure and size. There are 6,000 local authorities in Greece, of which 5,645 represent villages with less than 1,000 people, having practically no budget or staff to speak of. Local government is also heavily dependent on central government grants and this, together with the imposition of strict central controls and regulations concerning all aspects of personnel management and finance, makes it dependent on central government and subject to political control.

Central government itself is also highly centralised. Ministries have most of their staff located in Athens where decisions are made.

Most Ministries have regional offices in the counties (nomoi) but their powers are limited and they are subject to strong managerial and financial control from the centre. In spite of government policy to decentralise functions during the 1980s to local authorities and to government regional offices, public administration in Greece remains the most centralised in Western Europe.

Centralisation goes hand in hand with political control. Traditionally, in Greece, parties in government used their office to consolidate party-political objectives. This is facilitated by the centralisation of power and the existence of a civil service which has low status and low technical competence. In these circumstances, politicians and party cadres can take decisions and exercise influence without regard to processional or technical requirements or local considerations.

A high degree of centralisation such as that which exists in Greece, obviously facilitates the exercise of political influence by the governing party. This is exactly why centralisation is still so strong: a decentralised system of government would erode the influence of politicians and parties in government and would weaken the operation of the 'political clientele' system which has always dominated, and is still dominating, the political and administrative mechanisms of the Greek state.

The history of modern Greece has been seen by political scientists either as a 'facet of underdevelopment' (Mouzelis, 1978), or as an idiosyncratic evolution in institutions and structures within the state machinery, which has isolated Greece from the mainstream political activity of Europe against which it stands in sharp contrast (Tsoukalas, 1981).

One of the reasons for the peculiar road to development adopted by modern Greek society has been the excessive size of the state machinery. Tsoukalas points to three issues which are central to the role played by the state in the recent history of Greece :

1. For many decades the Greek State has withheld an extremely high proportion of the country's economic surplus.
2. This surplus is in turn redistributed among the agencies which formulate an excessively inflated government machinery.
3. The political staff, the top dogs of the bureaucracy, but also the civil servants more generally and the social groups which depend on state employment, make up a wide social class which appears to be privileged in relation to the rest of the population.

One of the main issues related to the social control of the state is the domination of political clientelism, which not only functions in the context of political parties but also within the state bureaucracy. As already noted, after the fall of the Junta in 1974 the social rift which had been created in the Civil War was deemed to have been bridged and the outlook of Greek politics changed drastically through the reformation of the two major political parties (the Conservatives and the Socialists) and the legalisation of the Communist Party. However, clientelism proved to be firmly embedded in the mentality and the practices of the new parties and to dominate many aspects of policy making both at central and local level.

Funding cultural activities or recreational and cultural infrastructure was, after 1974, one of the most favoured 'objects of exchange' among politicians or bureaucrats and their clients, the latter being usually local authorities or voluntary bodies. The popularity of such favours was explained by the upsurge of interest in and involvement with cultural activity in the mid 1970s following the suppression of most cultural activity during the dictatorship as subversive.

The new state of affairs was crucial for the development of two issues regarding leisure policy. The first issue concerns the recognition of the wider meaning of culture and the connection of the notion of culture with everyday life, leisure and the creative use of free time. This resulted in a recognition of the importance of leisure (in the sense of free time, entertainment, recreation) for all. This popularisation of culture acquired political connotations and became connected with leftist politics - initially with the Communists and later with the Socialists. In parallel the notions of leisure and free time for recreation and self-improvement became accepted as vital needs for everybody and an essential part of the quality of life. The notion of quality of life was in part to be defined by the opportunities for leisure and by the quality of the physical environment.

The second issue concerns the role of the State as a provider for these 'vital needs'. The Ministry of Culture, which is in the main public agency at central government level that assists financially cultural and recreational activity, increased its size and functions significantly in the 1980s by annexing departments from other Ministries which dealt with sport, youth and adult education, thus changing its image from that of a 'manager' for the archaeological service and the national (state owned) theatres to an 'umbrella' for activity aimed at the creative use of free time.

This last issue became one of the central points of the strategy of the Socialist party which governed Greece for most of the 1980s. Under the Socialists, with their commitment to decentralisation, local authorities were encouraged to become providers of art and leisure facilities. This was attempted by funding infrastructure, such as cultural centres, youth centres, multi-purpose centres or gymnasia, swimming pools etc., in the regions, and by financing the organisation of local festivals or single events, involving usually concerts or theatre/dance performances.

This effort became connected by many with populism, which dominated the ideology of the Socialist party and was condemned. However, local authorities were given the opportunity to develop a new type of activity which directly affected the quality of life in their localities, to involve themselves in substantive policy making, and to put decentralisation into practice at least in one sector of activity.

The results have been positive, in the sense that the above three aims were achieved by most local authorities which involved themselves in the provision of leisure facilities and cultural activities. The shortcomings have been many, as well. Among these one may note the haphazard and incidental nature of the provision, the reluctance of local authorities to invest in infrastructure (buildings) and their preference for organising single events or festivals which enhanced their public image and political capital in the short term, and finally the reluctance of local authorities to spend money from their regular budget for these purposes and their dependence on the Ministry of Culture for securing special grants.

Central Government and Leisure Policy

The notion of leisure policy has not been familiar to either politicians or government bureaucrats. As already noted, leisure as a term does not exist in the modern Greek language. The notion of leisure is conceptually close to entertainment and recreation, while culture (politismos) refers to self-fulfilment and self-actualisation through creative or intellectual activity. In this sense, leisure provision has been traditionally regarded as the preserve of private enterprise, while culture has been provided for by the state, either as 'high culture', or as preservation of the national cultural heritage.

The Ministry of Culture was created in 1970 to provide an institutional framework for the National Archaeological Service and to upgrade its status. Gradually it undertook further responsibilities as a patron for the Arts and was radically reorganised and expanded in 1985 to include alongside its established functions four separate Secretariats: for Sport, Youth, Adult Education and 'Greeks Abroad'.

The Ministry of Culture is the major policy-maker within central government in respect of leisure and cultural activity. It regulates the operation of, and subsidises the state-owned or other repertory (non-profit or experimental) theatres, the National Opera, the classical orchestra, innovatory cinema, and all museums and national exhibitions of visual arts. It also funds art festivals or cultural events organised by local government, the voluntary sector or other public or quasi-public bodies. It patronises major athletic events and sports meetings, and funds the building of facilities for all the above activities, including the arts. It funds adult education courses all over the country and grant-aid for cultural activities organised in foreign countries for the Greek immigrant communities.

The Ministry of Culture has been always allocated a minute budget, which usually ranges between 0.5 and 0.6 per cent of the National Budget and indicates the lowly position which it occupies within the Government's hierarchy of priorities. The Ministry's budget reached its maximum in 1988, when it represented 1.2 per cent of the National Budget. In that year, the allocation of funds to the Ministry and its 4 Secretariats was 32,350 million drs, of which 7,300 million were earmarked for investment in buildings and the remaining 25,050 million represented the regular expenditure budget of the Ministry. From the latter, the following sums were spent for the various activities of the Ministry and its two Secretariats (Youth and Sport), which bear a direct relationship to leisure, i.e. support recreational or cultural activity.

Table 8.1 Ministry of Culture Grant-aid for the Arts, Local Government Cultural Activity, Cultural Clubs and Societies

		% of Sections' budget
Ministry of Culture	3,169,740,000 drs	26.5
Secretariat for Sport	6,303,000,000 drs	90.0
Secretariat for Youth	3,200,000,000 drs	84.0
Total :	12,672,740,000 drs	50.6

As Table 8.1 illustrates, 50 per cent of the Ministry's overall budget is allocated to sports, recreation and cultural activity, which represents between 0.3 and 0.5 per cent of the National Budget. The remaining 50 per cent is mostly spent on salaries, including the archaeological service, and on special projects for adult education and Greeks Abroad.

The commercial sector which serves leisure needs (cinemas, theatres, restaurants etc.) falls into the jurisdiction of the Ministry of Commerce, which, however, limits its role to pricing policy and to the enforcement of regulations for public safety and hygiene. Many other Ministries or public organisations, including the banks, spend relatively small amounts on subsidies for cultural or recreational activities undertaken by local authorities, the voluntary sector or by their staff.

The size of the budget devoted to cultural activity, sport and recreation by central government reflects the attitude of the state towards a sector of public policy which traditionally has been considered to be marginal. However, this does not reflect the importance of culture and leisure as political issues after 1974, since they were regarded as particularly significant by the Socialists during their time in government in the 1980s. The problem of inadequate and unsystematic policy-making in the sectors of culture and leisure would seem to be a reflection of the gap which existed between rhetoric or ideology and political practice during the two terms of Socialist government in the 1980s rather than the discounting of leisure as insignificant in principle.

Table 8.2 Population, Area and Number of Cultural Events Staged by Greek Local Authorities						
City	Population	Area		1987	1988	1989
Egaleo	81,744	Urban	Attica	-	39	31
Koridallos	61,460	Urban	Attica	33	50	38
Ag. Paraskevi	32,724	Urban	Attica	53	36	25
Kifisia	31,988	Urban	Attica	27	36	15
Ag. Anargiroi	30,470	Urban	Attica	-	-	38
Kaisariani	28,897	Urban	Attica	31	10	35
Alimos	27,193	Urban	Attica	-	27	16
Giannitsa	23,202	Urban	Peripheral	-	51	38
Perama	23,073	Urban	Attica	-	16	38
Ptolemaida	21,278	Urban	Peripheral	12	46	18
Kastoria	20,973	Urban	Peripheral	11	12	10
Lavreotiki	9,993	Urban	Attica	-	-	34
Gravena	7,958	Semi-urban	Peripheral	11	10	11
Velventos	3,890	Semi-urban	Peripheral	21	11	12
Average				28	31	30
Standard Deviation				16.01	17.58	11.04

Local Authorities as Agents of Leisure Policy

The provision by local authorities of facilities and services for leisure has to date been optional in Greece. Local authorities first became involved in this sector during the period of general euphoria which followed the fall of the Junta. The voluntary sector which patronised and spread the 'cultural movement' in the 1970s was in some cases supported actively by a local authority. The reputation of these active local authorities (such as Hymmetus in Athens) spread and became a motivating factor for local authorities which sought to emulate them in sponsoring cultural and recreational activity.

However, local authorities started to have a more substantial role in this sector after 1981, when the newly elected Socialist government initiated its programme of funding cultural activities organised by local government. The extent of funding received, and the type of activities undertaken by local authorities, cannot be deduced from official statistics, and the National Secretariat for Research and Technology therefore funded research in 1990 to investigate these issues in detail, seeking to measure the involvement of local government in cultural and recreational activity and to identify the components of the corresponding policy.

Table 8.3   Percentage of Cultural Events for Chidren Staged by Greek Local Authorities

| | 1987 | | | 1988 | | | 1989 | | |
City	Total	Child	%	Total	Child	%	Total	Child	%
Ag. Paraskevi	53	0	0	36	3	8	25	3	12
Ag. Anargiroi	-	-	-	-	-	-	38	25	66
Egaleo	-	-	-	39	8	21	31	7	23
Alimos	-	-	-	27	6	22	16	0	0
Velvendos	21	1	5	11	1	9	12	2	17
Giannitsa	-	-	-	51	8	16	38	4	11
Grevena	11	0	0	10	2	20	11	1	9
Kaisariani	31	13	42	10	4	40	35	5	14
Kifissia	27	8	30	36	5	14	15	0	0
Koridallos	33	0	0	50	12	24	38	8	21
Lavreotiki	-	-	-	-	-	-	34	0	0
Perama	-	-	-	16	3	19	38	8	21
Ptolemaida	12	0	0	46	3	7	18	1	6
Average	25	3	10	29	5	17	24	4	14

At the time of writing, fieldwork had been completed in 14 local authorities and some of the principal findings are presented here. The 14 surveyed authorities, as Table 8.2 illustrates, range in population size from 3,890 to 91,794 and are located both in Attica (about two thirds) and in the regions. They are also evenly divided according to the political party which controls the Council majority. The data collected relate the type of activity undertaken by the authority, the volume of this activity, the types of public at which provision is

targeted, and the cost of the staff involved in the management of the
activity. Data was collected for three years, 1987 - 1989.

Table 8.4 Percentage of Free Cultural Events Staged by Greek Local Authorities								
	1987			1988			1989	
City	Total	Free	%	Total	Free	%	Total	Free	%
Ag. Paraskevi	53	53	100	36	34	94	25	22	88
Ag. Anargyroi	-	-	-	-	-	-	38	29	76
Egaleo	-	-	-	39	39	100	31	31	100
Alimos	-	-	-	27	27	100	16	6	38
Velvendos	21	20	95	11	9	82	12	11	92
Giannitsa	-	-	-	51	40	78	38	26	68
Grevena	11	11	100	10	10	100	11	11	100
Kaisariani	31	31	100	10	10	100	35	34	97
Kastoria	11	11	100	12	12	100	10	10	100
Kifissia	27	21	78	36	27	75	15	13	87
Koridallos	33	18	55	50	36	72	38	19	50
Lavreotiki	-	-	-	-	-	-	34	34	100
Perama	-	-	-	16	13	81	38	38	100
Ptolemaida	12	12	100	46	46	100	18	18	100
Average	25	22	91	29	25	90	24	20	80

Several problems were encountered in the collection of the data,
of which the most significant was that local authorities had not kept
account of the activities they organised especially for the earlier years
(1987-88) and some of the information had to be retrieved from files
of publicity material and programmes of past events. In the absence
of formal records, it was difficult also to establish the financial profile
of these activities even as a grand total. These problems highlight the
amateurish nature of local authority involvement in the organisation
of these activities. Indeed, no local authority had a culture and leisure
department and the organisation of their activities was undertaken by
staff with other responsibilities in other departments.

Ten out of 14 authorities had established Cultural Centres which
operated as separate legal entities and employed a small staff. Seven

of these Cultural Centres were housed in authority-owned accommodation. Cultural Centres, where they existed, organised the educational activities (arts and crafts) of the authority, might include a small library and might also organise some events (exhibitions or performances). Cultural Centres usually undertake the organisation of most of the authority's cultural (but not recreational) activity. Where such organisations existed, they were much better organised in terms of recorded information and appeared to operate in a much more effective way than the main municipal administration.

Table 8.2 shows the number of cultural events organised by these local authorities during 1987-89, and Table 8.3 indicates the proportion of events aimed at children. The data confirm that there is no continuity in the activity of the local authorities nor a consistent leisure policy maintaining a particular volume of activity, either overall or for particular sections of the population. The tables highlight the fact that there are certain 'active' local authorities, although variation in the level of activity from year to year is quite common. This fluctuation is unpredictable, and does not appear to follow any pattern or trend. A similar picture emerges from a comparison of the number of classes of sports programmes provided. However, the change in the volume of activity from year to year can be due to budgetary limitations or expansion (usually due to the reception of grants) and/or lack of availability of staff.

Table 8.4 shows a slight change in the commitment of local authorities to provide free entertainment and recreation for all by introducing paid entrance to some events, particularly theatre or music performances. This trend seems likely to grow as local authorities realise that they can compete with the commercial sector on the basis of the quality and accessibility of their services.

Table 8.5 presents information on the level of grants received by the authorities surveyed, from the Ministry of Culture in 1988 as a proportion of their total income and compares this figure to the proportion of the authority's budget allocated to culture and recreation (including open spaces). Three authorities received more in grants than they were able to spend for leisure and culture, but the majority spent substantially more than they received in special grants indicating that they fund these activities from their regular income. The proportion of the authority's expenditure which goes to leisure and culture varies from 1 per cent to nearly 20 per cent with a mean value of 11 per cent. This is an encouraging figure, which implies that local authorities have taken their role as providers in the field of leisure and culture seriously.

No significant relationships have been noted between the characteristics of local authorities and the amount and variety of services offered. However, two qualitative findings can be noted. Firstly, the role of the mayor appears to have been decisive in creating the preconditions for the authority's involvement in cultural and recreational activity. The 'active' local authorities reflected more the enthusiasm and dedication on the part of their leader than any other characteristic such as population size, budget, political complexion, or location. Secondly, there was a correlation between the volume of local authority activity and the active presence of the voluntary sector in the area. Towns which had an active authority in terms of leisure and cultural provision, tend to have active clubs and societies as well. This suggests that the local clubs have reacted to the 'competition' from their local authority with an intensification of their own activity, which in turn has often resulted in bigger grants being paid by local authorities to the clubs.

Table 8.5 Grants Received and Local Authority Expenditure on Leisure and Culture by Greek Local Authorities		
City	Ministry of Culture Grants (% of L.A. Income)	Expenditure for Leisure and Culture (% of L.A. Expenditure)
Ag. Paraskevi	5.0	11.4
Ag. Anargiroi	-	19.3
Egaleo	-	16.7
Alimos	2.0	13.7
Velvendos	9.2	3.5
Giannitsa	-	13.2
Grevena	0.6	5.9
Kastoria	-	2.4
Kifissia	3.6	1.0
Kaisariani	-	19.2
Koridallos	16.8	13.7
Perama	1.1	7.5
Ptolemaida	-	10.2
Lavrio	-	4.1

Concluding Remarks

Prior to the 1980s, leisure policy was practically non-existent in the Greek context. However, despite the introduction of central government grants in the 1980s, at both the central and local government levels the development of leisure policy has been both relatively marginal and uneven over the past decade. However, despite these short-comings, there have been signs of potential for significant development, particularly at the local level. This potential is a function of increasing awareness about the contribution of leisure to the quality of life, providing alternatives to increasing consumerism and passive recreation (such as television viewing), and opening up opportunities for activities which are not offered by the private sector. The excessive centralisation of the Greek state is a barrier to overcome, since there is little scope for a flexible and meaningful leisure policy designed at central level. Local authorities are much better placed to take initiatives to meet leisure and cultural needs in their localities. The right climate has been created for such initiative and the initial experimental period has passed. However, better levels of organisation, professionalism, financial commitment and consistency are needed in order to move from the amateurish operation of the present time to a more effective mode of provision.

REFERENCES

Mouzelis N. (1978) *Greek Society : Facets of Underdevelopment*, Athens: Exas.

Papageorgiou F. (1990) 'Leisure, Culture and the Political Economy of the City: the Case of Kalamata, Halkida and Argyroupoli', Paper presented at the European Conference on Leisure, Culture and the Political Economy of the City sponsored by the EC and the Mayor of Halkida, Halkida, December.

Tsoukalas K. (1987) *State, Society, Employment in Post-war Greece*, Athens: Themelio.

Tsoukalas K. (1981) *Social Development and the State*, Athens: Themelio.

Chapter 9

Elements of Leisure Policy in Post-war Poland

Bohdan Jung

Introduction

In its proper sense, leisure policy in post-war Poland has never existed as a concept[1] and could not be either elaborated or implemented. However, its elements can be found in the official and actual social and cultural policy of the state. It is the analysis of these elements (culture, media, recreation, sports, tourism) which constitutes the subject matter of this chapter. It has to be stressed from the beginning that these elements have never been analysed together as 'leisure' by Polish policy makers. For this reason, when reference is made to leisure policy later in this chapter, the term is used in the sense given to it in the West, and not the sense in which it was perceived by Polish policy makers, who referred separately to recreation (usually meaning social tourism and mass sports), culture (fine arts, mass culture with the media), professional competitive sports and commercial tourism.

The second introductory issue to be raised is the extremely close linkage between social and cultural policy, ideology and politics. This conforms to the general attitude of policy makers in communist countries, in whose eyes even leisure was essentially political (Wilson, 1988). The impact of political changes on state policy in the sphere of culture and recreation in post-war Poland were probably much more pronounced than in any other country (including the USSR) discussed in this book. In the post-war period Poland has gone through a number of distinct political phases, which entailed changes in the country's economic and social strategy for development[2]. The chronology of these changes provides the key to understanding trends in the evolution of leisure policy in Poland. An historical outline of

189

the political and economic situation in the post-war years is included later in the chapter to reflect the specificity of the approach to elements of leisure policy in Poland.

The third issue is the legacy of the communist approach to elements of leisure policy, which is still firmly rooted in the mentalities of policy makers, providers, social organisations and consumers of leisure. The importance of the past 45 years of a centrally-planned economy cannot be ignored. The attitudes of *homo sovieticus* are, and will continue to be, present in Polish society, and social policy in the sphere of leisure would both reflect them and be forced to take them into account.

The last introductory comment stems from the previous ones. Even when the centrally-planned economy in Poland was at its best, any elements of leisure policy (in the Western sense) would be characterised by fragmentation of efforts and scattering of resources. This fragmentation meant that even though a centrally-planned economic system offered potential possibilities for creating and implementing a complex and comprehensive policy, these opportunities were never fully seized. The tale of evolution of the elements of leisure policy in Poland continues to be an account of actions taken separately by diverse organisms and agencies, including different ministries, party committees, central boards, local government and enterprises.

Leisure and Social Policy Goals

Elements of policy in the sphere of culture and recreation can be found in the country's social policy. Definitions of social policy which dominated in the post-war period in Poland reflect the country's social, economic and political system, which until 1990 was that of communist government and centrally planned (command) economy. One such definition describes social policy as '...actions whose objective is to directly gratify important needs of wide strata of the society, especially of the working people (wage earners) and their families' (Rajkiewicz, 1979, p. 35). Social policy was also seen as an active instrument in shaping the new post-war society, or part of the social project to transform the Polish society into a communist one. Social policy was thus also defined as '... an active action to shape the value systems, means and conditions of existence through a global policy (national development strategy), as well as assure social and economic security' (Czykowska, 1990, p. 13).

The scope of social policy incorporated a concern for both the material conditions of existence and cultural needs of society (Rajkiewicz, 1979, p. 36). An exemplification of the elements included in such a policy offers clues as to the importance of its leisure component. These elements included such sub-policies as employment, income (from wages), environmental and labour protection, social security, health care, housing, organisation of recreation and time free from work, a policy of national education, and a policy of mass access to culture (Rajkiewicz, 1979, p. 47). Within each of these domains, a series of strategic and tactical goals was elaborated and had to be attained within the system of planned development. Social policy measures used to attain these goals included the shaping of income (including transfer payments from the state budget and social security funds), free access to goods and services (e.g. holidays subsidised by the employer out of a special fund), organisation and provision of services (including the functioning of cultural and sports centres), expansion of the social infrastructure serving collective consumption (such as national parks), organisation of collective behaviour and self-managing organisations (such as Polish Domestic Tourist Associations - PTTK).

In laying out theoretical objectives of social policy, much attention was given to the goals of cultural policy. These included the removal of the existing ecological, economic, educational and other barriers to cultural participation, thus providing equal access to cultural opportunities, especially with respect to basic forms of cultural activity. This was to be achieved through expansion of the cultural infrastructure, higher total circulation of publications, deliveries of cultural goods and services in quantity and at prices which allowed for their wide distribution, and application of a proper (i.e. subsidised) policy of pricing (Czykowska, 1975, pp. 153-156). Specific leisure-related functions of state policy were to 'organise vacations and provide opportunities for resting and cultural entertainment during time free from work on work days and holidays' (Szubert, 1973, pp. 52-53). This approach, which stresses state responsibility for culture and recreation both at central and local level (through state-owned enterprises, which act as employers for the bulk of the working population) is quite different from the notion of leisure policy in the West.

The element of ideological control was quite bluntly exposed in social policy goals. For instance, the main objective of national culture during the construction of socialism was to mobilise society around the dominant ideology, integrating doctrine with culture. This integration was to be assured through the country's leading political and social force (the Party) and the working class, which was to guarantee the fulfilment of the historical task of construction of a new social and economic system, both at home and abroad[3]. However, the predominance of ideological and political goals did not exclude the fact that much stress was placed on real democratisation and egalitarisation of culture and recreation, with the ultimate goal of eliminating disparities between cities and rural areas, and between various income, educational and professional groups (Czykowska, 1990, pp. 163-164).

The definition of policy goals in the sphere of physical culture, recreation and tourism reflected similar priorities. Democratisation (i.e. mass access), provision of services and expansion of the infrastructure were key priorities. One element which has often been stressed both in theory and in practice was the state (and employer's) responsibility for organisation of free time and recreation, implying that the individual was not capable of making his own 'proper' choices in this field.

Levels of Planning and the Financing of Leisure Policy

In a centrally planned economy, elements of leisure policy were featured in plans for both social and the economic development. The social plan included such policy elements as general access to culture and stimulation of cultural participation, as well as development of physical culture, recreation, sports and tourism[4].

The country's economic plan focused on such leisure-related issues as shortening of the working week and greater flexibility of work time (Strzeminska, 1988). In practice, this meant that two different planning attitudes were applied (roughly corresponding to the difference between planning economic development and social policy). The economists looked at time free from work as a burden on the economy. This burden was created by less time being made available for production and by the additional demand (caused by more leisure time) for goods and services that were in short supply or financed out of public consumption. Social planners (mainly sociologists) were concerned with long-range social and political goals, the implementation of which was to be dependent upon collective consumption. While cherishing humanist visions about the future of the Polish *homo ludens*, their concern with economic realities was slight. In the 1970s, when Western credit was giving the Polish economy relative prosperity, many social projections were developed, in which much expectation was placed on the changing personality patterns and value systems of the Polish population (Sicinski, 1977; Czerwinski, 1972, 1974; Jasinska and Siemienska, 1978). These changes were to lead to higher cultural participation and greater demand for 'high culture' in leisure patterns (Szczepanski, 1977; Suchodolski, 1977). The economic and political chances of fulfilment of these unquestionably noble cultural goals were very slim[5].

As the Eastern European countries nurtured the ambition to co-ordinate their development policies within their economic community (the Council for Mutual Economic Assistance - the CMEA), elements of planning in the sphere of culture and recreation were also developed on a supranational level. These referred to development of physical culture, tourism and recreation, as well as to the 'development of spiritual culture of society'. In the sphere of leisure, this coordination was either verbal or limited. It was restricted to signing protocols on cultural and sports exchange programmes, rather than common policy, projects and investment guidelines.

On a national level, the above policy goals were pursued through allocation of budgets to the respective government agencies, within whose competence different aspects of leisure would fall. Three central funds were created to implement state policy and to finance national projects in the field of leisure: the Central Fund for Culture (later called the Fund for Development of Culture), the Central Fund for Development of Physical Culture and the Central Fund for Development of Tourism and Recreation[6]. The three central funds accounted for 7 to 8 per cent of the finance made available for (target) central funds generated by the state.

The priorities given to social policy goals at central and ministerial levels were reflected in the composition of the collective consumption fund, or the share of public spending on leisure. In the post-war period the share of leisure (culture, recreation/social tourism, sports) in total current expenditure from the state budget (both central and local) was in the range of 1.5 to 2 per cent. Of this public spending, the ratio of spending on culture to spending on all other leisure-related activities was 4:1. Within the recreation/sports group, 90 per cent of the outlay of central and local government went to physical culture and sport[7].

Public money was generally helping to meet current financial needs of cultural institutions. Most went into subsidies for the performing arts, as well as for cultural clubs and centres (mainly youth centres). Roughly one quarter of the Fund for Development of Culture actually went into investment and overhaul. In the case of public spending on physical culture, sport, tourism and recreation, some three-quarters of the amount in question has gone into investment in sport and tourist infrastructure. The second most important spending item was subsidy for holiday centres belonging to trade unions[8].

Whereas the spending priorities could be deduced from the composition of public spending and the allocation of central funds, the division of competencies between the various agencies of central government in the sphere of leisure was not clear. From the perspective of leisure, there were many overlapping areas. A simplified scheme of the basic responsibilities is presented in Figure 9.1.

Figure 9.1 does not incorporate several other bodies which directly or indirectly received public funds to carry out policy goals which were related to leisure. Such organisations included trade unions and their representation at the national level, together with the Employees' Holiday Fund (FWP) - a powerful body which operated a network of holiday centres throughout the country and subsidised vacations for Polish holiday makers employed in the public sector (i.e. 80 per cent of all employees)[9]. Leisure activities were also financed by political parties, youth organisations, social associations, etc. There was little financial involvement of the Catholic church in this area. Political, youth and social organisations were fully or partially subsidised by the state and had extensive leisure programmes, many of which had a strong ideological component. One must also include the practical impact of the Office for Control of Publications (the Board of Censors) in the picture, which, through its function, set political and moral standards for cultural productions, entertainment and broadcasting.

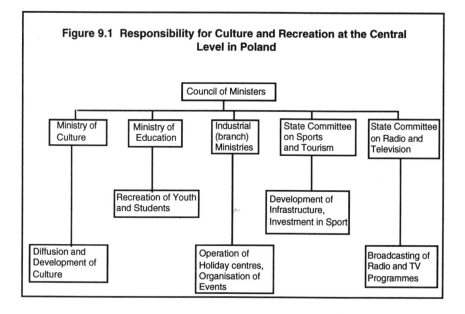

Figure 9.1 Responsibility for Culture and Recreation at the Central Level in Poland

Despite a number of central bodies and agencies with competency in the field of leisure organisation and planning, the practical implementation of cultural and recreational policy in Poland was really carried out at enterprise level. Besides its economic objectives, each enterprise had to fulfil a number of social objectives. As a part of the government policy to provide subsidies for many social activities, enterprises were obliged by law to generate a so-called social fund, which was used to entirely or partly cover the cost of many leisure activities of their employees.

The 'social activities' of enterprises were also subject to planning. The goals which enterprises had to attain in the sphere of leisure were a curious mixture of indoctrination with the socialist work ethic and genuine concern for recreation opportunities, especially for family holidays. These goals included (Frank, 1978, p. 311):

- improved employee attitudes towards individual and team work and towards their self-actualisation at work (through better work culture);
- the development of an *esprit de corps* within a given enterprise or branch of industry through better knowledge of the company's history, its 'work heroes' and achievements;
- combating the symptoms of de-humanisation of work (such as excessive glorification of technology);
- the development of continuous job education and training, organisation of reading contests etc.; use of the existing network of mass communication within the enterprise to diffuse information about cultural events;
- the organisation (or *management*) of employees' free time to allow them to spend more of it in cultural pursuits;
- the use of free time of workers living in workers' hostels to enhance their level of culture;
- combating the causes of social delinquency among employees.

Table 9.1 Composition of social fund in 1987

Spending item from social fund	% of total
Financing of vacation facilities for employees	36.1
Weekend recreation and tourism	3.6
Recreation of youth and children	18.3
Cultural activities	4.3
Sports activities	3.8
Transfers in kind	2.2
SUBTOTAL: SPENDING ON LEISURE FROM SOCIAL FUND	68.3

Source: Czyzowska, 1990, p. 79

To cope with these objectives, a centrally planned system obliged enterprises to create a special social fund, composed of write-offs equivalent to 50% of the minimum wage in the public sector per employee.

To have some idea about the use of this fund, originally set up to extend social assistance to employees in need, Table 1 provides a breakdown of the actual outlay from this fund made by Polish companies in 1987.

Over the first 45 years of the post-war period, the average consumer, himself / herself a wage earner in a state company, has come to identify social benefits provided by the above fund for his or her cultural and recreational activities with the concept of free time itself, especially with respect to his / her holiday-making patterns.

The Changing Political and Economic Situation in Poland and its Impact on the Periodisation of Cultural and Recreational Policy

Before attempting to describe stages in the evolution of cultural and recreational policy in Poland, it is necessary to describe their general determinants. These determinants were mainly of a political and economic nature.

After the end of the Second World War, the country's immediate preoccupation was with post-war reconstruction and creation of a new social and political system. The years in question were characterised by high rates of economic growth and rapid social advancement of the social strata which had been underprivileged before the war. After the initially democratic and prudent policy of the first three years (1945-1948) of a coalition government, a ruthless destruction of non-communist opposition became the priority goal, together with the imposition of a new ideology and extreme centralisation of policy decisions. The economy was subjected to centralised planning. Massive industrialisation began, which placed stress on the development of heavy industry and defence. This industrialisation was also linked to rapid urbanisation and the resulting diffusion of a city lifestyle among new city populations with predominantly rural backgrounds. Stalin and the USSR acted as the main sources of inspiration, both in terms of social policy and of culture. This period in Poland lasted practically until the mid 1950s. One of its features, characteristic of the command economy, survived until recent economic reforms - the nationalised economy was constantly plagued by shortages of capital and consumer goods. Demand always exceeded supply. This situation, known as the producers' market, placed a powerful source of influence into the hands of policy makers - the distribution of scarce goods, the allocation of which could be entirely independent of the actual needs of the economy. Political pressure could be used to 'persuade' planners to provide goods or funds to a given enterprise or ministry (this also applied to leisure).

After the death of Stalin in 1953 and the ensuing political 'thaw' in Eastern Europe, a series of brutally crushed workers' protests (in 1956) brought into power a new set of communist leaders in Poland. These men were jailed during the Stalinist days for being communists with deviant 'nationalistic' tendencies. These leaders were not trusted by Moscow, a fact which helped to establish their political credentials in Poland and generate universal support for their proposed reforms of communism to make it more 'human'. Their attempts to reform the system were well within the bounds of communist ideology. It was a reform 'from within', without abandoning any of the basic communist dogma. Partial democracy was encouraged within the structures of the Communist party. In the economy, priorities were shifted to the production of more consumer goods, but as years went by, the country's economic leaders again decided to launch themselves into gigantic, capital-intensive investment projects which successfully competed for funds with the production of consumer goods.

The era of 'communism with a human face', as this phase of reforms was called, ended in disgrace. The end of the 1960s in Poland marked a time of political frustration and economic stagnation. Student riots provoked by a censor's ban on one of the nation's most celebrated dramas (accused of containing an anti-Russian message) marked the formal end of the liberalisation of policy. An ugly anti-Jewish campaign, which took advantage of the Arab-Israeli conflict in 1967 (and which was in fact orchestrated by quarrelling factions within the Communist Party to mask the real struggle for power) gave rise to nationalism and obscurantism. This period culminated with the riots of 1970, in which, as their last gesture before being ousted from power, the communist leaders of that time ordered the army to open fire on the striking workers of the Baltic ports.

The new communist leaders who managed to dominate Poland's political scene for the next decade (1970-1980) deftly cultivated their 'enlightened' image in the West and used the available Western credit to give the country a period of economic expansion, political stability, and to widen international contact.

The era of relative economic prosperity brought about by Western credit came to an end in the late 1970s, when sources of cheap credit dried up, while Polish exports (expected to expand with the help of Western technologies and components) either failed to materialise, or were not able to find their way into Western markets. On the domestic market, rapidly growing consumer demand (including demand for leisure goods and services) outstripped supply and ended in widespread shortages, a bout of high inflation and a return to the situation of a producers' market. The initial credit of political confidence given to the new leaders rapidly vanished, as the authorities brutally suppressed workers' protestation over a drastic increase in food prices and took up a tougher stance with the country's intellectuals.

The new intermediate period, which lasted throughout the 1980s, began with the workers' strikes in the Polish shipyards. These strikes gave rise to the independent trade union and political movement of Solidarity. Even before martial law was imposed to crush this trade union and political movement in December 1981, the falling purchasing power of the consumer, widespread shortages of everyday necessities, and political inflexibility of the communist state had resulted in a widespread conviction that the communist system could not be improved from within. This growing de-mythologising of the communist welfare state also opened up the search for the means of transition to alternative social and economic systems, such as capitalism and self-management [10].

The outlined changes in Poland's political and economic scene in the 1945-1981 period are reflected in the stages of its cultural and recreational policy. The following sub-periods should be taken into consideration as being distinct for both their political and leisure context[11]: culture and recreation for the masses (1945-1955), communism with a human face (1956-1970), mass communist culture (1971-1979) and the intermediate period (1980-1989). The possible leisure policy implications of the most recent changes in Poland will be discussed later in this chapter.

Culture and Recreation for the Masses (1945-1955)

In the sphere of leisure, these years were characterised by the building of a system of centralised leisure provision, strict ideological control of culture, full censorship at all levels and the launch of a dominant style of art (socialist-realism) (Kloskowska, 1980, p. 320; Kossak, 1977, pp. 163-169). The propagandist role of the arts was stressed. Official preference was given to collective, organised, leisure experience at enterprise and central (workers' parades etc.) level. Leisure (in the Western sense) became yet another front of the ideological struggle, in which various leisure practices had to be labelled as being either 'bourgeois' (and therefore condemned) or 'proletarian'. Yet another preoccupational characteristic of cultural policy of this period was the struggle against cosmopolitan, decadent and individualistic forms of leisure. However, it must also be stressed that the policy goal of achieving a significant increase in the cultural and recreational participation of the 'masses' in selected areas was fully met, if not exceeded. Much success was also achieved in the democratisation of leisure (Strzeminska, 1988, p. 30). Basic culture and recreation for the whole population had virtually become freely accessible - a feature most Poles have come to accept as a part of the centrally-planned system, which offered this type of compensation in exchange for political indoctrination and oppression.

Attempts to Establish 'Communism with a Human Face' (1956-1970)

Together with modest political and economic reforms came the policy of more relaxed ideological control over culture, including opening it to more contact with the West. The impact of jazz (previously outlawed) and imports of high culture from the West helped to boost the cultural revival in Poland, which lasted until early 1960s. In reaction to the extreme 'Sovietisation' of the previous period, more national, religious and regional elements were incorporated into the communist model of culture and recreation without having to be justified in terms of their proper class and ideological content. Also noteworthy was the intellectual effort (with leisure policy implications) involved in the search to establish the meaning and core values of communist humanism. The cultural policy of the period successfully managed to merge Polish high culture with post-war mass culture, resulting in the generation of a modern mass media-based culture with high cultural standards (Kloskowska, 1980, pp. 427-452).

What leisure planners at that time did not foresee was the rapid expansion of a specific communist petty bourgeoisie and its model of leisure, which continues to prevail well after the downfall of communism in Poland (Jasinska and Siemienska, 1978, p. 253; Sicinski, 1977, p. 347).

Mass Communist Culture (1971-1979)

The idea of 'enlightened socialism' which prevailed in the cultural and recreational policy of this decade included the use of 'subtle persuasion' (mainly through highly professional use of the media) to build and reinforce a communist model of mass culture. The audience of the mass media had risen to unprecedented heights. The same was true of the number of holiday makers taking advantage of 'social tourism' or recreation in holiday centres subsidised by enterprises and trade unions, and of genuine tourists going abroad (Poles were for the first time allowed to cross borders with only their national identity cards, but this was restricted to travel to the neighbouring countries of East Germany and Czechoslovakia).

The 1970s were a period of considerable achievement for the 'socialist welfare state' in the sphere of leisure. A rich and prosperous state subsidised all forms of collective participation in culture and recreation generously. Perceptible growth in the standard of living created additional demand for leisure-related goods and services, and after nearly 20 years of stagnation, the working week was finally shortened through the introduction of long-overdue non-working Saturdays (one per month). The shift in consumer attitudes opened up a new debate on cultural and recreational policy. This debate focused on the elaboration of the *socialist model of consumption* and its programming by the state through economic policy, rather than ideological indoctrination as in earlier years. Priorities established (in the best 'enlightened' tradition) by economists and social policy makers included the expansion of television broadcasting and more weekend recreation, fuelled by mass car and summer residence (*datcha*) ownership (Wnuk-Lipinski, 1981, pp. 164, 166, 172). Culture and sport were also treated by the authorities as vehicles for building Poland's international prestige and local pride, continuing to feed the machine of propaganda with more evidence of the country's and its leaders' success (Hadzelek, 1981, pp. 61-76).

The 1970s were also a period of large investment projects. Culture and recreation continued to rank low on the list of priorities, but they too, nevertheless, profited from the general boom. Through local rivalry, political lobbying and competition between ambitious projects, the leisure infrastructure greatly expanded and became more differentiated to include both high and low segments of the leisure market (in contrast to the policy of providing a uniform mix of basic cultural and recreational products as in the early days of the communist regime).

Elements of Cultural and Recreational Policy in the Intermediate Period (1980-1989)

Despite an economic crisis which had began in 1976 and continued throughout the 1980s, leisure became a well-established element of household patterns of behaviour and spending. This was helped by further reductions in work time, which were part of the deal struck by Solidarity just after it was created in 1980.

The emergence of a unified opposition with its vision of an alternative civic society, as well as its own attempts at developing cultural policy (self-organisation, clandestine culture, independent publishing, etc.) and its following in Polish society had proved that the official line of cultural policy was extremely fragile despite many years of promotional propaganda. As less public and consumers' money was available for the pursuit of leisure and life became more home-centred , participation in all outdoor forms of culture and sport fell drastically (Jung, 1989). However, nearly all of the growth in free time shifted to watching television.

At the end of the 1980s, a new passport and immigration policy granted Poles unrestricted freedom to travel to the West, inciting many to break the home-centred pattern of leisure and engage in 'shopping tourism'. Some of this shopping was panic-buying of home electronics to get rid of money that was rapidly losing its value under very high inflation. The home-centred pattern of Polish leisure was thus reinforced through the purchase of more modern leisure equipment for the home. For the first time, private imports and individual consumer decisions (as opposed to centralised provision of culture and recreation subsidised and organised by the state), were beginning to shape the patterns of Polish leisure. The scope of state policy in the sphere of culture and recreation was minimal. It applied to the distribution of scarce (imported) paper among the various publishing houses and newspapers (here the old system of favouring those whose publishing policy was compliant with the political preferences of the Ministry of Culture was still operating). It also applied to the provision of subsidised holidays for children from low-income families. The lack of more ambitious goals for cultural and recreational policy on the part of the state (explained by a lack of resources to implement them as state spending was reduced) coincided with the period when official cultural and recreational policy was for the first time facing organised resistance. This challenge came from clandestine publishers (printing books outlawed by the censors) and the Roman Catholic church which, after the imposition of martial law, became involved in sponsoring independent culture (high culture and arts), as well as forms of recreation for children of the underprivileged (such as those who were imprisoned or had lost their jobs for political reasons).

Heading for Market Economy and Democracy - the Future for Leisure Policy

The Pattern of Leisure Inherited from the 1980s

Before seeking to explore the future of leisure policy in Poland, it is necessary to present some elements of the current pattern of Polish leisure. This pattern was shaped in the 1980s under the impact of the country's prolonged economic and social crisis. For the average Pole it was a time of Dumazedier's 'historic inversion', when daily discretionary time (270 minutes per day) became greater than time spent on work (235 minutes). This was due to the drop in the duration of the working week (from 46 to 42 hours) and to early retirement. In this sense the crisis has, in a perverse way, brought Poland one step closer to a poorer brand of a 'new leisure society' - poorer because food accounts for over 50 per cent of the average household budget (against 18 to 25 per cent in the EC countries), leaving little material means available for other needs.

Much of the time liberated from work was used up by the deteriorating conditions of daily existence, such as queuing for food and performing household chores which could no longer be purchased as external services. Even though there is no data on the use of time in the 1990s, it can be asserted that time spent on queuing has drastically dropped as shops have become better stocked. Nevertheless, high prices for external services (laundry, processed foods, etc.), higher (unsubsidised) charges for rent and electricity and, in general, free market prices coupled with wage controls imposed under the current programme of economic reforms are pushing households to increase work time in various sectors of the economy (formal and informal) to make ends meet. On the other hand, over the years 1990-1991, unemployment has gone up from zero to 10 per cent, which would probably also affect the national figures in time budget surveys.

In the years 1976 and 1984 (when the last two nation-wide time budget surveys were held), the structure of leisure time in Poland went through a transition which, in many respects, was more profound than changes in the total amount of time available for leisure.

The forms of leisure most frequently pursued in 1984 (see Table 9.2), and probably even more so in the 1990s, were low-cost activities requiring no special skills or equipment. The number of active sports participants had more than halved, cinema and theatre audiences had dropped by one third and the number of adults going to museums was down by 40 per cent. Half of a national sample interviewed in 1985 declared that they had not read a single book during the previous year. Only 30 per cent of the households reported having more than 30 books at home (GUS, 1987).

When analysing the change in the time spent on various leisure activities between 1976 and 1984, there emerges a trend towards a pattern that is highly reminiscent of that observed among the unemployed in the West. The leisure practices that have become more important are watching television, conversation, walking, reading newspapers, passive resting, listening to the radio and religious practice. Leisure patterns have thereby become more homogeneous and monotonous, with less scope for spontaneity, choice and innovation.

In the case of watching television , growth in the time spent on this activity accounted for over three-quarters of total growth in the use of free time. The shift in the use of time in Poland has been towards domination by television on an unprecedented scale. The time spent on mass media in Poland has risen from 120 minutes per day in 1965 to 122 in 1976, then up to 144 minutes by 1984, accounting respectively for 47.5, and then 53 per cent of total free time. In 1965 television accounted for just 58 per cent of time spent on the media but by 1984 the figure was 76 per cent (GUS, 1987a - all calculations are based on data from national time budget surveys). Out of the two state-owned channels only one is broadcast nation-wide (the second channel covers less than two-thirds of the country), which gives some idea of the homogenising effect of this most popular form of passing discretionary time. To this, one must add the rapid increase in video recorder ownership in Poland - from under 1 per cent in the mid 1980s to an estimated 25 per cent in 1991, which contributes to even more time spent in front of the television set (exact figures are difficult to establish as many video recorders have been brought into the country illegally).

The leisure activities most affected by the Polish economic crisis and its impact on the declining purchasing power of the household are holidays, travel abroad (as genuine tourists, as opposed to Polish *suitcase importers* and petty traders, posing as tourists for visa and customs officials) and the use of weekends. Poland's hotels and motels are oriented to foreign tourists, and their prices are prohibitive to Poles. Relatively inexpensive and subsidised accommodation in trade union holiday centres has declined by 50 per cent. A lack of financial resources is the reason most often given for not taking holidays. A simple two-week break at a holiday centre subsidised by a company or trade union for a family of four now costs the equivalent of four times the average monthly wage. (It used to cost a single months wages in the late 1970s.) Most blue-collar families, and other households in the low and medium-income brackets now send only their children on holiday. They use their own holiday time on home improvement, odd jobs and home-centred resting.

Increasingly passive, home-centred leisure should be set against the backdrop of a drastic deterioration in public health, especially for men. Between 1965 and 1985 the average life expectancy for a one year old child in Poland dropped from 69 to its 1950 level of 66.9 years, mainly due to a rapid rise in so-called 'civilisation diseases', such as coronary disease and cancer. However, Poland's abnormally high number of deaths due to injuries, accidents (including work accidents), and food poisoning points to low hygiene and safety in everyday life (GUS, 1986).

Another very crucial point in Poland is the acute problem of housing, which assumes an even more dramatic dimension when seen from the perspective of increasing home-based leisure. The basic type of housing provision in Poland used to be through state-subsidised cooperatives. Due to a variety of factors, the output of these cooperatives in the years 1981-1985, measured in cubic meters of living space, fell by one fifth. The standard waiting time for a flat for those who joined a housing co-operative was 29 years, practically a generation. The lucky ones who have waited through that period now see all of their earnings being eaten up by repayment of housing credits as state subsidies have now been largely removed from this area. In consequence, half of all young couples live with their parents in a typical flat with only 50 to 60 square meters of floor area. Three and even four generations living under one roof is common.

The Polish crisis has also coincided with a worsening ecological situation in the country. This is the consequence of the manner in which industrialisation was pursued under the command economy. In the 1960s one third of Poland's rivers and lakes were classed in the top group for water purity. By the 1980s the corresponding figure was 6.1 per cent. Forest area directly affected by air pollution has doubled (GUS, 1989). Other examples of this nature are plentiful. They all point to the gravity of Poland's social and economic problems and their detrimental effect on leisure. This demonstrates the complexity of future leisure policy and its linkage to the general course of economic and social reform which must be undertaken in Poland.

Perspectives on Leisure Policy under Solidarity rule

A new period in the country's post-war history was initiated when, in late 1989, Solidarity came into power. The country entered into a phase of political and economic transformation, which had important implications for leisure patterns and policy. The economic reforms introduced in Poland to bring it closer to a market economy follow the broad pattern of World Bank stabilisation and structural adjustment programmes inspired by monetarist economics. The liberalisation of prices and removal of state subsidies, coupled with strict wage controls, has led to a drop in consumer and investment demand. Living standards, already some 40 per cent lower than in the mid-1970s, plunged even further as purchasing power and savings eroded. A deep recession has set in, together with growing unemployment (for the first time in post-war history) and a rapidly rising crime rate.

Table 9.2 Use of leisure time in Poland (1984; in ascending order)

	Average time (hrs, min.)			% participating		
	Total	Men	Women	Total	Men	Women
Active cultural participation	0.00	0.00	0.00	0.1	0.2	0.1
Theatre, concert	0.00	0.01	0.00	0.3	0.4	0.3
Political, civic activities	0.01	0.02	0.01	1.0	1.5	0.6
Active sports participation	0.01	0.01	0.00	0.6	1.0	0.3
Cinema	0.02	0.02	0.01	1.4	1.7	1.2
Listening to music, playing music	0.02	0.03	0.01	2.8	4.0	1.9
Tourism	0.02	0.02	0.02	0.5	0.6	0.4
Hobbies	0.05	0.08	0.02	4.4	6.8	2.5
Radio	0.06	0.09	0.04	10.7	14.6	7.6
Conversation with others	0.07	0.07	0.07	13.2	13.4	13.1
Reading books	0.09	0.09	0.09	12.4	11.8	13.0
Religious practice	0.11	0.09	0.13	18.1	14.5	21.0
Walking	0.13	0.14	0.13	15.4	15.9	15.0
Conversation with family members	0.1	0.14	0.12	26.4	29.1	24.3
Reading newspapers and magazines	0.15	0.22	0.09	32.5	45.7	21.9
Passive resting	0.31	0.37	0.26	38.8	47.3	32.0
Social gatherings	0.37	0.39	0.36	24.1	23.8	24.3
Watching TV	1.48	2.07	1.15	80.3	84.6	76.8
Total free time	4.30	5.14	3.54	95.6	97.5	94.0

SOURCE: GUS, 1987a, pp. 138-149.

Political decisions sought to compensate for economic hardships of transition to a market economy. In the sphere of leisure, one important development was the abolition of censorship. The state also abandoned its monopolistic and centralised approach to leisure, encouraging pluralism and self-help. The normative visions of leisure patterns, characteristic of communist governments, ceased to be the object of concern of state policy.

In the initial two years of Solidarity rule, it was both state cultural policy and a natural reaction of the providers of culture to stress and even overplay national, patriotic and religious traditions suppressed by communism. Much coverage was given to the previously forbidden aspects of life. The two first years of post-communist Poland were thus marked by a rapid swing from a repressive to an extremely liberal state, in which political, cultural and religious organisations were expanding side by side with sex shops.

While it is difficult to comment on the perspectives of leisure policy in Poland after only two years of transition towards a new political and economic system, there are already some developments which cast a shadow over its future. For ideological and practical reasons, state policy is openly hostile to many elements of the welfare state and its practice of subsidising various social activities, such as leisure. In an attempt to curb inflation by maintaining an equilibrium in the state budget the government is seeking ways to cut its spending, especially since, under the impact of the recession, its revenue from state-owned enterprises (still producing some 80 per cent of manufacturing output) is falling drastically. The state outlay on culture, sport and recreation is not likely to maintain its current levels when money has to be found for unemployment benefit. While public provision of culture and recreation at the central level is likely to be seriously reduced, enterprises, which were the traditional providers at a local level, have in the meantime become too poor and/or disinterested in subsidising culture and recreation for their employees[12].

In a well-intentioned effort to end the preponderance of a centralised policy over a local one, a reform introduced wide scope for self-management at a local level. Many cultural, sports and recreational centres and institutions, which continue to be publicly-owned, have become local or 'communal' property. However, this reform provided wide local autonomy without providing for necessary funds to be generated at the local (commune) level. De-centralisation and local autonomy thus seem to be working to the disadvantage of leisure provision, since many of these institutions and centres have been shut down by local authorities, who are occasionally short of funds to keep schools and hospitals open.

Another set of problems seems to have been created by disillusionment among Polish intellectuals, who largely contributed to Solidarity's political triumph and who in exchange expected the new authorities to be more attentive to their own (and society's) cultural needs. Polish high culture, traditionally of very good quality throughout the 1960s and 1970s, has found itself given unprecedented artistic freedom, but little money and fewer consumers. Cultural preferences seem to have shifted to imports from the lower end of Western mass culture. Intellectuals were counting on financial concessions to stimulate artistic production, but the new authorities are more concerned with the economic ideology of the World Bank than aesthetic or intellectual considerations (Mirdzyrzecki, 1991)[13].

The immediate effects of economic reforms and of the 'laissez-faire' policy in most areas of social and economic life for Poles includes mass withdrawal from established patterns of holiday recreation and expansion of non-material (i.e. free) forms of leisure. After decades of egalitarianism in provision of culture and recreation, a phenomenon of a sharp polarisation of wealth has appeared for the first time on a wide scale. A sector of specialised petty private providers has emerged, which is highly successful in providing for leisure needs of the income elite - a new small entrepreneurial group of *nouveau-riche*. This elite is establishing its social position through ostentatious spending and luxury consumption, reminiscent of Veblen's description of the 'leisure class', and through its alternative set of status symbols (often consumer electronics, villas and cars). On the other hand, 'true' (i.e. capitalist, Western, as opposed to communist) work ethic is officially encouraged in order to improve living standards and stimulate the economy. A concern with economic survival, together with severe political and social problems in the transition period have resulted in reduced concern for leisure, even though shops full of imported leisure goods tempt the consumer with an unprecedented choice. These political and social problems include; youth as a 'lost generation'; high unemployment; the marginalisation of that part of society deprived of the extended social 'umbrella' of the communist state; and increased worries about the role of the Church, which is seen by some as seeking to exert unprecedented control over social life and ethics.

To further complicate any speculation on the future of leisure policy in Poland, the authorities also seem to be lacking a practical vision of how to handle the commercialisation and privatisation of leisure provision, which they regard as the ultimate solution for this sector. On the whole, Polish society is too poor to invest in the purchase of these facilities. Foreign investors have so far been very cautious about investing in Poland. Organisational changes, as exemplified by the recent creation of a central body, the Office of Physical Culture and Tourism (overseeing such widely different areas as commercial tourism and heavily subsidised professional sport, as well as amateur sport and social tourism) reflect an incoherent policy on recreation. This policy fails to make a distinction between commercial and profit-making forms of leisure and those which require special protection as part of social policy.

Invariably, in shifting from one extreme to another, much time will yet have to pass before the authorities realise that their trust in market mechanisms is excessive and that in the sphere of leisure, there is a state responsibility (with accompanying policy measures) for the quality and access to culture and recreation. So far, freedom of potential consumer choice and access to Western goods has had to be the only compensation for lack of a coherent leisure policy (Jung, 1990). It is thus likely that the foreseeable future will be characterised by a marked absence of state intervention in the leisure field.

REFERENCES

Czerwinski, M. (1972) *Przemiany obyczaju (Changing customs)*, Warszawa: PiW.

Czerwinski, M. (1974) *Ycie po miejsku (Urban lifestyle)*, Warszawa: PiW.

Czyzowska, M. (1975) *Spoleczny rozwój Polski (Social development of Poland)*, Warszawa: KiW.

Czyzowska, Z. (1990) *Polityka swiadczen socjalnych. Cele, zadania, realizacja (Policy of social benefits. Objectives and implementation)*, Warszawa: PWE.

Frank, M. (1978) *Planowanie spoleczne w przedsirbiorstwie (Social planning at the enterprise level)*, Warszawa: PWE.

GUS (Central Statistical Office) (1986) *Rocznik Statystyczny 1986 (Statistical Yearbook for Poland)*, Warszawa: GUS.

GUS (Central Statistical Office) (1989) *Rocznik Statystyczny 1989 (Statistical Yearbook for Poland)*, Warszawa: GUS.

Hadzelek, K. (1981) 'Sport jako czynnik tozsamosci narodowej' ('Sports as a factor of national identification'), in: Krawczyk, Z. (ed.), *Sport i kultura (Sport and culture)*, Warszawa: PWN.

Jasinska, A., Siemienska, R. (1978) *Wzory osobowe socjalizmu (Personality patterns under socialism)*, Warszawa: Wiedza Powszechna.

Jung, B. (1989) 'The impact of the crisis on leisure patterns in Poland', in: *Leisure Studies*, 9 (3).

Jung, B. (1990) 'More freedom, less leisure: the Case of Economic Reforms in Poland', in: *World Leisure and Recreation*, 14 (3).

Kloskowska, A. (1980) *Kultura masowa (Mass culture)*, Warszawa: PWN.

Kossak, J. (1977) *Podstawy polityki kulturalnej PZPR (Foundations of cultural policy of the Polish United Workers' Party)*, Warszawa: KiW.

Mirdzyrzecki, A. (1991) 'Dyktatura czy dialog?' ('Dictatorship or dialogue?'), in: *Gazeta Wyborcza*, March 18 (in Polish).

Rajkiewicz, A. (ed.) (1979) *Polityka spoleczna (Social policy)*, Warszawa: PWE.

Sicinski, A. (1977) 'Problemy przemiany w stylu zycia' ('Problems in transformation of lifestyles') in Szczepanski, J. and Besdid, L. (eds), *Badanie wzorow konsumpcji (Study of consumption patterns)*, Wroclaw-Warszawa-Krakow-Gdansk: Ossolineum.

Strak, M. (1988) *Kultura, polityka, gospodarka (Culture, politics and the economy)*, Warszawa: PWE.

Strzeminska, H. (1988) *Czas pracy i czas wolny w polityce spolecznej (Work time and free time in social policy)*, Warszawa: PWE.

Suchodolski, B. (1977) 'Problem celow i wartosci w zyciu spolecznym' ('The problem of objectives and values in social life'), in: Suchodolski, B. (ed.), *Kultura polska i socjalistyczny system wartosci (Polish culture and the socialist value system)*, Warszawa: KiW.

Szczepanski, J. (1977) 'Wartosci kulturowe, styl zycia i wzory konsumpcji' ('Cultural values, lifestyle and consumption patterns') in Suchodolski, B. (ed.), *Kultura polska i socjalistyczny system wartosci (Polish culture and the socialist value system)*, Warszawa: KiW.

Szczepanski, J. and Besdid, L. (eds) (1977) *Badanie wzorow konsumpcji (Study of consumption patterns)*, Wroclaw - Warszawa - Krakow - Gdansk: Ossolineum.

Szubert, W. (1973) *Studia z polityki spolecznej (Studies in social policy)*, Warszawa: PWE.

Wilson, J. (1988) *Politics and Leisure*, Boston: Unwin Hyman.

Wnuk-Lipinski, E. (1981) *Budzet czasu - Struktura spoleczna - Polityka spoleczna (Time budget - Social Structure - Social Policy)*, Wroclaw-Warszawa-Krakow-Gdansk: Ossolineum.

Statistical sources (GUS - Central Statistical Office, Warszawa)

GUS (1987) *Uczestnictwo w kulturze 1985 (Participation in Culture 1985)*.

GUS (1987a) 'Analiza budzetu czasu ludnosci Polski w latach 1976 i 1984' ('Time budget analysis of the Polish population in the years 1976 and 1984'), in *Studia i Prace* No.12.

GUS (1989) *Rocznik Statystyczny 1989 (Statistical Yearbook 1989)*.

NOTES TO CHAPTER 9

[1] In fact, 'leisure' as a word does not exist in the Polish language. When Veblen's *Theory of the Leisure Class* was published in Poland, the word 'leisure' was translated as 'idle'. The terms used are 'free time' or 'recreation' (*wypoczynek*), conceived broadly as all forms of rest.

[2] This is also true of the present course of reforms in Poland, where haste in moving from one extreme policy solution to another confirms the strong politicisation of this domain.

[3] For example, in late 1970s, the principles of the Polish United Workers (Communist) Party's cultural policy were still expressed in an orthodox Marxist rhetoric reminiscent of the Stalinist days some twenty years earlier (Kossak, 1977, pp. 83-85):

- recognition of the unbreakable links between politics, economy and culture, as well as the acceptance of the principle of unique leadership in the processes of social development. This leadership is provided by the Party, which acts as the *avant garde* of the proletariat;
- recognition of the crucial role played by education for revolution, and the basic role of education in the real democratisation of culture;
- recognition of the working class struggle for creation of new socialist culture, which would reflect their goals and aspirations;
- in creating its new culture, the working class does not turn its back on its national cultural heritage, but only appropriates it and reappraises it from the perspective of class interpretation of intellectual and artistic tradition;
- cultural activities of public agencies and social organisations cannot be limited to the creation of a market for culture, but should also stimulate the intellectual and cultural activity of the society;
- culture is an important domain of international co-operation; cultural exchange with other countries, which is an element of the country's foreign policy, helps to accelerate the process of integration of socialist countries and builds up support for countries combating imperialism.

[4] The actual issues which were examined included a variety of topics, ranging from those (labelled as 'challenging problems in the sphere of culture') dealing with the emergence of an educated and dominant middle class which could succumb to the trap of mass consumption lifestyles imported from the West, to the social consequences of the shortening of working hours, development of social infrastructure related to the growing use of free time, and spatial planning and development of areas from the point of view of their leisure and tourist functions.

[5] In the planning process in Poland, the competition for investment and subsidies was *de facto* open to various lobby groups. Those who had better access to real centres of power and policy makers were able to carry their projects through. In the post-war period, the most powerful lobby groups usually represented the interests of heavy industry, mining, defence and engineering. Under such a situation investment priorities were a measure of the real political power of the various interest groups. The sphere of culture, recreation and sport was thus usually given the lowest priority. However, due to its political role, the 'bargaining power' of the media was much stronger. The same was true of professional, competitive sports and some

elements of high culture, which were regarded as areas requiring special consideration due to their potential effect on the country's international prestige.

[6] The mechanism for generating these funds was through taxation. For instance, the Fund for Development of Culture was generated as a wage tax. In 1990 the Fund was scrapped and replaced with the National Foundation for Culture, voluntary contributions to which are tax deductible for individuals and enterprises.

[7] Source: *Statistical Yearbook for Poland* GUS, Warszawa, 1986, 1989 (in Polish).

[8] All figures based on data from *Statistical Yearbook for Poland*, GUS, Warszawa, 1989 (in Polish).

[9] The FWP was created in 1948 with the goal of making holidays away from home accessible to every working Polish family.

[10] This method is based on predominance of a political cycle in Polish cultural policy (Strak, 1988, pp. 171-72). Considering duration of work time alone, a different periodisation could be followed (Strzeminska, 1988, p. 67).

[11] At the time of writing, many aspects of the poor performance of the communist state previously carefully hidden from the public eye by state-controlled media, have received much coverage and public attention. These include factors such as drastic shortages of housing, the disasterous ecological and health situation of the country, its inflation and foreign debt, the impossibility of boosting production, breakdown in values, and the emigration of many young and educated Poles.

[12] Enterprises have become profit-making organisations, no longer interested in their social mission. While the core of the economy still consists of public enterprises, they are self-managing units, in which decisions on redistribution of net profits no longer have to take into account the social fund. In fact, the decisions are usually taken in favour of higher bonuses.

[13] Polish intellectuals describe the situation as an absence of dialogue between the financial and cultural lobbies in the government. The financial lobby clearly has the upper hand and can dominate any discussion.

Chapter 10

Leisure Policies in the Soviet Union[1]

Jim Riordan

The Geopolitical Background

Occupying a territory of 22,402,000 square kilometres (8,550,000 sq m), one sixth of the world's land surface, the USSR was by far the world's largest state, embracing half of Europe and a third of Asia, covering as many as eleven time zones, stretching a quarter way round the world, from the Gulf of Finland and the Black Sea in the west, to the Pacific Ocean in the Arctic, to the deserts of Central Asia and the Himalayan 'wall' thrusting four miles into the sky.

The ordinary citizen could ski and skate for almost six months of the year in the European part of the country (where the bulk of the population lives) without travelling more than half an hour from home, could gain a healthy suntan on beaches along the Black and Caspian seas, swim off the Baltic shores of Estonia, Latvia and Lithuania, hike almost to the ends of the earth in Siberia's taiga, fish in thousands of rivers and lakes, and experience cultures as diverse as the Islamic in Samarkand, Tashkent and Alma Ata, the ancient Armenian in the Caucasus, the Bhuddist Buryat on the shores of the world's largest lake, Baikal, in south-east Siberia, or the old Lutheran and Catholic cultures in the Baltic area.

What few ordinary citizens were able to do was to travel beyond Soviet borders for leisure-time activities. Leisure for the 291 million (1991) Soviet people meant, therefore, almost exclusively internal leisure-time activities, for which abundant opportunities existed, with limitations only dependent upon levels of health, free time, personal and public prosperity, urbanisation, state-provided facilities and security (e.g. hang-gliding was not permitted close to the Soviet frontier with one of the dozen states that are contiguous with the USSR).

Yet it has to be remembered that economically the USSR did provide stability and security for many of its citizens: no unemployment, no inflation for sixty years. The Soviet economy provided a base which enabled the USSR to pioneer space conquest, to provide the first artificial satellite, the first man and the first woman in space. By the 1980s the country had become the world's biggest producer of gas, oil and steel.

All this was no mean achievement for a nation whose revolution (like other socialist revolutions of the twentieth century) had taken place against a background of war devastation and capitalist failure, that had to contend with the heavy burden of socio-economic backwardness (80 per cent illiteracy, and overwhelmingly peasant population liberated from serfdom only 56 years before 1917) as well as military encirclement.

In political, social and economic terms, the USSR has undergone a metamorphosis: the Union (of Soviet Socialist Republics) has experienced rapid disintegration, the economies of the member states are in crisis, the polity is in tortuous transition from totalitarianism to democratic pluralism, and some of the republics have seemed to be on the brink of civil war. A major consequence of mass dissatisfaction with centralised control and the breakdown in supplies of basic goods and services was the resurgence of nationalism, and the rejection of the Centre and the Union. Ethnic tensions have resulted in frightening explosions of racial hatred, with thousands killed and over a million rendered homeless. Failure of the 20-24 August 1991 coup accelerated the demise of the old Federation and the progress to independence of several of the fifteen republics, particularly Latvia, Estonia, Lithuania, Georgia, Amernia, Azerbaidshan, the Ukraine, Moldavia and Belorussia. Thus, the former USSR has been reduced to the Russian heartlands.

The leadership became reconciled to accept what the country always was, despite its grandiose and messianic aspirations - one of the most advanced of the developing countries, in the 'second division' (the second fifty of world nations in terms of per capita GNP). The Soviet economy was therefore reasonably successful in building a basic industrial structure - the iron and steel plants, the coal mines, the hydro-electric stations, the railways, oil production and refining - i.e. the core of modern industrial and defence capacity. Such ventures lent themselves well to the central planning and administrative-command structure. Round about the mid-1950s, however, the old design began to founder; its leaders were unable to adjust it from quantity to quality, from production of things to production of ideas, from reacting to command to reacting to demand, to the consumer standards set by the more affluent West. Furthermore, the protracted Cold War imposed an increasingly stringent technological blockade and escalating military budget. The tasks of economic co-ordination became more complex as the economy advanced and the 'socialist camp' spread from Eastern Europe to Asia, Africa and the Caribbean. Access to Western technology was blocked and the earlier motivation was dimmed as cynicism and corruption set in under Brezhnev (who ousted Khrushchev in October 1964). By the time Gorbachov took over in April 1985, labour productivity was very low, waste of every sort high, and 'planning' mainly imposed a thoughtless incrementalism, with each plant seeking to increase its output of goods or services over the previous period. The economy simply had no mechanism for ensuring that resources were channelled to the most efficient and innovative enterprises. If the Soviet economic experience taught us anything, it was that economic innovation requires some form of competition and market regulator for responding to demand and ensuring efficiency.

It is against this background that we examine leisure policies and patterns of leisure that took shape in the final years of the Union's existence.

Post-war Trends in Leisure Patterns

So great was the change in all areas of Soviet society precipitated by perestroika and glasnost that it is necessary to divide any review of recent soviet history into two periods: before and after 1985 when Gorbachov took over and launched his twin policies of perestroika (restructuring and economy) and glasnost (openness).By the early 1990s, 'perestroika' seems to have signalled the disintegration of the Union and the onset of a painful attempted transition to a market economy.

Post-war Leisure Policies and Trends up to 1985

It was in the post-war period that a distinct pattern of leisure, similar to that in other modernising, urban-industrial societies, began to take shape in Soviet society. If the pre-war years had been marked by the industrialisation campaign, the forcible collectivisation of agriculture, terror and mass purges, the post-war years were, once the country had recovered from war, to see the fruits of the pre-war and wartime sacrifice and suffering.

However, it was not until the 1970s that, for the first time, the urban population exceeded the rural, that the state spent more on consumer than on producer goods, and that the standard five-day week was introduced for the bulk of industrial workers. The later post-war period also saw a fairly steady rise in public and personal prosperity, a marked growth in the range and quantity of consumer goods and a reduction in working time. All these factors, regardless of the nature of the polity, promote and predispose people to certain kinds of leisure-time activities which have, in turn, social and political consequences.

It was in this period that the government first elaborated an explicit leisure policy; indeed, it had first to produce and 'dust off' a word for 'leisure' itself, insofar as none had ever adequately fitted the bill, or actually been needed. In the 'time budget studies' that began to appear in the early 1960s, sociologists (then referred to as 'philosophers') started to use the term 'free time activities' and finally came to the hitherto unfamiliar word 'dosug' - meaning what one does in filling in time between work and sleep. Henceforth dosug was to designate 'leisure'. A new breed of social scientists was tutored to engage in 'problem solving' in relation to the new-found leisure time and activities, and to ensure that this time was spent in a constructive manner befitting a society building communism. It was hardly surprising that in a centralised command economy, edicts on leisure were made at the top of the Party hierarchy (as on all social matters), passed on to government agencies (the Soviets) and then passed down through the traditional chain of administrative command (see Figure 10.1). Most leisure policies were determined in the Committee on Physical Culture and Sport, in keeping with the 'cultural' role that leisure was intended to play.

Increasing prosperity

Figures published in the USSR indicate that both national income and consumption more than doubled in the two decades after 1960. Part of the increased personal income was undoubtedly being spent on recreation, on the pursuit of a growing variety of activities, particularly outdoor ones, and on personal durables such as skis, skates, tennis and badminton rackets, fishing tackle, tents and, to a lesser extent, on motor cycles, canoes, dinghies, yachts and cars. Higher national income also resulted in more substantial government allocation to leisure amenities and the development of a number of activities that presuppose a certain level of industrial development and economic surplus; for example, motor racing and rallying, yachting, karting, and various winter sports.

Increasing free time

The relationship of work and leisure also altered radically during the two decades from 1960 to 1980. In 1956, the standard (six-day) week in Soviet industry was of 46 hours; by 1961, it had declined to 41 hours, most workers having five seven hour days and one six hour day each week. In 1980, the average working week in industry was 40.7 hours and, in state employment in general, 39.4 hours in a five day week. Altogether, Soviet industrial manual workers had 95.4 days off during 1980, including annual paid holidays of 15 days for most workers.[2] Not merely had there been an increase in the amount of leisure time, but the reduction in the workday resulted in workers spending less time than previously in such institutional settings as factory and office. There was thus a shift in the expenditure of time from the public realm, which includes work, to the private.

The breakthrough which signalled the greatest revolution in the pattern of recreation, just as in other industrial societies, was the introduction of the long weekend. As a result of the government resolution in March 1967, for the first time in Soviet history the majority of industrial workers had their weekends free. Holidays with pay and long weekends enabled men and women to pursue leisure activities which cannot be enjoyed in an evening or even in a half-day's holiday. It is this pattern of leisure which made possible in Western Europe and North America the great growth in recreation which takes place far from the city streets and office blocks. A similar trend was taking place in the USSR from the late 1960s, a minor instance of convergence of the two systems. The boom in camping, fishing and hunting and, to a lesser extent, in rock-climbing, pot-holing, water-skiing, motoring and boating was partly accounted for by longer holidays with pay and partly by the developing cult of the weekend.

Increasing urbanisation

By the early 1980s well over half of the Soviet population lived in a relatively modern, urban industrial society, a human condition which, in itself, regardless of political values and policies, predisposes people to certain kinds of leisure activities. Whereas only 18 percent of the Soviet population lived in towns in 1926, 50 percent in the mid-1960s, as many as 64 per cent were urban-based by 1980.[3] At the same time as people migrated into the towns, the government followed a policy of high-density building in multi-storey blocks of flats. Despite the fact that town planning tends to allow for sizeable courtyard facilities for each block of flats, the problem of providing adequate outdoor amenities for leisure was becoming increasingly difficult in the most densely settled urban areas.

Facilities and opportunities, and their limitations, determine to a great degree not only what Soviet citizens actually do with their leisure, but also their aspirations. In developed Western countries, for example, the motor car had a considerable impact on the way families spend their leisure time. How great an impact the motor car would have on Soviet leisure patterns was already being forecast by some Soviet sociologists in the early 1970s :

> like the television set, the appearance of the family motor car
> will stimulate the emergence and development of a whole
> number of activities, will lead to a change of a whole number
> of activities, will lead to a change in habits and traditions and,
> ultimately, will transform the psychology of millions of
> people. When the car becomes part of everyday life, it is no
> longer simply a 'means of transport', it becomes a means of
> transforming everyday life, a weapon in the domestic
> revolution.
> (Gordon and Klopov, 1972, p. 275)

By 1985 the Soviet Union had some 15 million passenger cars - i.e. approximately one for every five families, still a long way short of all Western industrial states.[4]

Rising personal prosperity, an increasing amount of free time, particularly the long weekend, and the pressures of an urban-industrial environment, therefore, were bound to have implications for leisure. People were tending to form smaller groups for recreation and holidays, going on family rather than individual subsidised ticket (*putyovka*) trips. There was an increasing desire to 'get away from it all' rather than to 'get together'.

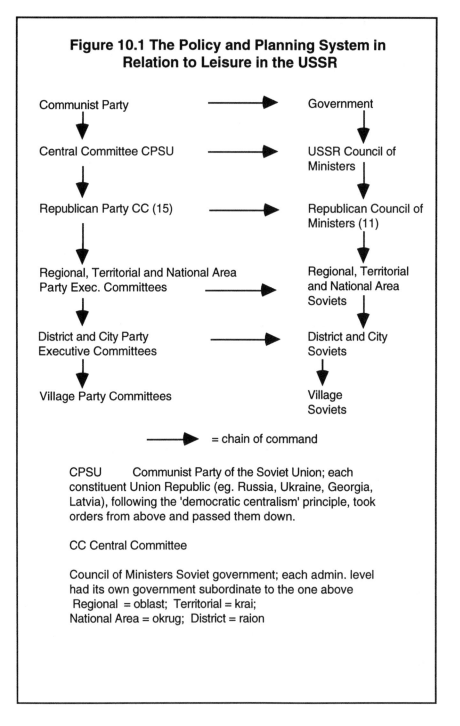

Figure 10.1 The Policy and Planning System in Relation to Leisure in the USSR

Communist Party ⟶ Government

Central Committee CPSU ⟶ USSR Council of Ministers

Republican Party CC (15) ⟶ Republican Council of Ministers (11)

Regional, Territorial and National Area Party Exec. Committees ⟶ Regional, Territorial and National Area Soviets

District and City Party Executive Committees ⟶ District and City Soviets

Village Party Committees — Village Soviets

⟶ = chain of command

CPSU   Communist Party of the Soviet Union; each constituent Union Republic (eg. Russia, Ukraine, Georgia, Latvia), following the 'democratic centralism' principle, took orders from above and passed them down.

CC Central Committee

Council of Ministers Soviet government; each admin. level had its own government subordinate to the one above
 Regional = oblast; Territorial = krai;
National Area = okrug; District = raion

On the whole, the leadership had tried to see to it that the facilities available to the population at large inclined them toward some form of public, collective recreation, mainly through the trade union club, the workplace, public park or play centre behind a block of flats. When workers gained the long weekend away from work, those production-based facilities no longer suited them because they were

> ill adapted to family forms of free-time activity or to the active
> leisure activities of a small group linked by personal and
> friendly rather than formal relations.
> (Gordon and Rimashevskaya, 1972, p. 115)

There was, therefore, a trend away from 'public and mass' leisure activities towards 'individual, domestic, family and passive leisure', especially watching television. 'Televiewing' actually became the single most important time-consuming leisure activity during the late 1960s :

> the amount of time spent in watching television in an urban
> worker's family exceeds the combined time spent on reading
> and visiting places of public entertainment and comprises a
> third of all time spent on culture outside work.
> (Gordon and Rimashevskaya, 1972, pp. 160-161)

It was felt officially that the social controls within the working *collective* were more effective than those embodied in formal institutions, and that conformity to social norms could therefore more readily be exacted through the collective. Collectivised leisure activities were seen as discouraging excessive individualism, introspection leading to doubt, and the development of tastes for privacy that might impinge upon loyalties toward the collective. That was considered particularly important in regard to young people. To the extent that, in all societies, the young are more concerned with active leisure activities than adults, the authorities were interested in using and guiding their leisure time, especially in view of the rebellious, deviant and anomic tendencies observable among some Soviet youth.

Another aim of the authorities was to see that free time generally was used in a *rational* way, that leisure should be socially functional. The prevailing functionalised conception of leisure stressed not so much the needs of the individual as those of society. Well-spent time on leisure activities was held to be important because of the contribution it made to production and the smooth functioning of society in general. It should enrich the individual so that he or she could enrich society. Only under socialism, it was argued, could that be possible.

Nonetheless, a number of pursuits existed which were clearly at odds with notions of 'rationality'. These included horse racing (as a spectator sport for gamblers), dominoes, lotto (bingo) and many card games. The position of dominoes particularly illustrates the ambivalent status that such games held. Some said,

> dominoes is a serious game, interesting, useful, intellectual. It
> has 'won its spurs' among such games as chess and draughts ....

Others maintain that the domino cult deals a blow at real mass
physical-culture work ... it is a notoriously irrational game and
not to be encouraged.
(*Sovetsky Sport*, 12 May 1971, p. 2)

Some Soviet sociologists seemed to believe that apparently wasteful
and irrational games such as cards and dominoes were an important part
of urban life, and that official sanctions would not, anyway, stop people
from playing them :

before campaigning against such non-sporting games, people
ought to realise that neither the cinema, books nor even
television can 'defeat' dominoes, because they all fulfil
different leisure functions.
(Gordon and Klopov, 1972, p. 2)

The authors do not specify these functions, but one may assume them
to include compensations for the lack of outlet for such motivations as
love of chance, successes and speculation, and a response to the needs of
the 'less cultured'. That such pursuits were tolerated is an indication that
the authorities were willing to compromise with the strong personal
desires of sections of the public on such matters, perhaps in order to gain
compliance, or at least lack of active resistance in other, more important
spheres.

On the whole, however, the leadership appeared to believe that
leisure was properly spent only when it was 'rationally' used. An official
spokesman put it thus :

The decisions of the 24th Party Congress oblige us to intensify
our concern over further improvements in the regime of work
and rest, over the rational use of free time and for people's all-
round mental and physical development. For most Soviet
people, free time is already filled with a rich content. It is
time used for active and multifarious social activities, political,
educational and professional studies, the tireless perfection of
specialised knowledge needed in highly productive labour,
active involvement in physical culture and sport. Philistine
notions of leisure as an idle, pointless pastime are alien to a
politically conscious Soviet person. The spending of free
hours in an empty way that is even harmful to one's health and
intellect contradicts the whole spirit of our society and can
cause serious harm to the person concerned. We cannot be
indifferent to that facet of people's lives, which some people
are still inclined to regard as purely personal.
(Teoriya i praktika fizicheskoi kultury, 1971, no. 7, p. 2)

It was the all-pervasive state 'control' over people's private lives, as
laid out in the prescriptions above, that was a contributory factor to the
revolt against the state and its institutions during the perestroika years.

Despite the tolerance of certain activities mentioned above (like
cards and dominoes, horse racing and bingo), others were attacked

because of their alleged 'irrationality' or exhibitionist nature or for the fact that they lend themselves to commercial exploitation. Such activities included women's soccer and women's wrestling. One can understand the official disquiet at such spectacles being arranged for male voyeuristic enjoyment, given the ideological disapproval of hedonistic sex and displays of public sexuality. Both women's soccer and women's wrestling were condemned because

> they aroused unhealthy excitement among male spectators ...
> and are harmful to a woman's organism in that they can cause
> harm to sexual functions, they can cause varicose veins,
> thrombo-phlebitis, etc.
> *(Teoriya i praktika fizicheskoi kultury*, 1973, no. 10, p. 62)

Another such doubtful activity was male body building; it had been particularly difficult to keep male body-building within state-desired limits. With an eye to the 'excesses' existing in the West, the authorities feared that it would become an excuse for exhibitionism and narcissism :

> egotistical love and dandified culture of the body and one-
> sided, unhealthy development of the organism are alien to the
> Soviet system of physical culture.
> *(Sovetsky Sport*, 25 January 1972, p. 3)

Other uncertain pursuits included hatha yoga, karate and bridge, all of which are condemned in a resolution passed in January 1973. Oriental pursuits such as yoga and karate were attacked because of their association with a philosophy regarded as alien to that of Soviet Society :

> yoga does not involve teamwork; it encourages individualism
> and advocates that its proponents should lead a closed, ascetic
> life outside society and even of the family .... It is based on
> idealist philosophy and mysticism.
> *(Sovetsky Sport*, 25th January 1972, p. 3)

Card games were regularly condemned throughout Soviet history as empty, time-wasting activities often associated with gambling and luck, so it was no surprise to see bridge condemned in 1973 as a 'perversion' of well-spent leisure activities. No official reasons were given, but one may assume that the game was regarded as a potential menace to productivity (people were supposed to go to bed early - hence the reasons for the closing of all cafes and restaurants by 10.30 p.m.), as an 'irrational' use of free time and as a game based on chance. All of these activities (bridge, yoga, body building, etc.) gained a hold, it is interesting to observe,

> because of the convenience, acquiescence and unprincipled
> position of certain administrators - instead of determined and
> daily work in ... organising the free time of workers, they
> became involved in charlatanism and roguery, helping to
> implant and popularise all number of 'fashionable' activities
> designed to excite the public and to encourage a spirit of profit
> that is detrimental to the health of participants and Soviet

society.
(Teoriya i praktika fizicheskoi kultury, 1973, no. 10, pp. 63-64)

The emphasis on the special interdependence of work and leisure stems from the paramount importance attributed to work in a Marxist-governed society and from the claim that it had acquired a uniquely satisfactory character owing to the lack of exploitation and alienation. Yet, as with other media of recreation and leisure - e.g. television and cinema - the official descriptions must be understood as arising largely from a desire to educate the public in the broad sense of the term and to prevent wasteful dissipation of energy and time, and not merely as logical extensions of the desire to control. By contrast with the view held by some Western intellectuals that television was the new opiate of the masses and by the masses themselves that television was merely a means of entertainment, Soviet television was considered not as a waste of time but as a centrally-controlled medium of education and propaganda.

The State and Leisure

In the pre-perestroika period, to sum up, the Soviet leaders appeared to opt for the following policies.

a) the organisation of the public in their leisure time to the maximum possible extent within the framework of a tidy hierarchical and functional structure;

b) the cultivation of competitive activities, as in sport (a leisure-time analogue of the competition between people at work designed to raise work performance) with again, as at work, material rewards for victors, the more effectively to improve people's readiness for work and to pre-train soldiers for the Soviet nation state;

c) using leisure, specifically, as a means of obtaining the fit, obedient, disciplined workforce needed for achieving economic and military strength and efficiency, in particular, in order to

- raise physical and social health standards, the latter meaning not simply educating people in the virtues of bodily hygiene, regular exercise and sound nutrition, but also combating unhealthy, deviant, anti-social (and therefore anti-Soviet) behaviour: drunkenness, delinquency, prostitution, drug-taking, even religiosity and intellectual dissidence;

- develop general physical dexterity, motor skills and other physical qualities useful in 'labour and defence';

- socialise the population into the new establishment system of values. Character training, advanced (so the Soviet leaders seemed to believe) by 'rational' leisure activities in such values as loyalty, conformity, team spirit, co-operation and discipline may well have encouraged compliance and co-operation in both work and politics, including the development of an uncynical attitude towards political leaders;

- encourage a population, in rapid transition from a rural to an urban way of life, to identify with wider communities: all-embracing social units such as the workplace, the neighbourhood, the town, district, region, republic and, ultimately, the entire country. By associating leisure activities or organisations with the workplace, the Party leadership and its agencies were better able to supervise, control and 'rationalise' the leisure-time activities of the public.

Despite the form into which leisure activities was cast, workers and peasants were still able to derive satisfaction from it (both that of simple fun and games and, for some, the derivative benefits of a competitive system). Leisure is one of the areas in which the systemic exigencies of official society confront the psycho-social imperatives generated by the conditions of life in industrial society. The results of that continuing confrontation increasingly came into sharper relief in the early 1980s and eventually caused a radical change in society's pattern of leisure.

Post-1985 Leisure Policies and Trends

During the early 1980s, radical changes began to appear in leisure trends and policies, thereby breaking the mould of the functionalised and bureaucratic (plan-fulfilment) structure. Until then not only had the state-controlled, utilitarian system hampered a true appraisal of realities that lay beneath the universal statistics and idealised veneer ('the worlds No 1 book-reading nation', 'a third of the population take part in the quadrennial Spartakiad', it had prevented concessions to particular groups in the population - the we know whats good for you syndrome by which men tell women what leisure activities they should and should not pursue; the fit tell the disabled that active leisure activities are not for them; the old tell the young they can only engage in leisure on their (old) terms, in their clubs, using their facilities.

In a way, the changes illustrate the diminishing ability of bureaucrats to enforce the Stalinist norms established at the end of the 1920s, when the Soviet Union embarked on its rapid industrialisation (and political 'straightjacket') programme. The following are some of the major changes brought about in the wake of the perestroika and glasnost policies.

Recreation for all

The Soviet leadership had always maintained in public that mass participation in leisure-time activities took precedence over professional application, and down the years it had produced regiments of statistics to prove the case: that millions were regular, active participants in all forms of recreation, that the vast majority of school and college students (as well as national servicemen) gained the Prepared for Work and Defence badge (originally based on the Scout proficiency badges), that rising millions (as much as a third of the population!) were taking part in the spartakiads, and that the bulk of workers did their daily dozen - 'production gymnastics' - at the workplace.

We now learn in this 'honesty's the best policy' era that these figures were fraudulent, and a show to impress people above and below and to meet present targets (each school, region, factory and farm received a recreation/fitness quota and incurred penalties and criticism if they fell short). It is now admitted that only 8 per cent of men and 2 per cent of women engage in recreational activities regularly (Dmitrieva, 1985).

It is further revealed that when put to the test only 41 out of 700 Moscow schoolchildren could meet the Prepared for Work and Defence (PWD) requirements (Kondratieva, 1986). Although swimming is an obligatory element in the PWD programme, it turned out that only 11 per cent of schoolchildren can swim and fewer than 5 per cent pass the PWD swimming norms (Belits-Gelman, 1987).

For most people many leisure activities remained out of reach. Even by the late 1980s, some two-thirds of workers were not members of any leisure organisation and it was recognised that 'their physical fitness [made] only a tiny contribution to raising productivity, reducing the sickness rate and resolving social and economic problems' (yet engaging in recreation had been said officially to promote these very functional ends) (Kondratieva, 1986).

After 1986 the spartakiads passed off in a low-key manner with no participation figures released for the first time since the Games were held. The 1991 Spartakiad had several sports cancelled (basketball, handball, water polo, women's volleyball) owing to lack of state cash, and the number of participants and the time schedule of the Games were drastically cut back 'owing to the new self-financing status of the State Sports Committee' and the country's dire economic situation[5].

Individual payment for leisure activities

Prior to 1985 most leisure activities were engaged in free of charge through trade-union subsidised clubs; after 1985 many clubs introduced charges for use of club premises, swimming pool, gymnasium, court and stadium. The state, including the various semi-autonomous governments in the republics, began to seek cost recovery from leisure facilities, removing all subsidies. Previously, for example, 'the cost of a holiday was purely symbolic; it was completely covered by subsidies'. Previously, half the average cost of a trade union holiday of 160 roubles, was paid by state subsidy, the rest by the person's trade union (the real cost being in the region of 350 rubles). By 1991 the cost of a trade union holiday had increased by more than four-fold, from 160 to 656 rubles (Voblikov, 1991). Another problem was that a number of republics had taken control of sanatoria, rest homes and leisure centres recently run from the centre, yet they had no money for their upkeep. This was the case in Georgia, one of the favourite Soviet holiday locations, especially on the Black Sea. The Soviet government also cut the budget of the USSR Sports Committee by some 900 million rubles to 2,000 million in 1991 (*Soviet Weekly*, 11 July 1991, p. 16).

Further, with official permission granted in 1987 for co-operative ventures to start up, a number of co-operative health, fitness and sports clubs began to appear. In Leningrad, for example, the Juventus Health and Sports Club came into existence in early 1988, with activities ranging from Aikido wrestling, skateboarding and break-dancing to tennis, swimming and weight-watching exercises. A month's membership cost about ten rubles (roughly one twentieth of the average monthly salary). The Club had a regular membership of 600 within months of opening, and had another 800 on its waiting list (*Soviet Weekly*, 7 May 1988). Down in the Caucasus, the former tennis champion Alex Metreveli opened a string of tennis clubs along the Black Seas coast and in the Georgian capital Tbilisi (*Soviet Weekly*, 18 June 1988).

A major change came over the trade union recreational clubs: in mid-1987 the eight leading trade union recreation societies amalgamated to form a single recreation organisation in an attempt to improve facilities and service to the public as well as to 'democratise the work of the recreation clubs'. They also declared their intention of diverting more funds to sport for all and to cater for a diversity of interest groups and health clubs (Balashov, 1988).

Independent youth clubs

Until recently, the Young Communist League or Komsomol had no official rival among youth organisations since all rivals were banned in the early 1920s; and since it controlled state facilities for youth activities - the media, club premises, theatres, sports amenities - it was only possible for young people to engage in non-approved activities by setting up an unlawful club and meeting clandestinely. That was precisely what had been happening on a wide scale since the mid-1970s. It was in an attempt to control this situation, which was rapidly getting out of hand, and bring young people back into the fold, that in early 1986 the Komsomol set up 'youth leisure departments' whose job it was to supervise all the 'informal groupings and associations'. When that did not work it approved a statute on 'Amateur associations and hobby clubs' in May 1986 which made non-Komsomol clubs legal as long as they had official sponsorship and premises. In practice they could become legal if they registered with the Komsomol which would then sponsor them and provide premises (Vasiliev and Rogozhnikov, 1987).

The glasnost policy revealed widespread disaffection by young people from Komsomol-led activities. Komsomol membership has plummeted from a peak of 40 million young people (between 14 and 28) in the early 1980s to 23 million in 1990 and 15 million in 1991. In September 1991, the Komsomol called it a day and, like several branches of its parent body, the CPSU, it disbanded itself. Some young people, freed from the social pressures of the Komsomol, began to seek an outlet for their energies in juvenile delinquency, drug taking and prostitution. Some are committing suicide as the old value system crumbles. Other are seeking enterprise and opportunity in co-operative business. Yet others, often 'politically active' young people, find no outlet for their political enthusiasm in an unreceptive and thoroughly-discredited Komsomol, and are forming or reforming youth associations like the Scouts, Young Anarchists and Democratic Socialists.

In the field of recreation, the youth clubs range from soccer fan clubs to groups for activities for which the government has been slow to provide facilities: aerobics, yoga, body building, jogging, karate and other combat sports. One of the first independent groups were soccer fans in the late 1970s and early 1980s, especially of Moscow Spartak, with their own distinctive red-and-white home-knitted scarves and hats. They were followed by combat sports clubs for both defence and offence in the spreading of street and soccer gang clashes.

The forced acceptance of such independent clubs is a radical departure for the Soviet authorities; after all, no groups free of Party tutelage had been tolerated from the 1920s up to 1986. Perhaps the current leadership is mindful of Trotsky's warning after the 1917 Revolution that 'The longing for amusement, distraction, recreation and fun is the most legitimate desire of human nature ... We must make sure this longing is given full reign and freed from the guardianship of the pedagogue and the tiresome habit of moralising.' (Trotsky, 1973, p. 32).

Women and leisure

Up and down the USSR women have long ignored the pontification of male leaders about their participation in 'harmful' leisure activities - body building, soccer, ice hockey, judo, weightlifting, water polo and long distance running. Within the space of a few years, however, Soviet women had held five national judo championships and hosted a world judo championship, and as many as 15,000 women were registered in judo clubs by the late 1980s (Merkulov, 1990). The first national soccer championship was held in August 1987 (eight teams took part in the first year, 20 in 1988, 50 from virtually all over the country in 1989 and well over a 100 in 1990) (Davletshina, 1991).

Moscow University formed its first women's water polo team back in 1982; the women's sport has now spread to several other cities and the Soviet women's team played its first international fixture in 1987 (Tsirlin, 1986). Weightlifting and body building developed apace: the first women's body building championships were held in 1988, and women have been members of body building clubs in the Baltic republics at least since 1986 (*Sobesednik,* 1988, no. 18, p. 6). Women's ice hockey reappeared for the first time since the 1920s, and women are doing the marathon, pole vault, triple jump and hammer throwing (Merkulov, 1990).

These changes came about thanks to a few women who were prepared to defy official sanction, ridicule and even persecution in order to establish their right to pursue the leisure activity of their choice. But profit and market are also strong motivators. Hence the first-ever women's boxing championships, held behind closed doors in Moscow in March 1990, followed by open championships in Moscow's Luzhniki sports complex watched by several thousand spectators in June 1991 (the winner earning 1,500 rubles) (Lomakov, 1991).

Leisure and the disabled

Another disadvantaged group to benefit from the wind of change was the physically and mentally handicapped, long neglected by the Soviet establishment.

> for a long time we pretended the problem did not exist. We thought: the state looks after the handicapped, social security provided living and working conditions for them. What else do they want?
> (Ponomareva, 1987)

In sport, for example, before 1988 the USSR had never held domestic championships at any level for any category of handicapped person. Two years after China had staged its first nation-wide games for the handicapped and in the year of the Seoul Paralympics, the newly-formed Disabled Sports Federation held its inaugural championship. This was the culmination of long years of campaigning by pressure groups, recently joined by the many thousands of maimed young ex-Afghanistan veterans. After a number of complaints that 'sport for the disabled has been developing around the world with virtually no participation from the Soviet Union', a team of thirteen blind athletes was sent to the Paralympics for the first time, at Seoul in 1988. Unlike its able-bodied compatriots in the Olympic Games, this team won no medals at all, but at least a start had been made.

Convergence

Yet another consequence of the 'new thinking' seemed to be the bringing closer of some facets of Soviet leisure activities to those in the West. For a start, commercial sports (in a professional, commodity sense) like golf, baseball, Grand Prix motor racing, Rugby League, even American football, arrived in the USSR. Moscow had its first golf course (nine holes) in 1988, partly designed for the foreign diplomatic corps and partly intended to prepare Soviet challengers for international golf tournaments (60 teenagers were registered at the club's golf school). A second golf course was being planned (in 1990) at Nakhabino, some 30 km from Moscow. With an eye to the inclusion of baseball in the Olympic Games, the authorities 'created' Soviet baseball clubs (just as they 'created' field hockey teams, by fiat, in the early 1970s expressly for Olympic participation - again without any grassroots tradition). The first baseball league came into being in 1988, a year after the first national championship. By 1989 there were thirty baseball clubs in the country and a special children's baseball school in Tashkent (Bezruchenko, 1990).

Following the holding of the first Grand Prix Formula 1 race in a then communist country, in 1988, the USSR embarked on the designing of a world class track and *Pravda* has called for the promotion of Soviet motor racing up to world standards[6]. A number of American football teams sprang up all over the Soviet Union, some of which played in Japan, France, Taiwan and the USA. In the case of the Moscow Bruins, much of their activity is said to be connected with the Soviet Mafia (Radyshevsky, 1990).

We have already mentioned that, largely as a concession to the public, horse racing in all forms (trotting, hurdling, steeplechase and racing on the flat - with betting on the state 'tote') has existed for most of the Soviet period, although 'no mention of it had been made in the press, simply because it was not accepted practice'; nor had it ever featured on television, despite the country's 3,000 racehorses and seventeen annual race meetings' (Dan, 1988). However, in 1987, the first dog (borzoi) races were held in Soviet times (they were very popular prior to 1917) - the first dog racing taking place at Moscow's Hippodrome Racecourse.

Other 'imports' and the resurfacing of old sports include snooker, darts, billiards the Chinese sport of wushu (martial arts; 52 cities are said to have wushu clubs with over 30,000 members) and body building. The first international body building contest, watched by 16,000 spectators, was held in Moscow in late 1988, jointly sponsored by West Germany's Armstrong Company and the USSR Sports Service. Soviet body builders, men and women, made their international debut at the world championships in the spring of 1989 (*Molodoi kommunist*, 1988, No. 4, p. 63).

Sponsorship, both foreign and domestic, became a common feature in a range of recreational activities, with soccer teams sporting the Dorna or the Ocrim Spa logo since the 1987/88 season, and, in the later 1980s, open professional sport was accepted. In soccer, cycling and basketball Soviet clubs and players have signed contracts with overseas firms and teams, and Soviet boxers and wrestlers are now permitted to join the professional ranks. In 1989 the USSR Boxing Federation signed a contract with North American promoters to take twenty four Soviet boxers to North America; similarly, eight heavyweight wrestlers were to perform in Japanese professional rings. It was even planned to stage bullfighting in Moscow's Lenin Stadium, with over thirty pedigree bulls being brought from Madrid for the spectacle during 1990. However, public protest successfully averted the blood-letting and forced the organisers (the Young Communist League) to cancel the show (*Soviet Weekly*, 6 June 1990).

Not everyone was happy about the convergence of Western commercial leisure-time activities and Soviet recreation. Nor were they happy at what was seen as a race for irrational glory in sport, the cultivation of irrational loyalties, the unreasonable prominence give to the winning of victories, the setting of records and the collection of trophies - a fetishisation in sport. In fact, this was a feature of popular antipathy to the pre-Gorbachov 'stagnation' period, with its tub-thumping, flag-waving obsession with international sporting success. A political commentator in the weekly *Moscow News* suggested the Soviet press should publish two tables: alongside that of Soviet Olympic medals should be a table showing the per capita provision of recreational amenities for each nation. If that were done, 'we would be in a very different position'. He cited the example of artificial skating rinks: Canada had 10,000, the USA 1,500, Sweden 343 and the USSR just 102 (Druzenko, 1988). The swimmer Salnikov contrasted the US total of a million swimming pools with the paltry Soviet figure of 2,500 (Salnikov, 1989). This was an indication of the relative paucity of recreational facilities available to the population at large, which sporting victories in the full gleam of world attention had done much to obscure.

Tourism

Although the Stage Agency Intourist was established in 1929 as an international tourist office, the traffic it had to deal with was almost entirely one way (into the USSR). As the Soviet Union entered a more liberal period after the death of Stalin in 1953 and the pursuing of a foreign policy of detente ('a peaceful coexistence between countries with different political systems') under Nikita Khrushchov after 1956, foreign tourism began to expand quite dramatically, even though travel outwards was confined largely to Eastern Europe. There was a four-fold increase in the number of Soviet citizens going abroad, rising from about half a million in 1956 to more than two million in 1974. The proportion travelling to the socialist states of Eastern Europe varied from 80 per cent in 1956 to 55 per cent in 1965 and 60 per cent in 1974. In the same period the number of foreign tourists entering the USSR rose from a million to two million in 1970, and to 3.7 million in 1975[7]. However, Soviet statisticians were coy about giving data on 'Soviet tourists' for, whereas they refer to foreigners holidaying in the USSR as 'tourists', they refer only to 'Soviet citizens (not tourists) travelling abroad' - the latter group including all Soviet people crossing the frontier, from Gorbachov on his way to a Summit, to an uncle visiting his niece in England. A more accurate assessment may be gleaned from the fact that Intourist (through which almost all Soviet holidaymakers abroad had to arrange their trips) arranged for fewer than 600,000 Soviet citizens to travel abroad in 1987, a tiny fraction of the 150 million Soviet tourists of that year (Konovalov, 1988).

In the perestroika period, pressure on the authorities to permit free foreign travel grew considerably and a 'free exit' policy was to be introduced in early 1992. It also led Intourist to introduce the open selling of 'tours' to some countries from 1 January 1988. Similarly, the youth tourist agency *Sputnik*, set up in 1958 and mainly concerned with incoming 'friendly' youth 'delegations', was urged to go beyond awarding its few foreign travel passes as a dividend of political rank (to high Komsomol officials) and 'as bonuses to those who excel in socialist production' (Andreyev, 1980). Sputnik introduced a scheme of individual tourism in 1989 (to what was then socialist states only); but each trip had to be sanctioned by one's employer, required a visa and cost between 400 and 600 rubles - no mean sum for students on a monthly grant of 45 rubles, or young workers receiving an average monthly industrial wage of 130 rubles. The greatest barrier to foreign travel by the beginning of the 1990s, was not political but economic: the state had no foreign currency to give travellers.

Conclusions

In the last two and a half decades Soviet society moved from the six- to the five-day week and entered a phase of relative leisure and prosperity (until recent times). This gave some people new diversions, new aspirations, new technology, new forms of emotional investment that conflicted with the old single-minded focus upon self-sacrifice and future orientation. The proud boast that the USSR led the world in volume of reading, for example, ignored the fact that this was largely due to the paucity of other leisure-time facilities. With brighter television and the video revolution - with the exception of the new, brighter and more liberal periodicals, reading was to decline.

Very often the new aspirations outstripped what the authorities had been able or prepared to make available in the way of leisure amenities, and this has resulted in a certain amount of frustration and bitterness, and an exaggerated perception of what was available in Western cultures.

Whatever the ramifications of recent political changes for various sections of the public, and whatever the future of post-Soviet society, there is no mistaking the significance of the changes in leisure which took place over the last two decades of the Union, with the dismantling of previously well-entrenched institutions and values. Individuals had increasing free time, an ever-wider range of amenities and equipment to pursue leisure activities of their choice, particularly in a non-institutional setting. How an individual spends his or her leisure time had become less ruled by the official utilitarian-instrumental approach, and more governed by the notion that adoption of an activity, for its own sake, should be the concern of the individual. However, the political uncertainty and economic difficulties which have pervaded the dramatic evolution of Arrangements in the former member republics, make it difficult to predict the future. For some, those with greater political stability and greater economic resources, the move to economic liberalism may be less painful. For others, it will be traumatic, if indeed it is accomplished at all. In such circumstances, leisure is likely to be relatively insignificant when compared with the more fundamental interests affected by such changes.

REFERENCES

Andreyev, A. (ed.) (1980) *The Komsomol: Questions and Answers* Moscow: Progress Publishers.

Balashov, V. (1988) 'Proizvodstvennaya gimnastika i proizvoditelnost', *Sport v SSSR*, No. 7.

Belits-Gelman, S. (1987) 'Lipa ne tonet', *Ogonyok*, 1987, No. 4, p. 27.

Bezruchenko, A. (1990) 'Soviet baseball moves on from first base', *Soviet Weekly*, 30 April [8].

Dan, O. (1988) 'They're off', *Soviet Weekly*, 30th April , p. 14.

Davletshina, R. (1991) 'Futbol i zhenshchiny', *Sobesednik*, No. 44.

Dmitrieva, O. (1985) 'Bokal protiv detstvu', *Komsomolskaya pravda*, October.

Druzenko, A. (1988) 'Olimpiyskaya slava', *Moskovski novosti*, November, p. 15.

Gordon, L.A. and Klopov, E.V. (1972) *Chelovek posle raboty* (Moscow) p. 275.

Gordon, L.A. and Rimashevskaya, N.M. (1972) *Pyatidnevnaya rabochaya nedelya i svobodnoye vremya trudyaschikhysya,* Moscow.

Kondratieva, M. (1986) 'Na uroke i v zhizni, *Molodoi konnunist*, 1986, No. 12.

Konovalov, I. (1988) 'Intourist to restructure its work', *Moscow News*, No. 8, p. 8.

Lomakov, D. (1991) 'Medveditsy na ringe', *Argument y Fakty*, No. 29.

Merkulov, V. (1990) 'Pressing on regardless', *Soviet Weekly*, 17 October.

Ponomareva, V. (1987) 'Yeshcho odna pobeda', *Sobesednik*, 37, 12.

Radyshevsky, D. (1990) 'The mafia and Soviet American football', *Moscow News*, 20-26 July, No. 8, p. 14.

Salnikov, V. (1989) 'Vremya nadyozhd', *Argumenty i fakty*, 1, 3.

Trotsky, L. (1973) *Problems of Everyday Life*, New York: Monad Press.

Tsirlin, V. (1986) 'Vodnoye polo dlya zhenshchin', *Sport v SSSR*, no. 8.

Vasiliev, A. and Rogozhnikov, M. (1987) 'Ideas for leisure', *Moscow News*, no. 13.

Voblikov, A. (1991) 'Otdykh-91 - eto dorogo', *Argumenty i fakty*, 29, 4.

NOTES TO CHAPTER 10

[1] [Editors' footnote] This chapter was first drafted in 1990 before the attempted coup of August of that year in the Soviet Union, and before the breaking away of many of the constituent republics of the Union. The chapter deals with the process of change over the period in which the political fabric of the USSR was being fairly rapidly unravelled. As a commentary on the shift from state controlled towards market liberal society, and the relationship of

leisure policy to this change, it represents a valuable insight into the relationship between the nature of the state and its leisure policy goals. Thus, though the Soviet Union no longer exists in the form it had since the Second World War, and which it retained when this chapter was originally conceived, nevertheless, an analysis of the changing relationship between the state, leisure policy, and civil society in this most significant of states in twentieth century history, was deemed highly appropriate in the context of this book.

[2] *SSRV v tsifrakh v 1980 godu*, Moscow (1982) p. 175.

[3] *SSRV v tsifrakh v 1980 godu*, Moscow (1982) pp. 7, 13, 14, 17.

[4] *Narodnoye khozyaistvo SSSR v 1985 g*, Moscow(1987) p. 547.

[5] See *Argumenty i fakty*, No. 21, June 1991, p. 8.

[6]' Motogonki', *Pravda*, 19 September 1987, p. 4.

[7] See *Bolshaya sovetskaya entsiklopediya*, Vol. 6 (*Sovetskaya Entsiklopediya*, Moscow, 1977), p. 637.

[8] For more details see Jim Riordan, 'Playing to new rules: Soviet sport and perestroika', *Soviet Studies*, Vol. 42, No. 1, January 1990, pp. 133-145.

Chapter 11

Leisure Policy: Supranational Issues in Europe

Peter Bramham, Ian Henry, Hans Mommaas,
and Hugo van der Poel

Introduction

The chapters of this book constitute a set of single nation case studies of the development of leisure policy. However, though the policy making unit on which the chapters focus is largely the nation state, this is not to say that the national level is the only significant level at which policy making takes place, nor is it to argue that policy making is effected within the nation state without wider mediating influences affecting policy goals and outcomes. Local, national, transnational and even global influences mediate policy in leisure as in other areas of government activity. The last two decades have seen fundamental changes in the world's economic, military, political and cultural systems. Some of these changes have been highly visible, symbolised by a single event or a brief, dramatic period of change, such as the tearing down of the Berlin Wall. Others have been more long term in their unfolding and subtle in their implications, such as the changing structure of the global economy. In both types of case the impacts of change are profound and have consequences for any form of policy analysis including analysis of leisure policy. What this final chapter aims to do is to review the nature of these changes, and theoretical accounts which seek to explain them, in order to establish whether and in what way, they affect, or are affected by, the context, goals, and development of leisure policies in individual European nation states.

The array of theoretical schemas aimed at explaining such change is impressive. Major structural shifts in cultural, economic, or industrial terms are explained in terms of a move from modernist to post-modern (Lyotard, 1984), but also from industrial to post-industrial society (Bell, 1974), from organised to disorganised capitalism (Lash and Urry, 1987), from mass production to flexible accumulation (Piore and Sabel, 1984), from industrial to consumer capitalism (Baudrillard, 1981) and from

Fordist to Post-Fordist economies (Boyer, 1986; Aglietta, 1979). These accounts, though drawn from competing and sometimes incompatible theoretical frameworks provide important insights into the nature of social change impacting on, and affected by, leisure policy. It is worth therefore beginning with some general points about these accounts before going on to locate our own view of the adequacy of explanations of social change and of the policy development within this changing context. The post-industrial theorist's account of the changing social structure in advanced economies points to the diminution of the traditional working class and the associated and proportionate increase in the middle classes of such societies, by virtue of the expanded service industries. Although regulation theorists reflect on the same type of industrial change as their post-industrialist counterparts, the implication for class structure is somewhat different, with the identification of the decline of traditional working class occupations resulting in the formation of an underclass made up of the unemployed and those who are underemployed in the new forms of flexible production and the new service occupations.

Post-modern theorists point to the fragmentation of class cultures which is attendant on the disappearance of traditional class structures. 'Modern' society, in the tradition of the Enlightenment, was deemed to have been premised on the development of rational thought applied to physical technology in industrialisation, and subsequently to social technology in the social engineering of the welfare state in developed industrial economies. The traditional modernist reliance on rational solutions to social problems has however proved to be misplaced. Technological advances have produced major disbenefits such as the Chernobyl, Five Mile Island and Bhopal disasters and the threat of global warming. Social technology has also failed in industrial societies as welfare settlements have been eroded in the light of the economic recessions since the 1970s. The communist regimes in Eastern Europe which constituted one of the great rationalist experiments in socio-economic engineering, have also collapsed.

Some theorists have concluded that this represents not simply a crisis of social planning but a crisis of rationality itself, with 'metatheoretical' analyses (or metanarratives), based on rational accounts of the way in which society works, doomed to failure (Baudrillard, 1981). Such metatheories are seen as representing not objective, detached, or neutral analyses of events and structures in the social world, but rather represent the imposition of one world view over another as an exercise in power of those employing and propagating such theories rather than an exercise in rational detachment (Derrida, 1982). This implies a relativist epistemology, in which descriptions of the world are not 'real' but are merely the assertion of one world view over another. Clearly there are power dimensions to the rehearsal of theoretical propositions, but this is not to dismiss all theories as relativist (Alexander, 1992; D'Amico, 1992). Our own account seeks to explain the demise of modernist thinking without descending into the nihilism of some relativist thinking.

We thus follow Bauman's injunction to derive an analysis of post-modernism rather than a post-modern analysis (Bauman, 1992). In other words we wish both to assert the existence of a real world, independent of our knowledge of it, and to acknowledge that our own account is founded in a particular moral-political and anthropological context.

A second point to make in relation to post-modernist accounts is that they may be taken to imply a break with the cultural and social structures of traditional industrial societies. This break, however, though evidenced in the fragmentation of lifestyle patterns in advanced contemporary capitalist societies, is not complete, nor is it universal. For many in such societies, traditional class, race and gender structures and identities remain firmly entrenched. The social, cultural, political and economic worlds may be in flux, but that is not to say that such flux is experienced uniformly by all.

Europe, however, is made up of more than advanced industrial societies, which suffer from the processes of restructuring. Even within the European Community considerable tranches of population live and work in relatively industrially undeveloped regions, such as the South of Italy, parts of Ireland, Greece, Spain, and Portugal, while outside the European Community in Eastern Europe social, cultural and economic, as well as the political structures are in disarray. The social and economic problems which leisure policy may be required to address in such circumstances are potentially of a very different order to those facing the advanced industrial economies. Indeed it is dangerous to generalise about the contrast between national groups since the heterogeneity of national populations may mean that similarities between social groups of different national backgrounds are stronger and more striking than the similarities within the populations of nation states. In the same way as it is dangerous to generalise about the relative affluence of one country vis à vis another (because affluent countries contain relatively impoverished groups), so it is dangerous to generalise about the nature of national cultures (since most societies are multicultural).

A final point to make as a preliminary to this discussion of the development of European leisure policies, concerns the nature of the relationship between transnational structures and influences, those of the nation-state, and those at the local level. Although we have focused on the importance of global change as the context of leisure policy development, we do not intend to imply that policy should simply be 'read off' as a product of such change, deduced in some kind of 'reductionist' analysis. National and local leisure policies are clearly influenced by such phenomena but also reproduce and modify their own structural context. Thus New Right or Green policies are not simply a product of wider structural forces, though they may be subject to transnational economic and ideological influences, and may contribute to the propagation of such ideologies themselves at both a local and transnational level. Policies reflect the actions of individuals and their intended and unintended consequences, but the resources available to those individuals to pursue lines of action are a reflection of wider social, economic, political and cultural structures. The individual chapters have focused on national leisure policy but in many instances the city may be a more significant unit of analysis. This may become increasingly evident as cities are able to negotiate directly with supranational bodies, such as the European Community and compete (and co-operate) directly over national borders.

The Nature of Global Change

The world economic, political and military systems in which we live were established in the period following the Second World War. The features of the *economic* system, such as the World Bank and the International Monetary Fund were established following the Bretton Woods agreement of 1946 at which the United States agreed to underwrite the system of world trade between liberal democracies by guaranteeing the value of the dollar in gold. The *military* system was essentially a stand-off between the two super powers, and the *political* system mirrored this with France, Britain and China, accorded the status of second order political powers as evidenced in their membership of the Security Council of the United Nations.

These three systems, the military, political and economic have collapsed, and are yet to be replaced by a new world order. Perhaps the most spectacular has been the military collapse of the Soviet Union as a super power. Essentially, after years of providing a solid and reasonably predictable enemy, suddenly the Union no longer exists, and NATO, set up as an American-Western European Alliance to oppose the Soviet Bloc, is faced with the prospect of the former communist nations of that bloc applying for membership of the very organisation constructed to oppose them.

The collapse of the political order is evident in the symbolism of the collapse of the Berlin Wall. Germany, having been occupied until the very point of collapse of East Germany, was able to decide the terms of its own unification with little or no input from the super powers or the other occupying forces (much to the chagrin of the then British Prime minister, Mrs Thatcher). The 1987 Single European Act (the most significant features of which came into force at the end of 1992) was constructed before German unification, but has resulted in the construction of a single market bigger than even the United States' domestic market, and with the demise of the communist bloc the centre of gravity in Europe has shifted to a European Community dominated in economic terms at least by a unified Germany.

The nature of the collapse of the economic system has been rather more subtle and long term. As we have noted the economic system in the post-war period was built on the stability of the American economy and on American military hegemony which guaranteed the international conditions required for stability in world trade. However, the American government had to meet the huge costs of the arms race, and military occupation in Europe, as well as the costs of the wars in Korea and Vietnam. This meant that the US had a growing federal deficit and a growing balance of trade problem. Given a resistance to increased taxation the only way to finance these was to print money. By the mid 1960s however, the United States no longer possessed sufficient gold reserves to guarantee the value of the dollar in gold. Hence in 1969 the decision was taken to float the dollar on the open currency market, abandoning the gold standard. The dollar decreased in value against other currencies triggering a world recession which was made worse by the oil producing countries forcing a four-fold increase in prices in 1973.

Thus the post-war economic system crumbled in the 1970s. America's preeminent economic position is now clearly under threat, in part by the new unified Europe which had all but eliminated internal tariff barriers by the end of 1992, and partly by Japan. Indeed, it is a measure of just how seriously the United States viewed this threat that President Bush chose to conduct part of his unsuccessful domestic presidential campaign in 1991-1992 in Japan seeking to persuade the Japanese government to open up domestic markets to American producers.

By the beginning of the 1990s, in terms of political, military, and economic power, the world had thus become a very different and less certain place than it had been even twenty years before.

Regulation Theory

The French regulation school of political economy has sought to analyse and explain the impact of these global changes on particular societies and their economies. Their argument is based on the notion that any form of economic organisation (or mode of accumulation), if it is to survive, will require a stable set of social arrangements (a regime of social regulation). Regulation theorists further argue that shifts in the global economy have resulted in fundamental change in the economies and societies of the advanced industrial nations. They term these changes a move from Fordism to post-Fordism. Our central thesis is that the breakdown of Fordist regimes implies a fundamental change in the rationales which nation states employ in developing leisure policy, and the function of much of this text is therefore to highlight ways in which leisure policies have embraced, contested, or been influenced by, notions of such a shift.

Table 11.1 is used here as an explanatory device to highlight the significance and direction of policy change. The label 'Fordism' is used to describe the nature of economic and social organisation in mature industrial societies. The term Fordism was coined to characterise Gramsci's account of the development of social and economic relations in industrial society. The term refers to Henry Ford whose car production plant in the 1920s provided the archetypal industrial system. Fordism is based on factory production. The efficiency of this system is achieved through economies of scale (mass production) and by breaking down production tasks into their simplest components, simplifying them and thus increasing productivity through increased speed and a reduction in errors. As a result workers jobs are deskilled as scientific management seeks to reduce tasks to their simplest level, eliminating any opportunity for craftsmen and women to practice their craft skills.

In order to achieve this highly ordered work scheme the industrial organisation itself had to be built on highly rationalised principles. Thus bureaucratic organisations, with long chains of command and tight control of workers were required to manage Fordist production. Workers in this system were inevitably alienated from their work so that their allegiance to their company, and commitment to their work, had to be ensured. This was to be achieved by payment of high wages by employers and by the provision of welfare services by the state. The social democratic state, the welfare state, is thus the result of the historic compromise between capital and labour. Leisure services are a feature of this compromise, with the state providing for health, education, housing and ultimately 'luxury' services such as sport and culture as part of this compromise.

A further central feature of the Fordist system is mass consumption. Henry Ford is credited as having realised that by paying his workers well (thereby forcing up wages in other factory-based work), and by producing his cars cheaply, his workers would be able to afford the very cars they were constructing. To reduce costs the cars were to be designed as standard, facilitating economies of scale, and the model T Ford was standard in every way, even in terms of colour (they were all black).

The key problem then of the Fordist system was worker alienation, which was to be managed by the promoting of compensation in the form of high wages, increased private (mass) consumption, and a welfare system based on universal rights of citizenship. Every citizen had not only political rights (the right to vote) but also social rights (to health services, education services and ultimately to leisure services). In most welfare states, local government was responsible for collective service provision. Liberal welfare professions such as teaching, youth work, social work and ultimately leisure services were developed, operating in local bureaucracies to provide a whole range of services.

The Fordist system however, reached a crisis in the 1970s. The system, having been shaken by the decline of the dollar and the steep rise in oil prices plunged into recession. This was a recession which could not be solved by traditional Keynesian economics, which had in the post-war years been almost universally employed in capitalist economies. Keynesianism implies a trade-off between unemployment and inflation, with states promoting demand in times of unemployment by increasing public sector expenditure. This fuelled inflation, and thus a balance was to be sought at which unemployment and inflation could be kept at an acceptable level. In the 1970s however stagflation occurred, with high inflation *and* high unemployment, together with nil or negative economic growth, a situation which could not be explained by traditional Keynesian economic theory. With such poor economic growth in the developed economies, transnational corporations sought to enhance their return on investment by reducing labour costs, transferring investment to low wage economies, with a resultant loss of employment in the developed economies. The kinds of manufacturing jobs which were retained in the high wage economies were those associated with automated production or those with high skill / technology requirements, which training and education in the developed economies might be better placed to serve. In addition, service sector jobs grew in volume and significance. Nevertheless such employment did not compensate for the loss of opportunities in developed economies and with an excess of labour over demand, there was no longer any necessity to retain the loyalty of the whole workforce by investing in high wages and social welfare provision.

If the key social problem for the Fordist system was dealing with worker alienation, the central problem for the post-Fordist system of flexible production of goods and services is dealing with the two tier workforce produced by economic change. The workforce is stratified into two tiers in the sense that 'core' workers in skilled positions, or in key industries whose roles are central to production, are able to command high wages and good conditions of service, while the unemployed, or low paid, part-time, peripheral, workforce do not need to be seduced to stay in post with high wages and social provision by the state. Their labour is not in demand and their compliance with the economic system is therefore not essential. In the post-Fordist system, the culture of welfarism is therefore likely to be replaced by an emphasis on enterprise culture. Welfare rights are likely to be dismantled and replaced by consumer rights, with a residual safety net of welfare provision for the peripheral workforce.

Local government provision of leisure services illustrates the shift to post-Fordism also. The focus of the efforts of leisure professionals in post-Fordism changes from one of a rationale for leisure provision as a social service, to one of maximising income and minimising costs in public services as public service budgets are cut. The emphasis on leisure policy is one on leisure as a tool of economic regeneration rather than as a tool of social development.

This then is an ideal-typical account of the kinds of shift in leisure policy one might expect, given the fundamental economic and social changes in developed economies. In emphasising the political and economic, we are not suggesting that there is not a cultural trajectory to leisure policy (which itself will carry political and economic implications). Nor are we suggesting that the global economy is simply a 'structural context' within which local agency operates. What we are arguing, however, is that the structurations/figurations which are the context/outcome of leisure policy have important political and economic dimensions at national and transnational level, so that governments are faced with the issue of how to proceed within a context which has important political, economic and cultural features.

Table 11.1 Ideal Typical Representation of The Fordist / Post-Fordist Distinction and its Implications for Leisure Policy

A) ECONOMIC RELATIONS

	Fordism	**Post-Fordism**
Manufacturing / Markets	Mass production Deskilled labour Mass consumption	Flexible production Skilled labour Market niches
Organisation Types	Mechanistic, 'tall', bureaucratic.	Organismic, 'flat', flexible
Management Type	Corporate management, centralised control	Deconcentration, autonomous roles to section / division managers, within organisations.

B) POLITICAL RELATIONS

	Fordism	**Post-Fordism**
Politico-economic System	Corporate policy making, involving business, unions, and government	'Strong state, free economy'
Central-local Relations	Local responsibility for service provision; central responsibility for economic planning	Service provision, taxation levels, economic , development centrally decided
Local Government	Large-scale, bureaucratic, corporate, policy-making	New flexible forms of management and control

Table 11.1 continued

(C) CULTURAL RELATIONS

	Fordism	Post-Fordism
Social Impacts	Worker alienation	Two tier workforce, 'core' and 'peripheral'
Dominant Culture	Welfarism	Enterprise culture
Rights of Individual	Universal rights of citizenship	Dual system; consumer , rights and 'safety net' welfare provision

D) LOCAL GOVERNMENT LEISURE POLICY

	Fordism	Post-Fordism
Orientation of Leisure Professionals	Bureaucratic, liberal welfare professional	Entrepreneurial, 'industrial' professional
Leisure Policy Emphasis	Social democratic, leisure as a right	Leisure as a tool of economic (or social) regeneration
Leisure Policy Rationale	Largely social with some economic benefits (externalities)	Largely economic with some social benefits

Source: Henry and Bramham, 1990

Leisure Policy and the Demise of Social Democracy

The thrust of our argument in identifying the shift from Fordist to post-Fordist approaches to policy is that there is a relationship between national policy systems and the global systems within which nation states operate. In particular the shift form Fordist to post-Fordist economies implies a shift in the mode of social regulation and therefore in the nature of national leisure policies. This is not to say that such a shift is a 'functional requirement' of post-Fordist systems, policy shifts are contingent actions rather than 'necessary' responses. However, the economic circumstances of the situation which gave rise to economic restructuring (or at least the way they are viewed) are such that national governments are less likely to feel able to finance the welfare systems that were characteristic of Fordist economies. Thus it is less important to establish whether a shift to post-Fordism has actually occurred, than it is to establish whether such a shift is assumed by government to be occurring. We will illustrate the demise of the social democratic politics of the Fordist period by reference to the development of leisure policy in four European Community member states, and one state from the former Eastern bloc. The first of the European Community states is Britain, which with its New Right dominated central government one might expect to actively embrace the post-welfare philosophy of post-Fordism. The second is the Netherlands, a country whose national governments have been Christian Democrat led coalitions in the 1980s and early 1990s but whose coalition make-up one might expect moderate the policy line, and weaken its rejection of welfarism. The other two European Community countries, France and Spain represent governments which have been socialist controlled for most of the 1980s and early 1990s, but which have nevertheless lacked the resources (financial and/or ideological) to pursue socialist or even traditional social democratic goals in respect of leisure and other areas of social policy. Finally, the Eastern bloc country, Poland, is cited to illustrate the consequences of shift from the universal welfare systems of state communism, to the attempted emulation of a neo-liberal economy.

Chapter 5 relating to the development of leisure policy in Britain provides an account of the growth of a social democratic consensus in the post-war period and the subsequent retreat from social democratic policy in the UK in the 1970s. Table 11.2 illustrates the structure of the changing rationales for state intervention presented in Chapter 5.

The account divides British policy in the post-war (and immediate pre-war) era into four periods, The first two taken together represent the growth and maturing of the welfare state. In the first stage the rationale for state intervention in recreation policy is described as traditional pluralism. The state became involved in sport, the arts, and countryside recreation to achieve certain benefits. National Parks were set up to conserve the landscape; an Arts Council established to preserve the 'cultural heritage of the nation'; and finally sport was funded because of the external benefits it was assumed to generate (specifically the provision of alternative and wholesome activities for troublesome youth, and the promotion of national prestige) rather than for the intrinsic value of sport itself. This support for state intervention on extrinsic grounds was evident right up to the 1960s.

The second stage of the growth of post-war British leisure policy is described as welfare reformism in that leisure forms were promoted not only for their extrinsic benefits but because access to the arts, countryside, sport and even tourism were recognised as intrinsically worthwhile. They were justified not simply on the grounds that they conserved landscape, or culture or national prestige, but in that period they were to be promoted as rights of citizenship, or welfare rights.

However, just as this process came to fruition, so the economic restructuring associated with the crisis of Fordism began to take effect. This painful economic restructuring was accompanied in some locations by serious urban social disorders and riots. Thus although the government sought to reduce welfare spending as it failed to raise the revenues to fund welfare programmes, nevertheless expenditure on leisure was retained and even increased in some programme areas, specifically those which were aimed at the groups implicated in the social disorders.

While in the later 1980s the problem of disorder had seemed to abate, state spending on welfare projects in general had begun to reduce in real terms. State services including recreation services were to be managed more like commercial companies on behalf of the state, with the danger that social policy goals were to be subverted by the requirements of economic 'efficiency'. Recreation spending in this new flexible state was to be justified primarily on the basis of its value as a contribution not to social welfare and development, but to economic regeneration.

Given the political history of Britain over the period since the late 1970s one might have expected the demise of social democratic policy goals. However, perhaps more surprising are the policy trajectories of those Western European nation states with differing or even contrasting political histories. Clearly important differences exist, but there are also important similarities between policy directions taken by different political regimes. Table 11.3 sets out some aspects of Chapter 3, by van der Poel, which describes policy change in the case of the Netherlands. The post-war period of reconstruction in the Netherlands saw both individual and collective consumption grow, with subsidy of public housing, social security and education spending being accompanied by state investment in recreational and cultural facilities. Van der Poel's account reflects a similar rationale to that experienced in Britain in the parallel period. Investment in culture was for the purposes of worker edification, investment in sport reflected a concern with alienated youth, and investment in recreation and leisure was to be channelled through the 'pillars' of Dutch society - Catholic, Protestant and non-religious sports and arts organisations - reflecting a similar use of the voluntary sector.

Table 11.2 Summary of Stages in the Development of UK Leisure Policy

(A) Traditional Pluralism (1937-1964)

Sport - state involvement limited to achieving externalities, working largely through the voluntary sector.

Arts - democratisation of culture / cultural élitism, and concern for the conservation of élite art forms.

Countryside recreation, promotion of National Parks in response to voluntary pressure groups and concern for conservation.

(B) Welfare Reformism (1964-1976)

Arts Policy liberalised (to some degree): growth of community arts and promotion of cultural democracy.

Countryside recreation: concern with access for all.

Sport and recreation recognised as a right of citizenship, part of social service provision

(C) Period of Economic Realism (1976-84)

Restructuring of state expenditure on leisure: attempts to reduce welfare spending and range of welfare rights - increased expenditure on inner city.

(D) Disinvestment and the Flexible State (1984 -1992)

Reductions in state spending on leisure.

Introduction of new flexible forms of state organisation: commercialisation of state provision.

Leisure seen as a tool of economic rather than social development.

Source: adapted from Chapter 5

The mid 1960s saw the establishment of the emblematic Ministry of Culture, Recreation and Social Work, marking the acceptance of culture and recreation as an element in the social services portfolio of the Dutch state. As a consequence the arts policy concerns of the immediate post-war period for 'democratisation of culture' were modified and the importance of 'cultural democracy' accepted. Culture was to be seen as not simply about edification, elevating the cultural tastes of the masses, but about development of the possibilities for cultural self expression. By the end of the period of promoting leisure as welfare policy, the Socialist led coalition were seeking to develop a fully articulated policy approach to leisure, calling for a thorough review of all problematic areas of social democratic leisure policy. However, by the time a review document was published in 1985 (*Vrije Tijd: een Visie*) the situation had radically altered.

Table 11.3 Summary of Stages in the Development of Leisure Policy in the Netherlands

---

(A) Post-war Reconstruction and Pillarization (1945-1965)

Growing state involvement but channelled through voluntary clubs and associations of 'pillarized' groups.

Use of sport and youth clubs for social integration of youth.

'Edification' of the masses through the spreading of high culture - the 'democratisation of culture'.

(B) Leisure as Welfare Policy (1965-1982)

1965 Ministry of Culture, Recreation and Social Work: indicative of welfare orientation of leisure policy.

Arts policy reflects wider cultural tastes: cultural democracy accepted alongside the spreading of high culture.

Strong growth of outdoor recreation and recreational sports policies.

Declining influence of pillarized groups on leisure provision.

(C) Growing Importance of Supply Side Policies (1982-1990s)

1982 Ministry of Culture, Recreation and Social Work disbanded. Culture absorbed into new Ministry of Well Being, Health and Culture; outdoor recreation absorbed into Ministry of Agriculture and Fisheries.

During 1980s, at national level, budget for outdoor recreation halved, for tourism budget trebled.

Arts policy becomes instrumental in terms of national and regional development.

Broadcasting one of the last strongholds of pillarized interests in leisure provision, and strongly influenced by European Community regulations.

Source: adapted from Chapter 3

The impact of the economic crises of the 1970s and 1980s on Dutch society was considerable, provoking an unemployment rate which peaked at approximately 20%. Van der Poel describes the welfare reformism of the late 1960s and early 1970s as giving way in the following decade to what he describes as mild Thatcherite policies, with an emphasis on supply side economics. In 1982 culture and recreation were separated out of the government ministry responsible for social work. Outdoor recreation was placed under a 'production' (rather than a collective consumption) ministry, the Ministry of Agriculture and Fishery, while culture was hived off into a new Ministry of Health, Well Being and Culture. The chapter highlights how government tourism policy came to be driven by the policy imperative of economic regeneration, while arts policy moved away from subsidy of production (subsidy paid to artists) to promotion of consumer sovereignty through a 'freer' market, and through policies employing arts for local and national regeneration.

Although the policy detail, and the enthusiasm for policy change may vary from one case to the other, clearly there are important similarities in the direction and trajectory of policy change in the British and Dutch cases. One might however argue that this is to be expected given that both were subject to governments of the right in the 1980s, Britain under Mrs Thatcher's Conservative leadership, the Netherlands under Christian Democrat led coalitions, partly in partnership with the economic liberals of the Liberal Party. However, some similarities may also be illustrated in socialist led administrations in France and Spain.

France is an interesting case because at the same time as policies of retrenchment were being introduced in Britain and the Netherlands in the early 1980s, the new Socialist administration was seeking in France to reject economically driven social policies, and to promote social democratic welfare spending during the recession. Table 11.4 illustrates aspects of the account of French leisure policy given in Chapter. 2 by Geneviève Poujol. Although the pluralist concern of working through local voluntary groups and Comités d'Entreprise reflects a similar post-war pattern during the period of economic reconstruction, the strength of the Conservative administrations during the De Gaulle era and in particular the influence of André Malraux's élitist cultural policy, and the rigid centralism of the Gaullist system, militated against the development of social welfare types of leisure policy in the mid 1960s and 1970s.

However, when the socialists came to power in 1981 they established a new Ministère du Temps Libre, introduced plans for decentralisation to local and regional governments with clear implications for leisure, and they sought to stimulate their economy by increased public spending, particularly on social programmes. The consequences of this approach were disastrous. There was rapid and alarming acceleration of inflation and a crisis of international confidence in the franc. Faced with the possibility of devaluation the Socialists imposed spending cuts. In Geneviève Poujol's review of policy for the remainder of the 1980s and early 1990s the emphasis of policy is on spending control, so that although decentralisation had taken place, it proved difficult for local and regional governments to take advantage of their new powers. Indeed some policies, such as the deregulation of French television seem to reflect the thinking of the economic right rather more than that of socialism. Among the few elements to survive the spending cuts over the 1980s were the 'grands travaux', the Musée d'Orsay, the Louvre Pyramid, l'Opéra de la Bastille etc. The level of *central* government spending on cultural projects over the period actually increased despite the squeeze on local authority budgets. However, the rationale for this spending has been rather different. The 'grands travaux' are cultural icons of the post-modern capital city. They reflect cultural investment in Paris which, as tourist attractions and as symbols of a vital, forward thinking socialism are of economic value in attracting tourism spending and inward investment for the growth service industries.

If socialist investment programmes were tried and failed in the case of France, the Spanish Socialist party (PSOE) has been under severe criticism for its failure to pursue socialist goals at all. Following its initial election success in 1982, Felipe González's PSOE government did not seek to achieve a socialist transformation of the Spanish economy, but rather sought to modernise the economy, and to rid Spain of its isolationist stance, pursuing policies designed to achieve entry into the European Community. In these endeavours, in the early 1980s, it met with some limited successes. In 1982 the PSOE inherited a growth rate of 1%, which they had boosted to 5% by 1987; inflation was cut at the same time from 14% to 5%; foreign debt was reduced and the trade balance improved. However the cost of this restructuring was to be felt largely in the form of unemployment, particularly among the young, with Spain recording twice the OECD average. Not only were there more unemployed people, but the Socialists failed in their avowed goal of extending social security payments to more than half those unemployed, and by 1987 only 30% of the unemployed were in receipt of such payments.

In the early years of the Socialist government social spending did rise, from 3.3 billion pesetas in 1982 to 6.3 billion pesetas in 1987, but education spending fell behind military spending, a proposal for a national health service was abandoned in favour of a much less ambitious scheme, and previous policies such as withdrawal form NATO were dropped. Wage restraint agreed with the unions in the mid 1980s was beginning to be seen by trades unionists as a pointless concession, since unemployment grew inexorably, government schemes for the unemployed were limited in number and generally temporary in scope. Moreover, in the face of world recession in the late 1980s and early 1990s, even some of the economic successes had turned sour. By 1992, the growth rate had declined to 2.5%, inflation was high at 6.5%, and in April 1992 unemployment benefits were cut as part of the Spanish plan for accommodating the convergence of markets and economies, proposed under the Single European Act and the Maastricht Agreement.

Table 11.4 Summary of Stages in the Development of Leisure Policy in France

(A) Post-war Reconstruction (1945-1959)

1946 Establishment of Department of *Culture Populaire*, promoting youth movements.

1946 Law establishing *Comités d'Entreprises* which promote leisure opportunities in work organisations.

1958 Haut Commissariat à Jeunesse et aux Sports: funding for local groups, and establishing of Maisons des Jeunes.

(B) Centralised Planning and Economic Prosperity (1959-1980)

1966-1979 Four laws reducing working hours.

Professional training introduced for those involved in animation (a new liberal welfare profession).

De Gaulle appoints André Malraux to a personal Ministry of Culture: Malraux promotes high culture but denigrates 'leisure'; democratisation of culture but within strict limits.

Pompidou inaugurates link between presidency and cultural projects (Pompidou Centre).

(C) Decentralisation and Socialism in a Hostile Climate (1981-1990s)

1981 New Ministry of Free Time established.

Mitterand appoints own Minster of Culture, Jack Lang, and continues the tradition of *grands travaux*.

1982 Law on Decentralisation shifts authority to local and regional bodies.

1983 Reversal of Keynesian policies of expansion led by public expenditure.

State monopoly of television ended, privatisation of some channels.

Increased cultural spending by central government with a strongly economic rationale, while local authority budgets squeezed.

Source: adapted from Chapter 2

Table 11.5 Summary of Stages in the Development of Leisure Policy in Spain

(A) Franco Dictatorship (1939-1975)

State seeks to control all aspects of life: work, leisure, religion.

1939-1950s Rural, agrarian Spain predominates: preindustrial leisure patterns.

1950s-1970s Economic development and modernisation: urbanisation, growing national income, industrial production, and consumer expenditure.

Dictatorship promotes:
- sports festivals to distract and entertain, promoting 'appropriate' values;
- cultural festivals, artificial folklore and customs to promote cultural identity;
- tourism for economic and ideological purposes, to earn foreign currency and to legitimate the dictatorship internationally.

(B) Period of Transition and Liberalisation (1976-1982)

Setting in place of democratic institutions.

(C) Leisure Policy under 'Socialism' (1982-1992)

Leisure as social policy for the elderly and the young

Cultural industries: concentration of ownership, multinational capital, diversification of large media firms.

Cultural policy: seeks to promote a Spanish culture but evident transnational influences promote cultural eclecticism.

Sport: *polideportivos* (municipal sports centres) constructed, raising sporting opportunity; but evident cultural heterogeneity, decline of community sports and rise of individualist activities (jogging, cycling, water sports, adventure sports); concern with health, fitness and the body.

Tourism policy: concern for decline of mass tourism products for mass markets; new strategies for product and market diversification.

Culture and urban regeneration: culture, tourism and leisure seen as major tools in promoting economic regeneration; 1992 Barcelona Olympics, Madrid European Cultural Capital, Seville World Expo.

Source: adapted from Chapter 7

A number of factors could be said to have generated the predominantly pragmatic form of restricted economic liberalism employed in Spain. Some of these are peculiar to the historical context of Spain's socialist government. The abortive military coup of 1981, for example, underlined the need for a cautious (conservative) approach to social change, to ensure social stability and render less likely any threat of intervention by the military. Indeed the prolonged success of the PSOE suggests that progress in democratic consolidation was rewarded in general elections, despite economic shortcomings. The influx into the party of young technocrats was another factor, with their fashionable (economic liberal) ideas of how to modernise the Spanish economy, initially to prepare for European Community entry and subsequently to achieve sustained development. Such technocrats were attracted perhaps less by the ideology of socialism (Marxism was officially abandoned in 1979 and there was no tradition of social democracy in Spain as such), than perhaps by the party's role in opposing the Franco regime. The second set of factors is external to Spanish circumstances. The lessons learned from the French socialist government's Keynesian experiments of the early 1980s counselled caution in support of social democratic policy goals.

Table 11.5 illustrates the account of the development of leisure policy in Spain given by González and Urkiola in Chapter 7. The development of leisure policy in the period of the dictatorship provides a contrast to the development of leisure policy for the other nation-states cited here. The governmental concern with leisure was dominated by its attempt to establish its own legitimacy; through the promotion of celebrations and festivals built around artificially constructed folklore and staged customs which fostered national identity through historical association; through sports festivals to distract, entertain, and promote appropriate values of competitive aggressiveness and community solidarity; through tourism development for economic purposes but also for the ideological purpose of legitimating the regime in the eyes of foreign visitors; and through a media policy built around moral and political censorship.

In the period of political control of the PSOE social policy goals for leisure have been pursued in limited ways. Certainly the establishment of *polideportivos*, municipal recreation centres, and programmes aimed at the elderly reflect such goals. However, in the case of provision of leisure as compensation for the effects of unemployment among the young, leisure policy is at least partially used for extrinsic purposes. Furthermore as a two tier society emerges in Spain (the division of tiers being those who benefit from, and those who suffer the consequences of, economic restructuring) so there is growing evidence of cultural heterogeneity, and the erosion of leisure as an occasion and indicator of community cohesion. This heterogeneity manifests itself in demand terms, for example, in the growth of individualist (rather than community-based) sports, and the concern with health, fitness and the body (rather than the social aspects of sport). In supply terms the development of oligopolistic control in the cultural industries, particularly by transnational firms also undermines the notion of local control over cultural products.

However, while expenditure on leisure as collective consumption is held on a tight rein, the most significant feature of leisure policy in Spain in the early 1990s is the growing governmental concern with leisure as a tool of economic regeneration. The failure of the Fordist, mass market, package holiday, in which Spain has specialised, and from which it has gained in terms of balance of payments, has encouraged government to foster tourism marketing plans. The major feature of these plans is the development of diversified tourist products which reduce spatial and seasonal concentration and which go beyond the appeal to the declining traditional, package holiday market. Thus in the Spanish context also, policy priorities are being heavily influenced by the economic imperative of adapting to the new economic structure emerging in Europe.

The development of economic liberalism in Europe is not of course limited to the European Community member states. Eastern European States are following the neo-liberal line, with Poland for example adopting the New Right prescription of 'the free economy and the strong state' in a qualified manner. Thus Bohdan Jung describes how the liberalisation of prices and the removal of state subsidies in Poland is coupled with strict wage controls to tie down inflation, deepening the recession and promoting growing unemployment, which is accompanied by a rapid increase in crime. In cultural terms the liberalisation of the economy and the polity has produced an expansion of political, religious and cultural organisations operating alongside 'seedy' elements of the commercial sector such as sex shops. State support for the high arts is in decline, as is consumer interest in the arts, which appears to have been seduced by Western popular culture. Management of recreation facilities has been devolved to local communities while local authorities are experiencing severe expenditure squeezes, and are unable to fund their operation.

The key elements of Poland's economic policy are plainly influenced by transnational organisation, in the form of the World Bank, which requires stabilisation of the macro-economy by the government's avoidance of fiscal deficit, and the management of available credit by strict controls on the internal banking system. At the same time price reform has been set in train so that prices approximate to 'real costs' of production of goods and services (Clague, 1992). Since the beginnings of the process of marketisation in the early 1980s in Poland, there has been a steady suppression of demand and Jung reports living standards 40% below pre-marketisation levels of the 1970s.

This restructuring process in Poland has also led to the development of a two tier society. While commentators on the effects of restructuring of Western European nations refer to a two thirds - one third society in advanced industrial nations, with the one third referring to the now redundant rump of the traditional working class in the newly restructured post-Fordist systems of production, in the Eastern European states the effects of restructuring are worse. The situation might more accurately be characterised as a one third - two thirds society (or one tenth - nine tenths society) since the group of *nouveau riche* benefiting from economic growth is considerably smaller than its equivalent in Western European states. This new leisure élite referred to by Jung is likely to be the major beneficiary of the projected annual growth of 5% predicted for the 1990s for Central and Eastern European nations by the World Bank. However, since the predicted growth rate for Western European nations is 3% for the same period it is estimated that it will take a lifetime at these respective rates for the gap in standards of living to be closed (Summers, 1992). However, it should be emphasised that even these projections are viewed as optimistic.

Current economic thinking reflects then the Schumpeterian notion that the advantage of the market economy is in its fostering of innovative activity rather than its allocative efficiency (Clague, 1992). However, the problems of allocative failure are such that they are likely to place severe strains on social cohesion, which result in for example the marginalisation of youth (on which Riordan focuses in his discussion of the former Soviet Union) and other groups, or even in the fragmentation of political entities such as the former Soviet Union itself. Nevertheless, it seems clear that economic liberalism, despite the scepticism of commentators such as Jung, remains the major ideology promoted by transnational organisations.

The European Community and the Europeanisation Project

In addition to the behaviour of transnational capital, perhaps the major transnational influence which represents the context and product of the policy interaction of the nation states is the Europeanisation project, that is the accelerating integration of the European Community and its changing relationships with other blocs and nation states. The Treaty of Rome which established the European Community, was essentially an economic and political treaty and had little to say about cultural matters. Nevertheless the integration process, albeit primarily economic and politically motivated, invariably exerts influence on the cultural dimension, and therefore on leisure policy.

The history of the foundation and development of the European Community reflects a tension between those who are concerned to develop a supranational body, and those who would wish the Community to act as an intergovernmental organisation, with power retained by individual nation states. In effect the events of the late 1980s and early 1990s have reflected the dominance of those with a more federalist, supranational vision of the Community. The Single European Act of 1987 not only introduced the single market, but also incorporated wider powers for the European Parliament, and brought in for a variety of policy concerns, qualified majority voting in the Council of Ministers, allowing individual nation states to be outvoted on certain issues. Similarly the Maastricht Treaty, with its promotion of a single currency, and shared limits to fiscal debt and inflation among member states, implies less room for policy manoeuvre at national level. Britain's opt out clause and Denmark's rejection of the original terms of the Treaty in a referendum, are symptoms of the remaining tension between the intergovernmental and supranational camps.

The Community was conceived in the hey-day of Keynesian economic thinking. Thus, although it was ostensibly set up as a 'common market', reducing state imposed tariff barriers, some of its policies were markedly interventionist. The Iron and Steel Community, the precursor to the formation of the European Community was both interventionist in social policy in attempting to alleviate the cost of rationalisation in the iron and steel industries, but was also conceived in a manner which was premised on the use of economic interests to achieve political goals (integration between France and West Germany to ensure political and military stability). The Common Agricultural Policy of the Community involved considerable distortion of markets to alleviate the costs of restructuring. The European Regional Development Fund and to a lesser extent the European Social Fund have also involved considerable social spending in an attempt to compensate for the operation of market forces within the Community. These activities, in a sense, formed part of a transnational approach informed by Keynesian logic. By contrast the Maastricht proposals, with their fiscal balance and anti-inflation requirements form much more of an economic liberal approach. It is ironic therefore that the British Conservative Party, dominated as it has been by the economic liberals of the New Right, should provide some of the most vehement opposition to the proposals for economic union.

In considering the implications for leisure policy of the Europeanisation project, there are perhaps two facets to consider. The first is to identify the role which the European Community itself will play in terms of generating policy at the Community level. The second is to consider the ways in which Community policy will mediate leisure policy at the level of the nation state. An answer to the first of these questions is bound up with a consideration of the principle of subsidiarity which asserts that policy should be formulated and implemented at the lowest possible governmental level. Thus questions of leisure policy, whether dealing with sport, outdoor recreation or cultural policy, one might expect to be the preserve of the nation state, or of regional or local groups within the nation state. There are, however, some important exceptions to this principle. In relation to sports policy for example, there are policy matters derived from the free movement of goods, people and capital which imply a Community interest in sport. These include the free movement of sportswomen and men, the mutual recognition of professional qualifications among member states (for coaches, managers etc.), the movement of sports equipment and animals (e.g. guns and horses), cross border transmission of television sports broadcasts and so on. In addition, action at the Community level is deemed appropriate in respect of safety in stadia, standardisation of facilities in stadia, drugs in sport, applied research in sport, the application of new technology, and the environmental impact of sport.

These concerns are unsurprising given the economic nature of the Community. However, there is a further strand of European Community sports policy which goes beyond the realm of the economic, for the Community has recognised the role which sport can play in the ideological task of, fostering a European identity. The Adonnini Report (1985) considered measures which might bring about greater public awareness and commitment to the process of European integration. The report promoted the notion of a European Community flag, and the Euro passport, but it also gave consideration to proposals to establish a European Community Games, European Community teams for international competition (with subsequent discussion of the role of national teams in the Olympic Games), the establishment of a European Community standard for sports equipment with approval displayed in the form of a Euro logo on all approved items, as well as a European Community programme of sport for the disabled and a partnership with sports organisations in combating violence. Thus the promotion of European unity as 'natural' was seen as requiring some legitimation in the cultural realm and sport provides an important cultural tool for such purposes. Although many of the concerns of the Adonnini Report have not been acted upon, the Community has increased funding of European wide sports events, assisting 57 such events in 1991, and a European Community presence was maintained at the Winter Olympics in Albertville and Barcelona.

EC interest in media policy is rather more readily understandable, since broadcasting across national boundaries is commonplace. Fears that the single market in television will generate disbenefits, principally the concentration of ownership of the media and the homogeneity of cultural products on television, underpin the European Community directive *Television without Frontiers* (1989), while the Community's MEDIA programme of financial aid (Measures to Develop an Audio-visual Industry) reflects its concern to protect the national cultures of the smaller member states. Here again there is a tension between the aim of protecting 'national' cultures (see for example Burgelman and Paulens, 1992 on strategies for cultural protection of small states), and the claim that an expanded broadcasting market will foster market niching, thus protecting significant minority cultures (see van der Poel, 1991, for the promotion of a market led solution).

A third area in which European Community involvement in leisure policy is significant is that of regional policy. European Community regional policy currently identifies three types of regions as priorities for grant aid under the European Regional Development Fund. The first is underdeveloped and peripheral regions, incorporating the whole of Spain, Portugal, Ireland, Northern Ireland, Greece and Southern Italy. The second type of priority region is that group of regions affected by industrial restructuring, incorporating the Basque Country, the Ruhr, parts of Belgium, the UK and Northern Italy. These regions are characterised by loss of traditional industries and high unemployment. The third type of region is that suffering from rural deprivation, depopulation and the decline of agriculture. In each of these types of region leisure investment is part of the regional redevelopment strategy. The peripheral areas contain many of the Mediterranean tourist destinations and the traditional package tourist industry has been seen as part of the key to redevelopment. In regions suffering from the effects of restructuring, however, leisure and cultural provision has been seen as a means of changing the image of the region, and its major cities rendering their infrastructure more attractive to the new service industries for which industrial location decisions might be made on cultural attractiveness criteria . The third group of regions has been assisted by the development of farm tourism, and also by provision of cultural facilities to make small communities culturally viable. Thus regional funds per se and to a lesser extent funds for the restructuring of agriculture, have significant implications for leisure investment.

Leisure policy or leisure-related policy at the Community level is only one side of the coin. Of potentially major significance for leisure policy at the nation state level, are the Maastricht proposals for economic and monetary union, since they imply a stricter fiscal and anti-inflationary discipline than might be agreed by individual governments, one which is likely to require spending on services to be curtailed. The room for manoeuvre in public spending will thus be limited, and leisure policy edged further towards a post-Fordist pattern.

Conclusion

The processes of globalisation and transnationalisation are not unidirectional 'forces' imposing themselves as structural constraints on 'local' agents. These processes are reproduced and challenged by such agents. A failure to grasp the specifics of local political, economic and cultural histories and forces can have tragic consequences, as the war in Bosnia demonstrates. Thus while developing the major transnational themes of this conclusion, we wish to remind the reader that the conclusion is designed to be read alongside the other constituent chapters. The richness and diversity of the local/national policy context should not be underplayed. Thus this conclusion can only represent a complement to he detailed individual nation-state studies which focus on that diversity. It should not be understood as a summary of their arguments. Understanding policy processes and outcomes requires a multi-layered analysis, one to which we hope this text will have made a positive contribution.

REFERENCES

Aglietta, M. (1979) *Theory of Capitalist Regulation: the US Experience*, Verso: London.

Alexander, J. (1992) 'General Theory in the Post-positivist mode: the "Epistemological Dilemma" and the Search for Present Reason', in Seidman, S. and Wagner, D. (eds) *Postmodernism and Social Theory*, Oxford: Blackwell.

Baudrillard, J. (1981) *For a Critique of the Political Economy of the Sign,* Telos Press: London.

Bauman, Z. (1992) *Intimations of Postmodernity*, London: Routledge.

Bell, D. (1974) *The Coming of Post-industrial Society, a venture in social forecasting*, London: Heinemann Educational.

Boyer, R. (1986) *La Theorie de la Regulation: un Analyse Critique*, Paris: Editions de la Decouverte.

Burgelman, J-C. and Paulens, C. (1992) 'Audio-visual Policy and cultural identity in small European states: the challenge of a unified market', *Media, Culture and Society*, 14, 169-183.

✳ Clague, C. (1992) 'Introduction: the Journey to a Market Economy' in Clague, C. and Rausser, G. (eds) *The Emergence of Market Economies in Eastern Europe*, Oxford: Blackwell.

D'Amico, R. (1992) 'Defending Social Science Against the Postmodern Doubt' in Seidman, S. and Wagner, D. (eds) *Postmodernism and Social Theory*, Oxford: Blackwell.

Derrida, J. (1982) *Margins of Philosophy*, Brighton: Harvester Press.

Henry, I. and Bramham, P. (1990) 'Leisure, Politics and the Local State', in Botterill, D. and Tomlinson, A. (eds) *Leisure Policy: Ideology and Practice*, Brighton: Leisure Studies Association.

Lash, S. and Urry, J. (1987) *The End of Organized Capitalism,* Oxford: Polity.

Lyotard, J-F. (1984) *The Postmodern Condition, a Report on Knowledge*, Manchester: Manchester University Press.

Piore, M. and Sabel, C. (1984) *The Second Industrial Divide*, London: Basic Books.

Summers, L. (1992) 'The Next Decade in Central and Eastern Europe', in Clague, C. and Rausser, G. (eds) *The Emergence of Market Economies in Eastern Europe*, Oxford: Blackwell.

van der Poel, H. (1991) 'Media Policy in Europe: compromising between nationalism and mass markets', *Leisure Studies*, 10 (3), 187-201.

Index